God, Caesar, and the Constitution

God,
Caesar,
and the
Constitution

*The Court as Referee
of Church-State Confrontation*

Leo Pfeffer

Beacon Press

Boston

Copyright © 1975 by Leo Pfeffer

Beacon Press books are published under the auspices
of the Unitarian Universalist Association

Simultaneous publication in Canada by Saunders of Toronto, Ltd.

Printed in the United States of America

9 8 7 6 5 4 3 2 1

Library of Congress Cataloging in Publication Data

Pfeffer, Leo, 1910–
    God, Caesar, and the Constitution.
    Bibliography: p. 359
    1. Religious liberty—United States   2. United
States—Constitutional law   3. Ecclesiastical law—
United States.   I. Title.
KF4865.P44   342'.73'085   74–210
ISBN 0-8070-4480-6

To Hy and Shari Rosen

Contents

Chapter 3.   The Family   82

Chapter 4.   The Military   138

Chapter 7.   The Community and Its Welfare   298

Chapter 8.   Where Do We Go from Here?   343

Chapter One

The Contestants, the Stakes, the Referee, and the Rules

God and Caesar in a Democratic Society

In a theocracy there is no conflict between God and Caesar. Caesar is captain of the Lord's host and as a loyal and faithful officer he sees that the soldiers obey the Lord's word as conveyed to them by His priests. He who disobeys the commands of the priest is punished just as he who disobeys the captain's commands, for both come from the same ultimate source.

Nor is there conflict in Erastianism. There too the ultimate source is the Lord, but it is the monarch rather than the priest who determines what is God's will (as in England in 1927 when the Parliament refused to approve a change in the prayer book sought by the Church of England).

Colonial America experimented with both types of government: a theocratic establishment in Massachusetts and an Erastian in Virginia. Neither lasted very long; the individualism and egalitarianism of the frontier, the rationalism which in the 18th century swept westward from France, and other factors combined to make American society hostile equally to authoritarianism of church and state. It has had little room for either theocracy or Erastianism.

Conflict and trouble are, however, inevitable when God and Caesar part company and set up independent es-

1

tablishments. In the first place, they compete in the same market. Each demands supreme loyalty from the same people, even when God takes the form of individual conscience and Caesar that of a democratic state. Moreover, it often happens that they issue contradictory commands. God told the Mormons that everyone must take to himself several wives; Caesar forbade more than one at a time. God decreed that thou shalt not kill; Caesar sent you to Vietnam and demanded body counts to make sure you were killing effectively. God forbade avoidance of conception by any means other than consultation of the calendar; Caesar's hospitals and clinics provided contraceptive devices and instruction for all. In these circumstances, it is impossible to render unto God that which is God's and to Caesar that which is Caesar's for the simple reason that both claim exclusive dominion over the same territory.

What makes the situation even more complicated is that, because we have rejected both theocratic and Erastian solutions, we allow God to take many shapes and speak in many tongues: Protestantism with its many divisions, Catholicism, Judaism, and many smaller sects, denominations, and faiths. When last counted in 1936 these amounted to over 250; today the total may be twice that. All have prophets proclaiming "Thus saith the Lord": the Reverend Billy Graham, the brothers Berrigan, the Black Muslims, and the Hassidic rabbis of Brooklyn. Moreover, the same prophets often speak disparately at different times. Protestantism once preached that contraception was sinful; today it asserts that not to practice it may be wrong. For a century, American Catholicism fought to keep the Bible out of the public schools; later it bitterly attacked as secularists those who successfully sued to remove it from the schools; then it took the view that perhaps it was best that the Bible had been removed, or, in any event, that a constitutional amendment allowing it to be brought back would not be wise. Most recently it returned to stage 2 and again urged an amendment restoring both Bible and prayer to the

schools. Jews long opposed governmental financing of parochial schools; today the Orthodox wing of Judaism, with
some support within the Conservative and some even
within the Reform branches, strongly favors it.

The result has been conflict and competition not only
with the state* but within religion itself. What, however,
has been most remarkable about religious conflict and competition in the United States is that on the whole it has been
singularly peaceful. This does not mean that no blood has
been shed, violence experienced, or persecution suffered.
Mormons, Catholics, Jehovah's Witnesses, Black Muslims,
and others have been victims of all. Nor does it mean that
resolutions of the conflicts, even when peaceful, were not
accompanied by bitterness and divisiveness. It means only
that compared to most nations, the United States has succeeded in keeping religious conflict in check and working
out a modus vivendi which, while not completely satisfactory to any group, is one with which all groups have found
they can live.

Nevertheless, the conflict continues; religion and the
state have demands upon each other and are likely to continue to have them so long as we maintain a democratic
society in which God and Caesar are allowed to compete
with each other. The United States, of course, is not the
only nation with a democratic system of government, and
friction between church and state is hardly unique here.
However, here the conflict is carried on in the frame of
reference of a written constitution which sets forth the
basic rules for its resolution and a Supreme Court which interprets and applies these rules. It is the purpose of this
book to examine the conflict and how the Court** has acted

---

*Throughout this book "state" is used as a synonym of government; "State"
as one of the 50 constituents of the United States.
**Throughout this book, whenever "Court" is used, the United States
Supreme Court is referred to. If a different tribunal is intended, "court" is
used, unless its official name which includes "Court" is given, as "the New
York Court of Appeals."

to resolve it in six specific arenas. Our major concern will be with the contemporary scene, with the historic background set forth to the extent necessary to clarify the situation as it exists today. It need hardly be added that the Court's resolution in each case is of uncertain duration. This is so not only because the religious situation is dynamic and the nature of the conflict between religion and state is ever changing, just as religion and state are ever changing, but also because the Supreme Court itself is not a static institution and its decisions reflect these alterations in conditions as well as in the Court personnel. Moreover, constitutional principles, which are simply the Court's interpretations of the words in the Constitution, do not come full grown from a particular case but are developed by the Court from decision to decision. Hence, as we examine the confrontations between religion and state, we will become aware of the developing constitutional principles that govern their resolutions. However, before we can do this, we must first give some consideration to the nature of the contestants, the stakes, the referee, and the rules.

The Contestants

The contestants are, of course, religion and the state, but their characters have changed considerably since 1787 when we wrote a constitution for a new nation. It was written in the light of conditions as they then existed, but was fashioned with the expectation that it would last for a long time, if not, as John Marshall thought, forever. This indeed it did; it is today the oldest written constitution governing any nation in the world. It has been amended only sixteen times (the first ten amendments were really part of the original document, added to make it acceptable to the people). Of these, only the fourteenth effected a radical change in the relationship between the nation and its citizens in the context of the conflict of religion and state, and this perhaps only by interpretation of the Supreme Court rather than by the intent of those who framed the amendment. We will return to this and examine it more fully, but first we turn to the other contestant, religion, as it was in 1787 and is today.

God in 1787

What is most significant about religion in 1787 is the unimportance of the church. Undoubtedly the great majority of Americans, if asked, would have professed a belief in God and would have considered themselves religious. If pressed further, they would have identified themselves as Protestants, but affiliation with a particular church was the exception rather than the rule. According to the most reliable estimates, less than 15 percent of the population were members of churches when our republic was founded, as compared to almost 65 percent today.

Of the Protestant denominations, the two most prominent were the Congregationalist in New England and the Anglican (Protestant Episcopal) in the South. These were established churches; that is, they enjoyed a special, preferred status. However, though they both were established religions and professed Protestantism, they had little in common theologically, culturally, politically, or economically.

The Congregationalists brought to America the Puritan values of 17th and 18th century Calvinism. They were obsessed with the dogma of original sin. Men were inherently evil and, with the exception of a few whom God selected to save, were doomed to damnation. Accordingly, the idea that men should be free in matters of faith and morals was completely unacceptable, for if they were free to choose they would invariably choose error and evil, and, for the same reason, men of state must be subject to men of God. The Congregationalists' theocracy did not last long in America, but their church in Massachusetts was the last to become disestablished, and when this was finally achieved in 1833 it was over the strong opposition of the church elders.

Politically, the Congregationalists were the backbone

of the Revolution. Economically, they represented the rising trading and commercial classes. They espoused middle-class virtues—thrift, diligence, austerity, and truthfulness—and eschewed middle-class evils—lewdness, covetousness, vanity, and idleness.

Congregationalist Calvinism played a tremendous role in shaping America's cultural patterns, but the contributions of Anglicanism were comparatively insignificant. The religion and culture of Anglicanism suited the needs of the Southern plantation aristocracy (as they had those of the Tudor and Stuart aristocracies); whatever influence Anglicanism might have had on American culture vanished along with the disappearance of the plantation aristocracy. The Protestantism of the South was to become that of the popular denominations: the Baptists, Methodists, and other dissenting sects. Aristocratic Anglicanism had little to offer either the poor white tenant farmer or the poorer black slave. Besides, the Anglicans chose the losing side in the Revolution. Most of their clergy were not merely unsympathetic to it, but were ardent and active Loyalists, and with the success of the Revolution, followed quickly by the disestablishment of their church in Virginia, Anglicanism (renamed Episcopalianism) rapidly lost whatever influence it had previously exerted on Southern cultural patterns and moral standards.

Today, Episcopalians constitute a comparatively small, elitist group within Protestantism; and Congregationalism has completely disappeared as a separate denomination, having merged in 1957 with the Evangelical and Reformed Church to form the United Church of Christ. For a variety of reasons the expanding American frontier was not suited to established churches. It was the unestablished or dissenting sects, principally the Baptists and the Methodists, that enlisted the many millions who today make up American Protestantism.

The dissenting sects reflected a wide spectrum, from fundamentalist Baptists in the South to the Unitarians and

Universalists in New England and the Presbyterians, Mennonites, and Friends in the Middle Atlantic States. What they shared in common, aside from considering themselves part of Protestantism, was opposition to church establishment in the States and above all in the newly founded nation. Their opposition went far beyond a system of formal and preferential ties between the government and a particular church; they opposed any involvement of government in religious matters and were convinced that man's relationship to God was not and should not be within the scope of governmental concern.

Outside Protestantism, but within the conventional definition of recognized religions, were a small number of Roman Catholics and an even smaller number of Jews. Primarily, the former had come from England and France; the latter from Spain and Holland. There was, surprisingly, a rather friendly relationship between these groups and the Protestants; the anti-Catholicism of the 19th century and the anti-Semitism of the 20th were to come as aftermaths respectively of the influx of Irish in the 1830s and '40s and of East European Jews at the turn of the 20th century. Nevertheless, although Jews helped finance the Revolution and a Catholic was one of the signers of the Declaration of Independence, neither group played a significant role in shaping the new nation's political and cultural patterns.

The group which, along with Calvinist Congregationalists, made the greatest contribution to American cultural and political development was one that in 1787 could be called religious only by a most generous definition of the term. Variously called deists, humanists, and rationalists, they accepted the existence of God so long as He kept His hands out of human affairs. Strongly anti-clerical, they were at best indifferent to organized religion. One indication of their influence on the course of American development is the fact that none of the first seven Presidents was at the time of his election a member of any church, and, perhaps even more important, that the two basic documents of

American freedom, the Declaration of Independence, and the Bill of Rights, breathe the spirit of deistic humanism.

Deism was almost the diametrical opposite of Calvinism. It rejected the concept of original sin and asserted the inherent goodness of man. It assumed that given freedom—of belief, thought, speech, and association—men would choose the right thing. From that romantic and optimistic assumption flowed the other aspects of deism: its individualism; its anti-authoritarianism in church and state (it was the French-influenced anti-Federalists who were most opposed to and suspicious of strong government); its anti-clericalism; its secularism (concern only for this world); its egalitarianism ("All men are created equal," said the deist Jefferson in the Declaration of Independence); its faith in reason; its commitment to voluntarism; its libertarianism; and its insistence that religion is a matter of free election rather than inherited or imposed status. "No man," said John Locke, whose influence on American thought was immeasurable, "by nature is bound unto any particular church or sect, but everyone joins himself voluntarily to that society in which he believes he has found that profession and worship which is truly acceptable to God. A church is a society of members voluntarily uniting to that end."

God Today

We have noted that while only a small fraction of Americans in 1787 were affiliated with organized religious groups, today almost two-thirds of our population are in that category. The host of God has expanded tremendously, but for all things there is a price which even God has had to pay, and that price has been the acceptance of deism as one of His legitimate children—and perhaps even His favorite if not His first born. He has even had to suffer His long loyal and faithful children to debate whether He is or is not dead.

The influence of deism upon the conventional religions is most clear and dramatic in Protestantism. In colonial Massachusetts the legislature decreed that it was "the duty of the magistrate to take care that the people be fed with wholesome and sound doctrine"; pastors who preached in unauthorized churches were subject to appropriate penal action by the grand jury; Anne Hutchinson was exiled to her death because she affirmed a "covenant of grace" rather than a "covenant of works"; and, as late as the eve of the Revolution, Baptist preachers in Virginia were whipped, arrested, fined, and imprisoned on bread and water for preaching a theology deviating from that of established Anglicanism.

Today it seems Protestantism couldn't care less about theology, at least as that term is traditionally understood. In the Protestant camp the banner is ecumenicism and the cry is for union, not only within Protestantism but also with that ancient arch-enemy, Romanism. Protestants' main concerns today are not with theology and doctrine, but with war and peace, poverty, race relations, drug addiction, abortion, equality for women and homosexuals, and kindred social problems.

Of course, this is not the first time that Protestantism has been concerned with these problems. But the nature of that concern has changed sharply over the years, and the change has brought normative Protestantism away from Calvinism and close to deism. Nor does it mean that all Protestants have abandoned the old-fashioned religion and the traditional virtues; Billy Graham is still the most popular preacher in Christendom, and Jesus movements, particularly among the young, have been springing up all over the land. Indeed, it is these conflicts and tensions between the new and the old within religion that have been coming to the courts in increasing numbers for resolution in accordance with the Constitution as interpreted and applied by the Supreme Court.

Of the three major faiths in the United States, Judaism made perhaps the most far-reaching accommodation to deism. Proportionate to others (they make up less than 3 percent of the total population) far fewer Jews than Christians regularly attend religious services. Conversely, far more of them are actively engaged in civil rights movements, radical and liberal politics, and other libertarian causes, particularly in opposing censorship and seeking to maintain the separation of church and state.

Recently, there appears to be some backsliding within Jewry. On governmental aid to parochial schools, Orthodox Jewry has completely changed its position and now strongly favors it. Only Reform (liberal) organizations expressed consistent opposition to our involvement in Vietnam, Conservative (center) organizations remained quiet, and among the Orthodox the consensus probably favored a hawkish position. Jews have in the past been the most loyal and active allies of the Negroes in the latter's struggle for equality, but here too there has been a noticeable cooling of ardor, and with increasing frequency Jews find themselves opposing rather than supporting blacks in specific arenas such as racial quotas and preferential treatment in employment and education. The reasons for this change are manifold: the virtual disappearance of anti-Semitism, which makes the Jews' need for allies much less urgent; the explosion of nationalism resulting from the establishment of the State of Israel, which undercut a dovish position in respect to Vietnam and liberals' natural anti-Nixonism; the comparative affluence of Jews, which naturally enhances their stake in the existing order; and the resurgence of fundamentalist Orthodoxy, which is pushing not only Conservative but even to some extent Reform Judaism toward more traditional liturgy and ritualist practices just when Protestantism and Catholicism are moving in the opposite direction.

It is by no means certain that these changes are encompassing all Jews. On the contrary, there is good reason to believe that young Jews—of whom the overwhelming majority are in colleges and universities—maintain their loyalty to the libertarian ideals in which they were brought up by their now backsliding parents. What we may be witnessing is a widening gap and polarization between generations of American Jews.

Of the major faiths, Catholicism has been by far the most resistant to deistic change. Fortified by an ecclesiastically controlled educational system from elementary school through college, it was able for almost a century and a half to erect a wall around the faithful, insulating them from corrupting influences outside. Initially the Catholic community did not take willingly to this confinement, but Protestant and nativist hostility made of Catholic schools and other institutions places of refuge, and fostered an unquestioning loyalty to the priests and bishops, as well as to the doctrine they taught and the values they inculcated.

Nevertheless, even Catholicism could not remain unaffected by the deistic spirit of American political and social culture. During the 19th century there was a strong though ultimately unsuccessful effort by the Catholic community to democratize the structure of the Church and transfer much of the hierarchy's power over its temporal assets to the laity. At the end of the century, another effort at liberalization was brought to a sharp halt by an apostolic letter from Leo XIII condemning what he called "modernism" and "Americanism," and asserting that Americans, no less than all the other faithful, must adhere to the immutable doctrines of the Church which could not be set aside by individuals to conform to modern ideas of civil liberty. In the 1950s another attempt at modernization and liberalization emerged under the intellectual leadership of John Courtney Murray and led to thinly veiled accusations of heresy against him by the theologians on the faculty of Catholic University, particularly in respect to his efforts to modify the dogma that there is no salvation outside the Church.

The breakthrough occurred with the ascension of John XXIII and his call for the modernization of the Church, followed by the deliberations and decisions of Vatican Council II, which pointed to ecumenicism, liberalization, and democratization. A somewhat alarmed Paul VI tried to slow down, if not halt, the ensuing dynamic changes within Catholicism, but his efforts have been no more successful than those of King Canute in commanding the waves to recede from the shore. Within two decades after Pius XII proclaimed as infallible truth the bodily ascent into Heaven of the Virgin Mary, responsible Catholic theologians began seriously to re-examine the doctrine of the Virgin Birth itself and to hold formal dialogues with atheists; priests advised their parishioners to ignore an explicit papal encyclical and continue to practice contraceptive birth control, demanded an end to clerical celibacy and the right to elect their bishops, disrupted State legislative sessions because not enough attention was being paid to the needs of the racially and economically disadvantaged, poured animal blood or red paint on the records of draft boards in protest against the Vietnam War, and allegedly conspired to kidnap Henry Kissinger and blow up the underground heating system in the nation's capitol.

Nor have the Sisters been far behind. Many changed their traditional garb for the ordinary clothes worn by their lay sisters and enrolled in mixed classes at secular graduate schools. One can imagine, too, the feelings of Cardinal Spellman had he lived to see nuns picketing his St. Patrick's Cathedral in protest against the failure of the Church to speak up vigorously for an immediate end to the Vietnam War. Nor would he have been happy about the increasing number of them leaving the convents to get married (often to ex-priests) or to become actively and militantly involved in the affairs of the secular world.

The picture should not be overdrawn. Catholicism is still not Unitarianism, and an institution which has weathered two thousand years of storms and turmoil is not likely soon to disappear in a sea of deism.

Notwithstanding rising dissatisfaction within the Catholic community, the Church does not appear ready to abandon its parochial school system or political efforts to maintain it with tax-raised funds. Catholics are militantly active in opposing liberalized abortion laws and are generally unsympathetic if not hostile toward laws supporting equality for women. The Church is engaged in defending itself against invasions from without and convulsions from within, and the result often is the conflict which finds its way into the courts for resolution in accordance with the Constitution.

In considering encounters between religion and state, it should not be assumed that only the conventional religions—Protestantism, Catholicism, and Judaism—are the contestants. As will be seen throughout this book, it is often the less conventional faiths, those with few or even a single adherent, which clash with Caesar and appeal to the Supreme Court for the vindication of their rights. Moreover, the Court appears to be honoring the mandate in Deuteronomy not to be a respecter of persons in judgment. Indeed, it seems on occasion to be more solicitous of the claims of sects and sectarians outside the mainstream of American religion than of those within; the Catholic Church probably envies the successes of the Jehovah's Witnesses, the Amish, and individualistic conscientious objectors to military service in their appearances before the Supreme Court.

Caesar in 1787

Within the context of this book, Caesar in 1787 meant the national government. Not that there were no conflicts between religion and government in the States or that these did not reach the courts. But the new Constitution was intended to control primarily the operations of the national government rather than those of the States. Thus, although the First Amendment forbade the establishment of religion, Massachusetts retained its own Congregationalist establishment until 1833 and ended it then on its own volition without coercion or influence by the national government. In 1845 a priest was convicted of conducting funeral services at a chapel which was not licensed in accordance with

Louisiana law. He appealed to the United States Supreme Court claiming that this violated his right to the free exercise of religion as guaranteed by the First Amendment, but the Court, in the case of *Permoli* v. *New Orleans*, rejected his appeal on the ground that the amendment guaranteed a citizen's rights only against the Federal government, and, as far as the Constitution of the United States was concerned, the States were free to establish religion or prohibit its free exercise as they saw fit.

There were during this period some instances of tension between the national government and religion. In 1798 President Adams signed and the Senate ratified a treaty with Tripoli which stated in its preamble that "the government of the United States is not, in any sense, founded on the Christian religion." (These words were omitted from a superseding treaty entered into eight years later.) Unlike other Presidents, Jefferson and Jackson refused to proclaim days of national prayer or fasting, asserting that this was God's business, not Caesar's. Madison as President vetoed a measure which granted Federally owned land to a Baptist congregation for a church site, giving as his reason that this would violate the First Amendment's clause forbidding establishment of religion. In later years he indicated his opinion that the same clause made it improper for the government to exempt church-owned property from taxation. In 1829, Richard M. Johnson enhanced his popularity, helping later to achieve the vice-presidency, by chairing a Senatorial committee which rejected petitions that the mails not be delivered on Sundays. It based its rejection on the ground that our government is "a civil and not a religious institution."

However, none of these conflicts or similar ones came to the Supreme Court for resolution. It was not until 1878 that the Court first acted in its role of referee in encounters between religion and the national government when, in the case of *Reynolds* v. *United States*, it ruled that the Free Exercise Clause of the First Amendment did not prevent the government from prosecuting Mormons for violating territorial laws against polygamy.

Caesar Today

In 1868, although it may not have been recognized at the time, the foundation was laid for a great extension of the domain of the referee and the applicability of the rules in contests between God and Caesar. In that year the Fourteenth Amendment was added to the Constitution. Neither its background nor its wording gave much hint of any relevance to the relationship of government and religion. Its background lay in the Civil War, and its wording indicated only a purpose to insure the newly emancipated slaves full equality as American citizens. It forbade States to make or enforce any law abridging the privileges or immunities of American citizens, or to deprive any person of life, liberty, or property without due process of law, or deny to any person in their jurisdiction the equal protection of the laws. This says nothing about religion and it was not until 1940 that the Supreme Court held, in the case of *Cantwell* v. *Connecticut*, that the word "liberty" encompassed liberty not only of body but also of conscience.

Although the First Amendment said that *"Congress shall make no law . . . prohibiting the free exercise"* of religion, neither could the States make such a law. (Earlier the Court had held that under the amendment the States were forbidden equally with the Federal government from abridging freedom of speech or of the press.) Seven years later, in *Everson* v. *Board of Education*, the Court held that "liberty" included freedom from established religion, and therefore States could no more make laws respecting an establishment of religion than could Congress.

It is difficult to overestimate the significance of this development. Most points of contact and, hence, arenas of potential conflict between religion and government are in the field of State rather than Federal activities. (Almost the only occasions in which the Supreme Court intervened in confrontations between religion and government involved Mormons in the territories, and, in respect to territories, Congress stood in the same position as the legislature in a State.)

Education, for example, is a prime source of conflict, since it covers religion in the public schools and governmental financing of parochial schools, and education has traditionally been primarily the responsibility of the States. It is therefore not surprising that the overwhelming majority of cases reaching the Supreme Court concerning the relation of religion and government have involved States rather than the Federal government.

Another factor helps explain why appeals to the Supreme Court to referee and determine conflicts between religion and government have become so numerous in the 20th century. Contacts between government (Federal and State) and individuals have multiplied tremendously. If we have not yet become a welfare state, we are not too far from it and are apparently approaching it rapidly. Matters which have long been considered private are increasingly becoming the concern of government. Universal public education, which marked the beginning of this development, was of course a product of the 19th century; but health, poverty, family relations, race relations (beyond the abolition of slavery), and other areas of welfare are now accepted as being within the scope of governmental responsibility.

When Caesar thus expands his boundaries, encroachments upon what God has traditionally deemed to be His territory necessarily multiply. What happens when Caesar commands parents to provide inoculations or blood transfusions for their children and God commands the contrary; when Caesar dictates you shall send your children to school and there they shall learn about evolution, and God says "thou shalt not" to both; when Caesar says you must not for your health's sake work on Sunday, and God says the sabbath must be on Saturday? What happens, of course, is that these and similar conflicts of commands are apt ultimately to come to the Supreme Court for resolution, as these in fact have.

But it is not only in the area of welfare that contacts and attendant conflicts between church and state have multiplied in recent years. War, like welfare, has become a way of American life. Since 1941 our nation has been at war for almost twice as many years as it has not. (In the 154 years between 1787 and 1941 we were at war for only 11 years, and those included the 4 years during which we were at war with ourselves.) Even during the years when we are technically at peace, we are preparing for war; peacetime military conscription, which would have shocked the fathers of our Constitution, is accepted as perfectly permissible today. And here again the consequence is often a conflict between a pacifistic God and a militaristic Caesar to be resolved by the Supreme Court.

The Individual Against God and Caesar

While we have been primarily concerned with conflicts between God and Caesar, there are many instances in which they appear to be allies. These situations, too, reach the Supreme Court and are accepted by it for determination even though the rules (the Constitution) expressly provide that the referee (the Court) may not intervene unless an actual conflict ("case or controversy") is presented to it. As we shall see, the Court has found that a conflict does exist in these situations warranting its intervention.

On the face of it, the conflict is between the individual on one side and both government and religion on the other. His grievance may be that the taxes he is forced by government to pay are used by it to propagate the teachings of religion in public or in private schools. Or it may be that because government relieves religious institutions from paying taxes on the property they own, his own enforced contribution to the upkeep of the government is thereby increased. Or he may have no use for religion at all, considering himself no part of it, and objects to being pushed into it by the government, of which he is a part.

The conflict, however, may be looked at in another way. America assumes that God can and does speak through deism (which literally means Godism) as well as through Christianity or Judaism. According to deism, God, if He does exist, created man and the world and told them thereafter to solve their own problems. When, therefore, government involves itself in religious affairs it is violating the command of the deists' God no less than it violates the Jehovah's Witnesses' God when it orders them to provide blood transfusions for their children.

It really does not matter how the issue is put. Conflict there is, and in our democratic scheme of things it must be resolved peaceably and in accordance with the rules as interpreted and applied by the referee.

The Stakes

For God

Religious groups are what political scientists call interest groups and what laymen call pressure groups. Interest groups are associations of individuals that share some common attitude and engage in continuing, structured activity to protect and advance their own position in society and to promote the attitude they share. Some interest groups concentrate on the former objective: the traditional bread-and-butter trade unions strive to raise the wages and improve the working conditions of their members; the National Association for the Advancement of Colored People (NAACP) seeks to protect and advance the interest of Negroes; the National Organization for Women (NOW) is concerned with achieving equality for women; the National Association of Manufacturers (NAM) strives for more profits for capitalists. These and similar associations may be called self-interest interest groups.

Other interest groups emphasize the second objective —promoting the attitude they share, or, in less technical language, seeking to reform society. A league to abolish capital punishment is not likely to have any members who will personally benefit from the abolition of the death penalty, and it may be assumed that the members of the Women's Christian Temperance Union are all teetotalers. Such groups are known as ideological interest groups.

Religious groups partake of both characteristics. When Catholics seek funds for their schools, or Christian Scientists lobby for the exemption of their children from attending the required health science courses in the public schools, or Seventh-Day Adventists urge amendment of Blue Laws to allow them to keep their stores open on Sundays, or Black Muslims claim the right to send their ministers into prisons to provide their faithful with spiritual assistance, or Orthodox Jews demand kosher food in the public school lunch programs, they are in all cases acting as self-interest interest groups. On the other hand, when Catholics lobby against liberalization of abortion, or Protestant denominations withdraw their deposits from banks which invest in South Africa, or Unitarian Universalists publish the Pentagon Papers, they are all acting as ideological interest groups.

In the encounters with government which find their way toward resolution by the Supreme Court, religion has great stakes in both capacities. Orthodox Jews intervene on the side of the defense in suits challenging governmental aid to religious schools because they believe that without such aid their schools cannot survive, and without their schools Judaism cannot survive. The National Council of Churches filed a brief as *amicus curiae* (friend of the court) opposing a challenge to the tax exemption of church-owned property because it claimed that without it many churches could not survive. Jehovah's Witnesses do not object to flag salute exercises in the public schools, but want to insure that their children not be compelled to participate (else they risk their salvation).

These are great stakes—survival and salvation—and it is quite understandable that religion strives for them not only in the political but in the judicial arena as well. But these are not the only stakes in the controversies between religion and government which are brought to the Supreme Court. Churches and even religions are not ends in themselves; they are instruments to achieve God's will on earth. Court suits are brought and defended to protect these instruments and to enable them more effectively to carry out their sacred missions.

Religious groups, avowedly or not, seek to translate their own hierarchy of values into categorical imperatives for the society at large, including those members of the community outside of their respective folds. Each religious group, consciously or unconsciously, attempts to shape the culture of the community according to its own concept of the good life. Catholics, or at least those in the mainstream of traditional Catholicism, hope for an America in which, if not all will be Catholics, all will adhere to Catholic values: no divorce, no contraception, no abortion, no obscene books or pictures, no homosexuality, everybody worshiping God in his own way, government solicitous of and helpful to religion, and children and adults equally obedient to their parents and to lawful authority. Fundamentalist Protestants and Orthodox Jews probably share most of these hopes. Others—liberal Protestants, liberal Jews, and deists—seek a different America: one in which individuals enjoy maximum freedom of thought and expression, contraception is used and encouraged to control population and avoid the birth of babies that are unwanted or cannot adequately be cared for, women's right to control their own bodies is recognized and respected, the sexual practices of adults, whether of the same or of different sexes, are of no concern to anyone but themselves, governmental institutions avoid manifestations of religiosity, public schools are free of sectarianism, and citizens are not forced to fight in a war they deem immoral or in any war.

Since government is the most effective means of translating particular values into universal rules of conduct, religious groups will quite naturally seek to prevail upon government to accept their values and impose them on all. When the Supreme Court upheld the conviction of Mormons for polygamy, it said that such practices were not acceptable in a Christian nation; but the classic example is Protestantism's temporary success in achieving adoption of the Prohibition Amendment. Another is to be found in the anti-gambling and anti-lottery laws which still exist in greater or lesser degree in all States in the Union, with the possible exception of Nevada, and which clearly reflect Calvinist values. Indeed, the typical State penal code, particularly in its provisions concerning sexual morality, is an Old Testament code mediated through Puritan Calvinists (who branded women found in adultery but did not stone them) and now most ardently defended by Roman Catholics.

For Caesar

This, however, is a two-way street. As religion seeks to use government to further its purposes, so does government try to use religion to promote governmental ends. Often religion will be as willing a partner in a governmental enterprise as government in a religious one, as when religion supplies chaplains for the armed forces or members of its clergy preach sermons supporting some specific national policy. Sometimes religion proves to be an unwilling partner or even an antagonist, as when a church body issues a resolution calling for the withdrawal of armed forces from Indochina or sends food and drugs to North Vietnam through Canada.

Government, however, seeks to utilize religion for broader purposes than such a specific enterprise as a particular war. A reasonable argument can be made for the proposition that in a democracy government should not have or promote values, but should limit itself to insuring an open society in which all groups and individuals are free to promote their own values and persuade others to adopt them. This is probably what President Eisenhower had in mind when he expressed lack of sympathy with anti-discrimination laws and asserted that racial prejudice could not be eliminated by force of law.

Governments, however, are made of men, and men do have values which they cherish deeply and believe should be embraced by all. Even in a democracy it will be inevitable that they will seek to utilize the instrumentalities of the government to universalize these values and make them the policy of the commonwealth. One of these values in the United States has been anti-communism, and we have used the Voice of America, Radio Free Europe, and countless other communication organs to promote it. Another is democracy itself, and there is hardly a civics textbook in use in any public school in the nation which does not propound its virtues. Racial equality, especially in the Northern States, is another such value, and the public school textbooks reflect that, too.

It is therefore not surprising that as religion seeks to enlist government in the effectuation of religious ideology, government will make a corresponding effort to effectuate its ideology through the substantial influence that religion exercises on the millions who profess allegiance to both. Hence, dominion over the values for which men live and sometimes die is the great stake for both God and Caesar in the contest between them.

There is another dimension to the contest. Government is power and it is the nature of power to expand. Those who wrote our Constitution (not only the 1787 text, but also the 1791 appendix, popularly known as the Bill of Rights) recognized this, feared it, and sought to guard against it. They did this by such devices as separation of powers, checks and balances, and, in the Tenth Amendment, the express reservation in the States and the people of all powers not delegated in the Constitution to the national government. They did it also in another way: in the Establishment and Free Exercise clauses of the First Amendment, which they intended to be a mandate to the government to keep its hands off religion.

In a totalitarian state there are no such restrictions; by its own definition the totality of man's life is within the power of the state, and this includes his religious life. Even in Communist states, where religion is deemed the enemy of the people and therefore to be destroyed, as long as it exists it is subject to government control and utilization. In a democracy, and particularly the American democracy, some areas of man's life are deemed too important or sacred to be entrusted to government, and chief among these are his relations to God—therefore, the Establishment and Free Exercise clauses.

But clauses in the Constitution are not self-enforcing; they can become what Madison once called a parchment barrier. The thirst for power is a potent force even in a democracy, and the state will be tempted and will yield to the temptation of seeking to exercise dominion over religion for no other reason than because it is there. Thus, in a real sense, what is at stake in the contest between God and Caesar is not only ideology and value but power as well.

The Referee

Inevitably religion will attempt to use government for religious purposes. Such efforts will be resisted by other religious groups or by individual citizens, but, whichever side is successful in the legislative and executive branches, the controversy is likely to end up in the courts. Following the Supreme Court's decision in 1968 upholding a New York law that provided for public financing of textbooks used in parochial schools, there occurred an explosion of State legislative enactments to subsidize the operations of these schools, followed almost immediately in most instances by a lawsuit challenging the enactment. On the other hand, when the Missouri legislature refused to enact such a measure, claiming it would be violative of the State constitution, and the executive department (through the commissioner of education) refused for the same reason to assign publicly employed teachers to perform their services within parochial schools, the Catholic Church in each instance sponsored or supported a suit in the Federal courts challenging the refusals.

In Connecticut, the legislature refused to repeal or even liberalize the State's anti-abortion law, and a lawsuit was brought challenging the constitutionality of the statute. In New York, the legislature did pass a repealing law, and a Catholic professor instituted a suit challenging the repealer. Efforts to persuade legislatures to repeal laws making homosexual practices penal offenses proving unsuccessful, homosexual groups have petitioned the courts to declare the laws unconstitutional, and in one case have sought (unsuccessfully) to obtain a court order compelling an unwilling municipal clerk to marry two males, and thus confer upon them the legal status of conventionally married couples.

What all this signifies is that in the confrontation between religion and the state both parties look to the judiciary as the final arbiter whose judgment will be honored by both. Both could well ask, as the Israelites asked of Moses, "Who made you a prince and judge over us?" If the question were asked, many historians and constitutional scholars would say that the only honest answer would be "I," the "I" being John Marshall in his 1803 decision for the Supreme Court in *Marbury* v. *Madison*. Certainly nothing in the Constitution can be read by ordinary laymen (by whom after all it was adopted and made the supreme law of the land) to empower the judiciary to declare invalid an act of the legislature or the executive, State or Federal.

It is particularly paradoxical that religion should accept the courts, and specifically the Supreme Court, as the referee in its contests with the state, for the courts are part of the state. The justices of the Supreme Court are appointed by the President and confirmed by the Senate; their salaries are paid out of the Federal treasury in amounts fixed by Congress, which retains the power to remove them from their office through impeachment. It is unusual, to say the least, for a referee to be in the employ and pay of one of the contestants.

Moreover, the authority of the referee in the contest between God and Caesar is exceptionally broad. He not only applies the rules but interprets them, and since the rules basically consist of but sixteen words ("Congress shall make no law respecting an establishment of religion or prohibiting the free exercise thereof"), the authority is practically open-ended; in fact, his function as he carries it out seems more to be making the rules than interpreting them. If this were not enough, it should be noted that he does not formulate the rules all at one time but seems to make them as he goes along to fit each case as it arises, and manifests little hesitation in changing them from case to case as the occasion presents itself.

Despite this, religion does on the whole accept the Supreme Court's decisions, sometimes over some bitter protest, and sometimes with efforts to evade them; but accept them it does, in the sense that it does not call upon its faithful or upon the state openly to defy them. On the contrary, its leading spokesmen will on occasion urge both not to seek to nullify them by constitutional amendment (as in the case of the Bible-prayer decisions).

There are a number of explanations for this. In the first place, the Supreme Court is the ultimate arbiter not only of controversies between religion or religious individuals and the state; long before religion was summoned to it, the Court had established its authority to determine conflicts within the state (i.e., between the national and State governments or between different branches of the same government) and between citizens and the state in matters having no relation to religion. In the second place, both the Constitution and the justices of the Court have as much as possible sought to remove the justices from control of the state. The Constitution does this by withholding from the President the power to remove the justices he has appointed, and from Congress the power to lower their salaries once they have been fixed. The justices have done this by scrupulously avoiding involvement in political affairs or (with a few exceptions) even advising the President or Congress on the wisdom or constitutionality of measures they are considering adopting.

Finally, there is really no alternative; avoidance of internecine warfare in the inevitable and continuing conflicts involving God and Caesar depends upon the availability of an arbiter in whom both parties have trust and to whom they can turn. This is so whether the conflict is between them or within the ranks of either. Take, as an example, a conflict within the ranks of Caesar.

In the 1840s, the poor people of Rhode Island, unenfranchised by reason of a pre-Revolutionary charter which limited the right to vote to landowners, decided to take the Declaration of Independence seriously and established their own government. Bloodshed could have been avoided if the Federal courts, which enjoyed the trust and confidence of both sides, had accepted responsibility for deciding which was the legitimate government of Rhode Island. They refused to do so; the Supreme Court ruled (in the 1849 case of *Luther* v. *Borden*) that the question was a political rather than a legal one and hence not within the courts' competence. The result was riot and bloodshed before the controversy finally was determined by force of arms.

For an early example of a case of conflict between church and state we go back to the reign of Henry II in the 12th century. The controversy between Henry and Thomas à Becket, Archbishop of Canterbury, revolved primarily on their differences regarding the proper domains of church and state. One aspect concerned ownership of estates which the Church claimed (and Henry denied) had been willed to it by the deceased owners. Neither Henry nor Becket would of course accept the other as arbiter, and one who was of neither church nor state was obviously not obtainable. A solution was found in referring the disputes to a judge who owed fealty to both parties, and therefore being bipartial could be impartial. What was done was to select twelve subjects, loyal to both king and church, and abide by their decision in each case (a procedure which ultimately developed into the jury system).

Another aspect of the controversy was not amenable to so satisfactory a settlement. It involved Becket's refusal to accede to Henry's claim that clerics, like all other persons who commit secular crimes, were to be tried in the king's courts. The dispute culminated in the assassination of Becket and the ensuing bitter conflict between Henry and the Papacy.

In 11th century England the rivalry between Erastian nationalism and theocracy was still unresolved, but by the 16th and 17th centuries the struggle was just about over. No nation would accept religion as final arbiter of conflicts between the two, or even of conflicts within religion. The Peace of Augsburg of 1555, whereby Lutherans and Catholics in the German states effected a compromise according to the formula (*cujus regio, ejus religio*), whereby the religion of a province was determined by that of its prince, was based on the Erastian concept.

The American Constitution rejected both theocracy and Erastianism. Moreover, neither the Henry-Becket resolution by assassination and excommunication or the Augsburg formula could work. Since there were in the nation and in the States many religions, but in each case only one government, the people by necessity had to assign to government the responsibility of determining conflicts between the two and within each, with the hope that the men of government chosen to discharge it would divorce themselves to the utmost possible extent from the rest of the government and from their own predilections—political and religious.

By and large the choice of the judiciary as final authority in resolving conflicts between God and Caesar has worked well. We have avoided the suppression of religion that has been the experience of totalitarian states, fascist and communist. We have avoided, too, the bloody inter-religious conflicts of Northern Ireland, India, Pakistan, and other countries. We have not suffered, in the arena of religion, the terrible bloodshed of the Civil War in a still unfinished history of resolution of racial conflict. Despite their strong differences on the issues which are the subject of this book, religious groups in the United States live harmoniously with each other and with the nonreligious and even anti-religious. There are a number of explanations for this happy history, not the least, of course, is the pervasive deist ethic in which religious differences and religion itself play a minor role. (It was not so long ago that, when a white girl in what is known as the "Bible belt" related to her mother that the Bible had not been read that morning in school, she might be told, "Don't bother me now; don't you see I'm busy?" whereas if she said, "A black boy sat next to me in school today," the mother might faint.) Nevertheless, a significant part of the explanation lies in the trust which both God and Caesar have reposed in the Court to apply the rules of the conflict, and in the way it has justified that trust.

The Rules

Written, Unwritten, and Rewritten

As has been indicated, the rules of the contest are basically the opening words of the First Amendment: "Congress shall make no law respecting an establishment of religion or prohibiting the free exercise thereof." But these words added nothing in substance to the Constitution as written four years earlier, nor were they intended to. Instead, they made explicit what was implicit in the original document, namely, that Caesar was to have no traffic with God or, as Madison phrased it, that there should be "a separation between religion and government" (a broader and more accurate phrasing than Jefferson's "separation of church and state").

That this was the intent of the framers of the Constitution is evidenced by the fact that during the four months the members of the constitutional convention met in Philadelphia, not once did they engage in prayer. More important testimony is the text of the Preamble to the Constitution, which, in listing the six purposes of the new government, deliberately and carefully limited itself to secular purposes and did not even include, as the radical Declaration of Independence did, an invocation to God and an acknowledgment of man's dependence upon Him. Indeed, the Constitution itself does not mention God; it is literally a "Godless" instrument. It does once mention religion, or more accurately "religious," but only because it was necessary to do so in order to exclude it. Article VI requires that all government officials take an oath to support the Constitution, but lest Congress be tempted to add a religious element, it provides further that "no religious test shall ever be required as a qualification to any office or public trust under the United States." (The phrase "So help me God," often added by oath takers, is purely a matter of custom; it neither is nor can be required by law.)

The reason the Constitution itself did not forbid establishment of religion or prohibition of its free exercise was that it was not deemed necessary. The Federal government would have only such powers as were delegated to it in the Constitution, and nowhere in that instrument was there any grant of power to deal with religion by way of its establishment or its exercise. The same rationale explained the absence from the Constitution of any provision for the safeguarding of other rights, such as freedom of speech and press, but the explanation did not satisfy the people to whom the Constitution was presented for approval. They were not satisfied with security by implication; they demanded and won a promise by the promoters of the Constitution that a Bill of Rights, expressly securing the people's freedoms, would be added by amendment. The promise was kept, and so it came about that government (originally only Federal, but later State as well) was forbidden to make laws establishing religion or prohibiting its free exercise.

Under the scheme of things envisioned by Marshall in *Marbury* v. *Madison,* when a controversy between God and Caesar reaches the Court regarding a law passed by Congress, all it need do is examine the law to see whether it is one respecting an establishment of religion or prohibiting its free exercise, and, if it finds that it is either of these, it declares the law invalid, thus ending the matter. Unfortunately, its task is not quite so simple. The words "respecting an establishment of religion" are not clear and precise or self-defining. While the words "prohibiting the free exercise" are no doubt clear, they certainly cannot mean literally what they say; the constitutional fathers could not have intended to forbid Congress from prohibiting human sacrifice by a religious cult in the District of Columbia. Since the words of the Constitution cannot in all cases be clearly understood, there had to be a Supreme Court to interpret and apply the written rules governing encounters between church and state.

The Court does not merely interpret the rules; it expands them, as indeed it must in view of their cryptic incisiveness and the ever-multiplying and changing nature of the confrontations between religion and government which the Court must resolve. How else, for example, can the Court determine the constitutionality of religious teachings or practices in the public schools in accordance with rules written when there were no public schools? On occasion the Court must even rewrite the rules. In the 1961 case of *Torcaso* v. *Watkins,* it ruled that to deny an atheist the right to be appointed to the office of notary public would violate the clause against prohibiting the free exercise of religion, thus rewriting the amendment to encompass the free exercise of nonreligion or anti-religion.

In short, while the Constitution provides formal methods for its amendment, the Supreme Court can be considered a *de facto* continuing convention expanding or rewriting the Constitution as the need arises. This, of course, applies not only to the Establishment and Free Exercise clauses but to all other parts of the Constitution, and explains why it has remained, with so few formal amendments, a vital and viable charter for almost two centuries.

Free Exercise

It was the Free Exercise Clause which first reached the Court for interpretation and application. This occurred in 1878 when the Court ruled against the polygamous Mormons in *Reynolds* v. *United States*. The Constitution, the Court said, assures freedom to believe, but actions remain subject to governmental regulation; the Mormons can believe anything they want, but engaging in marriage constitutes action and as such is subject to restriction by the state to conform with the moral standards of the community.

This belief-yes–action-no rule, however, proves unsatisfactory for a number of reasons. In the first place, it is directly contrary to the written rule, which protects the free *exercise* of religion, a word that surely connotes action. In the second place, if only belief is encompassed, the amendment offers little help to the nonbeliever, for, as the common law adage had it, the Devil himself knows not the thoughts of man, and all the nonbeliever need do is to keep his thoughts to himself.

In two cases, the Court held that expression of belief, and even associating with persons of the same belief, may constitute action subject to governmental restriction. In *Davis* v. *Beason*, decided in 1890, the Court upheld the constitutionality of a statute which deprived not merely the practitioners but also the teachers of polygamy of the right to vote in general elections. Moreover, the Court affirmed the conviction of a Mormon for voting even though the indictment under which he was convicted did not charge him with practicing polygamy or even teaching it, but only with voting in an election while he was a member of the Church of Jesus Christ of Latter Day Saints, a sect that he knew taught and counseled polygamy. In the second case, *In re Black*, the Court in 1955 refused to disturb a decision by a Utah court depriving parents of the custody of their children because they persisted in teaching them the orthodox Mormon tenets respecting polygamy.

Even if the Court had decided otherwise in both cases and upheld the right to teach or associate with those who teach, the Free Exercise Clause would have added little if anything to what the First Amendment otherwise protected, namely freedom of speech (as in both the *Davis* and *Black* cases) and freedom of association (as in the *Davis* case). Therefore, if the Free Exercise Clause is to have any effective significance, it must mean something different from or in addition to believing, expressing what you believe, and associating with those who share your beliefs. Finally, even if expression and association were protected by the Free Exercise Clause, it would still mean that while a Cromwellian legislature could not forbid attendance at mass nor recital of the prayers therein, it could forbid partaking of the bread and wine, for surely that is action.

Another effort at defining the Free Exercise rule was made by Justice Frankfurter in 1940 in the case of *Minersville School District* v. *Gobitis*. The clause, he said, goes beyond protecting merely freedom of belief, even if that includes expression of the belief and associating with those who share it. It forbids laws aimed at specific religious actions or religious groups, but it does not forbid general, secular laws which happen to impinge upon the beliefs or practices of a particular person or religious group. According to Frankfurter, the anti-polygamy law in the *Reynolds* case was upheld not because it concerned action rather than belief, but because it was a valid, general law regulating the secular practice of marriage. Thus, a law forbidding drinking wine at mass would be unconstitutional, but there would be nothing unconstitutional in applying to priests at mass a general law forbidding all persons to drink intoxicating liquors including wine. For this reason, Frankfurter held in the *Gobitis* case, children of Jehovah's Witnesses could constitutionally be expelled from public school for refusing because of religious reasons to participate in the patriotic (secular) program of flag salute.

While all but one member of the Court agreed with Frankfurter in the *Gobitis* case, the general or secular rule was found to be too constricting and failed to give religious freedom the breadth which it was believed the constitutional fathers wanted it to have, and to which American libertarianism thought it was entitled. In any event, the *Gobitis* decision was itself overruled within three years (in the case of *West Virginia State Board of Education* v. *Barnette*), and the rule on which it was based does not seem thereafter to have been applied again, or strongly urged even by Frankfurter. Instead, the majority of the Court borrowed the "clear and present danger" rule from the decisions interpreting another freedom of the First Amendment—that of speech.

That freedom too is set forth in the amendment in absolutist and unqualified terms: "Congress shall make *no* law . . . abridging freedom of speech." Yet, the Court said in a classic case, this cannot mean that freedom of speech is absolute, any more than freedom of religion can be absolute; it cannot mean that one may not be punished for falsely crying "Fire!" in a crowded theater. What the amendment means is that no person may be punished for speaking, unless what he says and the situation in which he says it constitute a clear and present danger of causing grave harm to the state or the people, as death and injuries in a groundless panic. Applying this rule to the Free Exercise cases, it can readily be seen that refusal of some Jeho-

vah's Witness children to participate in the flag-salute exercise does not give rise to a clear and present danger to the
nation's security, whereas such a danger to the safety of a
community would be presented by the refusal of Christian
Scientist children to be inoculated during a raging epidemic.

Frankfurter was never satisfied with the clear and
present danger rule; he proposed instead a different rule,
also taken from other freedoms secured in the Bill of Rights.
When a person complains that his constitutional rights have
been infringed upon by some law or action of the state, it
is the responsibility of the courts to weigh the importance of
the particular right in issue as against the state's interest
upon which its law or action is based. For example, the right
of an objector not to violate his religious conscience by engaging in war must be weighed against the nation's interest
in defending itself against foreign enemies, and, in such
weighing, the latter interest must obviously be adjudged the
heavier.

The majority of the Court appears to have accepted
Frankfurter's rule but, after his retirement in 1962, added
an element which has almost turned it around. Frankfurter
was of the view that a citizen who challenged the constitutionality of state action had the burden of convincing the
court that his interest was more important than that of the
state and should therefore be adjudged paramount. When
can an individual's right be superior to the state's interest?
This was a particularly heavy burden to carry, but it was
made even heavier by Frankfurter's insistence that any
doubt as to the relative weights must be resolved in favor
of the state, and only where its action is patently unreasonable may the courts set it aside.

The majority members of the Court have taken a more
libertarian approach in recent years. It is the state, the
Court has held, that must persuade it that the values the
state seeks to protect are weightier; the state must, in the
language of the decisions, establish that it has a compelling
interest that justifies infringement upon the citizen's right

to the free exercise of his religion. If it fails to do so, its law or action will be adjudged unconstitutional.

Two cases, decided within two years of each other, vividly illustrate the difference in the approaches. In *Braunfeld* v. *Brown*, one of the four Sunday Law Cases of 1961, the Court upheld the constitutionality of a Sunday closing law which made no exception in favor of Sabbatarians who kept their places of business closed on Saturdays. The opinion, which, though written by Chief Justice Warren, clearly reflected Frankfurter's views, was based upon the determination that the state's interest in insuring effective enforcement of its closing law by requiring everybody to observe it was weightier than the Sabbatarian's interest in opting for Saturday closing, and that the state did not act unreasonably since it would be difficult to insure that persons opting for Saturday closing do so for religious rather than economic considerations. On the other hand, after Frankfurter retired from the bench, the Court held in the case of *Sherbert* v. *Verner* (in an opinion written by Justice Brennan, who had dissented in the *Braunfeld* case) that the State of South Carolina had not established a compelling interest sufficient to justify its denial of unemployment compensation benefits to a Sabbatarian who refused to accept a position requiring her to work on Saturdays.

It is the compelling-interest rule to which the present Court appears committed. It was by this rule that the Court, in the 1972 case of *Wisconsin* v. *Yoder*, held, in expressly rejecting the belief-action rule, that Amish parents could not be prosecuted for refusing to send their children to school after they had completed the elementary grades. "Only those interests of the highest order," the Court said, "and those not otherwise served can overbalance the legitimate claim to the free exercise of religion." Thus, where action is based on sincere religious (rather than intellectual or philosophic) belief, it may not be forbidden by the state unless it endangers a secular interest of the highest order (such as the preservation of life) which can be protected

in no other way. How long the rule will prevail no one
can of course predict; but so long as it does, it appears to
afford a degree of freedom for the exercise of religion
but little short of an impossible holding that the freedom
is absolute and subject to no government regulation or
restriction.

Establishment

It was almost three-quarters of a century after the
Court first started exploring for a workable rule under
the Free Exercise Clause that it embarked on a similar ex-
ploration for the Establishment Clause. The outcome, however, was startlingly different. Whereas in the *Reynolds* case
the Court announced a rule (belief-action) which rendered
the Free Exercise Clause practically meaningless, in the
Everson case in 1947 it proclaimed a rule for the Establishment Clause which, at least according to its critics, was
unrealistically and impractically absolutist. Here is the rule
in the words of its author, Justice Black (who consistently
asserted that the First Amendment rights were absolute):

> The "establishment of religion" clause of the First Amend-
> ment means at least this. Neither a State nor the Federal
> Government can set up a church. Neither can pass laws
> which aid one religion, aid all religions, or prefer one reli-
> gion over another. Neither can force nor influence a person
> to go to or remain away from church against his will or
> force him to profess a belief or disbelief in any religion.
> No person can be punished for entertaining or professing
> religious beliefs or disbeliefs, for church attendance or non-
> attendance. No tax in any amount, large or small, can be
> levied to support any religious activities or institutions,
> whatever they may be called, or whatever form they may
> adopt to teach or practice religion. Neither a State nor the
> Federal Government can, openly or secretly, participate in
> the affairs of any religious organizations or groups and
> vice versa. In the words of Jefferson, the clause against
> establishment of religion by law was intended to erect "a
> wall of separation between church and state."

This rule has variously been called the "*Everson*," "no aid," "absolute," and "wall of separation" rule or test. In essence it imposes two obligations upon government: (1) to maintain neutrality not merely among religions ("prefer one religion over another") but also between religion and nonreligion ("aid all religions"); and (2) to avoid involvement in religious affairs ("participate in the affairs of any religious organizations or groups").

Neither of these commands, critics contend, is possible or even desirable. Suppose a congregation splits and each faction claims to represent the true faith and hence is entitled to possession of the church land, building, and other assets. The only way the state can avoid becoming involved is by letting the controversy be decided by the jungle law of force, which obviously in a civilized society it cannot do. Or, to take an example suggested in the *Everson* decision itself, if a fire breaks out in a church, is the city forbidden to send its firemen and apparatus to put it out lest it thereby "aid" the church?

Because of criticisms such as these and because the Court's general dislike for absolutes (Black's understanding of the First Amendment never won the acceptance of a majority), the *Everson* rule, although quoted fully as above in three other decisions before 1963, has not been so quoted since (although individual phrases from it have been cited). In its place, the Court in that year formulated a new rule (though based on language in *McGowan* v. *Maryland*, one of the Sunday Law decisions, which quoted in full the *Everson* rule), which too merits quoting in full. It appears in the opinion written for the Court by Justice Clark in the case of *Abington School District* v. *Schempp* as follows:

> The test may be stated as follows: what are the purpose and primary effect of the enactment? If either is the ad- vancement or inhibition of religion, then the enactment exceeds the scope of legislative power as circumscribed by the Constitution. That is to say that to withstand the strictures of the Establishment Clause there must be a

secular legislative purpose and primary effect that neither advances nor inhibits religion.

This rule has been quoted in full and applied only in one other case, *Board of Education* v. *Allen*, decided in 1968. There the Court upheld the constitutionality of a law allowing a State to furnish free textbooks for use in parochial schools because both its purpose and primary effect were secular (i.e., helping children get a better secular education), and neither advanced nor inhibited religion. Barely two years later, the Court expanded the *Schempp* purpose-effect rule. In *Walz* v. *Tax Commission*, the Court, speaking through Chief Justice Burger, announced another rule. The Establishment Clause, he said, forbids governmental action which (a) has as its purpose the advancement or inhibition of religion, or (b) the principal effect of which is the advancement or inhibition of religion, or (c) results in excessive government entanglement with religion.

The Rules and the Referee

What does this all mean? Indeed, does it really mean anything? Rules, after all, do not decide cases; judges do, and an examination of the cases discussed in this book seems to lead to the conclusion that judges do not let rules stand in the way of deciding a particular case the way they want to. They can, if they wish, simply ignore the rule they themselves propounded. This, in fact, is what the dissenting justices in the *Everson* case charged Black with doing. After declaring that the Establishment Clause forbids all governmental aid to religion, he held nevertheless that the State of New Jersey could constitutionally pay the costs of transportation to parochial schools, which certainly aided those schools and thus the Catholic religion. Or, if a rule is too conspicuous to be ignored, it can easily be changed, as we have seen in respect to the rules under both the Free Exercise and Establishment clauses.

Judges decide cases, and judges are not immortal. Within three years after the *Gobitis* flag salute case was decided two justices left the Court and were replaced. The result of this (together with a change of mind by three of the remaining justices) was a completely contrary decision. A year after Frankfurter retired, the Court began expressing and applying a considerably more understanding and sympathetic approach to the rights of Sabbatarians and other religious minorities.

Does this all mean that, notwithstanding their sound and fury, rules signify nothing, and that frankness impels a conclusion that judges do decide cases the way they wish? Not at all. It must always be remembered that the basic rules are not the ones promulgated by the Court but those implicit in the Constitution and explicit in the First Amendment. To the extent that they are expressed, in the Establishment and Free Exercise clauses, it is in broad generalities; yet they point clearly the direction in which the nation and the Supreme Court should go.

On the whole, the Court has been faithful to these basic rules and has traveled in the direction to which the constitutional fathers pointed. The rules fashioned by the Court are not so far apart as they might seem to be; a reasonable argument can be made for the proposition that the no-aid, purpose-and-effect, and no-entanglement rules say substantially the same thing in different terms. Judges, of course, are human beings and as such will differ with each other; but it seems, to this writer at least, that an examination of the cases discussed in this book shows that both the rules and the referee have held up remarkably well.

Chapter Two

The Church

The Church in a Secular Society

It may appear somewhat strange that the church,* which after all is an institution of God, should itself be an arena of conflict between Him and Caesar. Yet it very much is, and has been ever since they parted company and set up separate establishments.

There are several reasons for this. In the first place both claim sovereignty and do not take kindly to rivals, particularly when both claim jurisdiction over the same domain. During the Middle Ages popes asserted and exercised the right to enthrone and dethrone princes. By the time our republic was established, the tables had turned, and European governments exercised the power in respect to the princes of the church. In 1783 it was quite natural for the papal nuncio at Paris to address a note to Benjamin Franklin, American ambassador to France, suggesting that since it was no longer practicable to maintain the previous status in which American Catholics were subject to the Vicar Apostolic at London, a Catholic bishopric should be established in one of the American cities. Franklin transmitted the note to Congress, which directed him to notify the nuncio "that the subject of his application to Doctor Frank-

*Throughout this book the term "the church" is used to designate institutional religion generally. When a specific religious body is intended, most often the Catholic, "the Church" is used.

lin, being purely spiritual, it is without the jurisdiction and powers of Congress, who have no authority to permit or refuse it, these powers being reserved to the several States individually."

The last phrase is interesting. Congress acknowledged that it had only powers delegated to it by the States and that powers spiritual were not among these. Yet, it could not quite get itself to disavow such powers on the part of its constituent States. Very much later, in the *Everson* case, the Supreme Court, as we have seen, held that the States too were lacking in these powers. Nevertheless, the temptation for the state to meddle in church affairs (and vice versa) is difficult to resist. Theodore Roosevelt, when President, lobbied (unsuccessfully) with the Vatican to have Archbishop John Ireland of St. Paul elevated to cardinal. And with intermeddling, inevitably, comes conflict.

Secondly, church and state can be quite useful to each other in carrying out their respective missions and functions. According to Jeremiah S. Black, a noted jurist of the 19th century, it was "the manifest object of the men who framed the institutions of this country, to have a state without religion and a church without politics—that is to say, they meant that one should never be used as an engine for the purposes of the other," and ". . . for that reason they built up a wall of complete and perfect partition between the two." This, however, is an ideal and not always realizable. Religion has ideologies which it seeks to universalize and for this the state can be very helpful. So too has the state, and it similarly will often be sorely tempted to use the church to effectuate them. The result is a church in politics and a state in religion, and, in either case, conflict.

In the third place, the church is an institution in a secular society, and as such possesses assets temporal as well as spiritual. The enormous wealth of the church is universally taken for granted; to what extent this is more legend than fact is uncertain but for our purpose irrelevant. The fact that the church is believed to be wealthy is sufficient for the state to cast covetous eyes in the direction of the church and to seek to appropriate whatever it is the latter may possess. To achieve this, the state may find it necessary to set up a rival church (as did Henry VIII) or to seek to destroy the church completely (as in the Mexican, Russian, and many other revolutions). In either case, the church becomes an arena of conflict between religion and state.

Even where, as in this country, the state does not seek to appropriate the assets of the church, their existence gives rise to conflict. The lands, buildings, facilities, and other possessions of the church receive from the state protective benefits (such as fire, police, sanitation, and safety) enjoyed by all institutions. Other institutions, however, contribute to the cost of these services through taxation, while the church has traditionally been exempt. As the services expand and the costs increase, the privilege of exemption becomes less acceptable and begins to face challenge by nonreligious institutions and citizens upon whom the tax burden becomes ever heavier.

Finally, because the church is a collective institution, internal tensions and conflicts are inevitable. Who, for example, determines the dogma, doctrine, liturgy, and practices of the church, and who controls its temporal assets: pope, bishop, synod, priest, trustees, congregation? What happens when some in the congregation charge that others have strayed from the true faith and are guilty of heresy? Who is to pass judgment on these charges? Who is to act as referee, and by what rules is the issue to be decided?

According to Locke, as we have seen, a church is neither more nor less than an association of members voluntarily uniting toward the particular end of professing and worshiping God. In that sense it is not basically different from associations uniting to make profits, popularly known as partnerships or corporations. Internal conflicts within such associations are common, and society has learned how to manage them. The ultimate referee is the judiciary, and the rules are the secular laws of partnerships and corporations.

Religious groups often take the forms of corporations; yet it is a fiction to equate them with business corporations. A court of law can handle a dispute as to whether a corporation is making a profit or losing money, and, if the latter, whether the cause is mismanagement by its board of directors and officers; or whether it is complying with its charter of organization or deviating from it. Suppose, however, the dispute is not about profits but about prophecy, and the real charter is not a legalistic many-paged document filed in the office of the county clerk, but a dozen simple words, "Thou art Peter and upon this rock I will build my church." The referee in each case, we know, will have to be the same; that is, a court of law. But are the same rules to be applied, and if so will they work?

Theological Disputes in Common Law Courts

This indeed was how church disputes were resolved at common law, that thousand-year-old system which was brought to these shores and is still the basis of Anglo-American law. The English judges did not hesitate to pass on arcane questions of doctrine and theology, and American judges followed suit. In England, which has no constitutional requirement or tradition on the separation of church and state, this seems to present no substantial problem, but in the United States it does, and can lead to some strange lawsuits.

An illustrative example occurred in New York City in the 1930s. The rabbis of the city were divided about the requirements that had to be met in order that a chicken could be marketed as kosher for consumption by Orthodox Jews. A state court action was brought in which rabbinic experts on both sides presented voluminous Talmudic and other rabbinic authorities, going back hundreds of years, most of whose technical and esoteric works had never been translated into English from the original Hebrew and Aramaic, and which, even if they had, would never have been understood by any but the most specialized of rabbinic scholars. The judge listened patiently throughout the long trial, and reserved his decision. Weeks later, he handed down his opinion and judgment, consisting of many pages of careful examination and discussion of the fine points, with liberal quotations from the scholarly works, and a judgment in favor of one group of rabbis against the other. Accordingly, he issued an injunction forbidding the latter to certify, as kosher, chickens which did not comply with the requirements as fixed by the former. By chance, the judge happened to be an Irish Catholic (not that a Jewish judge would have done any better) who, it may be said with all due respect, neither wrote the opinion that bore his signature nor even understood what any of it meant.

The one manifest advantage of the procedure used in this case was that the referee in the intrareligious dispute was obviously impartial and that accordingly his determination could be accepted by both sides. Aside from this, the procedure appears quite unsatisfactory and, as we will see shortly, was strongly disapproved by the Supreme Court as improper under a constitutional system that mandates a separation of religion and government.

How did this unsatisfactory situation come about? Why did not the rabbis resolve the controversy themselves? Certainly that would have been preferable to calling upon a Catholic judge to decide what are the true Mosaic rules and regulations for kosher chickens. The answer lies in the fact that the rabbis (and in other cases ministers and priests) were not willing to rely exclusively on spiritual sanctions for compliance with theological doctrine. In the 1920s they prevailed upon the State legislature in New York, and later in other States, to enact a law making it a penal offense to sell, as "kosher," foods which did not comply with Orthodox Jewish requirements. In 1925, in the case of *Hygrade Pro-*

vision Co. v. *Sherman*, the Supreme Court upheld the constitutionality of this law, but that was before it was ruled in
the *Everson* case that the Establishment Clause of the First
Amendment applied to the States, and the decision was based
on grounds not related to the separation of church and
state. The constitutionality of kosher laws under the recent
decisions interpreting the Establishment Clause is far from
certain.

Resort to secular law to enforce ecclesiastical doctrine
is not limited to rabbis. As we will see, it is a practice engaged
in far more often by Protestant ministers and Catholic
priests. There are, however, occasions when resort to governmental courts to resolve theological disputes seems to be
unavoidable, as when ownership of the material assets of a
church depends upon its adherence to theological doctrine.

When such a situation reached a pre-*Everson* court, i.e.,
one uninhibited by Establishment Clause limitations, it decided the controversy in accordance with analogous common law rules and principles. Suppose, for example, a man
left land and a building to a university to be used for the
teaching of humanities, and a number of years after his
death the university trustees installed chemistry and phys-
ics laboratories in the building. If the question reached a
court, it would decide whether or not chemistry and phys-
ics were "humanities" and enforce the will accordingly.

Suppose, similarly, a man left land and a building for a
church to be conducted according to the doctrines of Roman
Catholicism, and many years after the donor's death, a
young priest, with the support of a majority of the congregation, but against the will of a vocal minority and the
bishop, introduced jazz and English into the mass and administered the sacraments to divorcees who had remarried.
Suppose the bishop removed the priest but the majority of
the congregation hired a lawyer to get an injunction against
the bishop and to assure the priest control of the church
building and equipment.

In England, the judge to whom such a case is presented

will simply consult the Catholic canon law and recognized Catholic theological authorities and will determine whether the church is being conducted in accordance with the orthodoxy of the Catholic faith. The rationale behind this approach is that when people leave property or money or make contributions to a church, they do it in trust, which means that the property or money is to be used only in accordance with the religious doctrines of the church at the time the bequests or contributions are made; it is the responsibility of the courts to see to it that the trust is kept. In the United States, following the common law, many courts did exactly the same thing, and so we find innumerable State court decisions delving into theological doctrines and ecclesiastical practices.

Some courts, finding it uncomfortable to be catapulted into the thicket of theological niceties, modified the common law rule substantially, and adopted what became known as the departure-from-doctrine rule. This meant that the courts would not intervene in quarrels regarding specifics and details of doctrine and practice unless there was shown to be a substantial departure from the faith of the church. This is obviously a compromise and, as is often the case with compromise, does not meet the real issue that divides the contestants; a secular court, often in the person of a judge who is not an adherent to the particular faith in controversy, must still decide what is and what is not substantial or fundamental to that faith.

This is hardly an easy decision to make. Those who feel deeply about a particular aspect of doctrine, discipline, or liturgy are likely to deem it fundamental, while those seeking its elimination or modification will naturally insist that it is merely secondary and expendable. In 1972 the United Church of Christ ordained an avowed homosexual to its ministry; Leviticus 18:22 calls homosexuality an abomination and condemns to death those who practice it. A major constituent of the United Church of Christ is the former Congregational Church, direct descendant of the Puritans whose Calvinist ethic made sodomy a secular crime in every State in the Union. Has the United Church of Christ been guilty of a substantial or fundamental departure from doctrine?

Or take another example which has led to considerable litigation in State courts. The traditional practice in Orthodox Judaism is for men and women to sit separately at synagogue services with a curtained partition between them. In many synagogues, particularly in suburban areas, members of the younger generation dislike the practice, and when they become a majority of the membership, discontinue it and institute mixed or family seating. Should a State court, at the instance of the older members, issue an injunction against the change on the ground that it is a fundamental departure from Orthodoxy?

Power and Control in American Catholicism

Independent of theological differences, church disputes often revolve simply around the question of control, and these, too, frequently reach the courts for resolution. The early days of Catholicism in the United States witnessed a long and often bitter internal struggle for the control of church property and the appointment of parish priests. The deism of the 18th century and Jacksonian democracy of the early 19th could not fail to have their effects on the Catholic Church. On the other hand, the Church was a hierarchical institution headed by an absolute monarch, jealous of his absolutism and fearful of the rise of national churches. Under Catholic dogma, at least before Vatican II, the obligation of the faithful was one exclusively of obedience, an obligation due rulers from their subjects.

Casting an envious eye upon their American brethren in the Congregational churches, Catholic congregations began to claim ownership of church property, the right to select their own priests, and, through lay trustees chosen by themselves, to manage the church and all its temporalities.

These claims received a sympathetic ear from Jeffersonian State legislatures. There was, however, something of an ambivalence or internal contradiction facing them when it came to framing appropriate laws to help the faithful. On the one hand, Jeffersonian and deist separationism mandated a hands-off policy in respect to church affairs. On the other hand, the legislators deemed the principles of political democracy and the fear of central authority as relevant to both church and state governments. The result was that the same statutes which granted or recognized the right of self-government in churches also provided how such government would be chosen and controlled in each individual church.

These conflicts between congregations and legislatures on the one hand and the hierarchy on the other led to many excommunications and lawsuits. The judges were faced with the same ambivalence as the legislators and the decisions varied from State to State. In time, however, the separationist spirit, combined with the growing political power of the Catholic Church, led to a resolution which proved quite satisfactory to the Church; the legislatures required Catholic churches to adopt the secular forms of corporations and associations, but allowed and indeed encouraged administration which preserved power and control in the hierarchy.

In New York, for example, the law requires each church to be controlled by five trustees, including two laymen. These laymen, however, are to be chosen by the other three trustees, who are the bishop of the diocese, its vicar general, and the church rector. Since the latter two are appointees of the bishop, this means that for all practical purposes control is vested exclusively in the bishop. In other States, even this pretense at democratic control is dispensed with. The law requires that the church be incorporated but permits use of the "corporation sole," i.e., a single person who, in all cases, is the bishop of the diocese. A number of States provide generally that all property bequeathed or donated to a religious body shall be held and administered in accordance with the appropriate church or canon law; and a few States simply enact into law a corporate structure drafted by each denomination for its own governance.

The upshot of all this is that separationism has prevailed over concepts of political democracy. The law to a great extent allows each church or denomination to control its own destiny and be master of its polity, whether authoritarian or democratic. (As we will shortly see, the Supreme Court reached the same conclusion as a constitutional mandate under the Establishment Clause.) Of all the major faiths, the Catholic Church benefited most from this development, but even it was unable to withstand the winds of change. The first Vatican Council, held in 1870, sought to set up a fortress of protection for papal authoritarianism, but in the second the wall was breached under the banner of collegiality. While only the bishops launched the attack, and the extent of their victory in the struggle for a share of power remains contested and uncertain, democracy has a way of seeping down. The Magna Carta was wrested from an unwilling monarch by nobles and barons for their own benefits, but ultimately its rights and privileges became the possession of all commoners. So too, priests, particularly in the United States, are increasingly articulate in their demands to share power with the bishops, and they are even forming ecclesiastical equivalents of labor unions to bargain collectively with the bishops. The faithful are not far behind; while it is much too early to expect congregationalism in American Catholicism, it is likely that this is the road to the future.

Control and Theology Under the Constitution

It was not until 1872 that the Supreme Court became involved in internal church disputes and found itself called upon to referee conflicts of control and theology. Although this occurred after the adoption of the Fourteenth Amendment in 1868, it was long before the Court ruled in the *Everson* case that the amendment forbade States from making laws respecting an establishment of religion. The Federal courts' intervention in the controversy was therefore not based upon a claim that the Federal Constitution had been violated; instead, it came about by accident. The Constitution provides that a suit may be brought in a Federal court if the plaintiff and the defendant live in different States, and it so happened that while the Walnut Street Presbyterian Church was located in Louisville, Kentucky, some of the congregants resided across the Ohio River in Indiana.

The controversy which brought the children of God into the courts of Caesar had its roots in the question of slavery. In 1845 the General Assembly of the Presbyterian Church declared that slavery was not sinful, but in 1861 it reversed itself and ruled to the contrary. The Louisville Presbytery, supported by the State Synod, condemned the decree of the General Assembly as schismatical and heretical; and the congregants of the Walnut Street Church, split down the middle, found themselves in the Federal court with each faction claiming that it represented true Presbyterian doctrine and therefore was legally entitled to possession of the church building and assets.

When a case comes to a Federal court because the contestants live in different States, the court decides the suit in accordance with common law principles. This would have required the Federal court in Kentucky to examine Presbyterian doctrine from the Westminster Confession to the time of the trial to determine which faction represented the true faith and which was heretical. This, said the Supreme Court in *Watson* v. *Jones* (as the case was called when it reached that tribunal), a State court may do, but a Federal one may not for it is restricted by the Establishment Clause of the First Amendment. That clause forbids Federal agencies, judicial, legislative, or executive, from making theological judgments or deciding what is orthodox and what heretical in any faith.

Yet the courts could not wash their hands of the controversy; some impartial tribunal had to decide which faction should have possession of the church and its assets, else the issue would be decided by physical force. Federal judicial intervention, the Supreme Court recognized, was unavoidable, but it had to be kept at a minimum and could not in any event encompass theological determinations. All that a court could and should do was to accept the determination of the appropriate ecclesiastical tribunal as to which faction represented the true faith, and direct its marshals to enforce it.

Even this necessitated some involvement in church affairs, for a court would have to decide which was the appropriate ecclesiastical tribunal or judicatory; was it the minister of the Walnut Street Church, the majority of its congregants, the Louisville Presbytery, the Kentucky Synod, or the General Assembly? The Supreme Court found it necessary to examine Presbyterian polity and from the examination reached the conclusion that the appropriate ecclesiastic tribunal, or highest judicatory, was the General Assembly; it accordingly held that the faction which had the support of the assembly was legally entitled to possession and control of the Walnut Street Church and its assets. Had the church been Baptist, Congregational, or Jewish, the judicatory would have been found to be the majority of the congregation; had it been Roman Catholic the Court would have found it to be the bishop of the diocese. In any case, a Federal court, reluctantly but necessarily, would examine the denomination's canon or church law in order to reach its determination.

Four score years after *Watson* v. *Jones*, the Supreme Court was once more called upon to act as referee in a bitter ecclesiastical controversy, and again the cause was not theological but political and social. In 1924, after the Bolshevik Revolution, representatives of a number of American churches affiliated with the Russian Orthodox Church in Moscow, held a "sobor" or convention and established the "Russian Church in America" to care for the faithful until such time as conditions in Russia would permit free and independent action by the Patriarchate in Moscow. Not all Russian churches in America joined the new group; some continued their loyalty to the Moscow Patriarchate. In 1945, a metropolitan or archbishop was sent by the Moscow Patriarchate to take over as archbishop of North America and, as such, obtained possession of St. Nicholas Cathedral in New York City. During the same year, the New York legislature passed a law which declared that the Russian Church in America was the recognized church and therefore legally entitled to possession of all the assets of the Russian Orthodox Church. That faction thereupon brought a suit in New York court to recover control of the cathedral from the Moscow-appointed archbishop.

By this time the *Everson* case had been decided and when, in 1952, the suit reached the Supreme Court, under the title of *Kedroff* v. *St. Nicholas Cathedral*, that Court held that under both the Free Exercise and the Establishment Clauses, New York could not legislate that the Russian Church in America represented the true faith of Russian Orthodoxy. The highest judicatory in the Russian Orthodox Church was the Moscow Patriarchate, and its determination had to be accepted by the State legislature, just as the General Assembly's ruling was binding upon the Federal court in *Watson* v. *Jones*.

In 1969, the Supreme Court found it again necessary to referee a contest within the Presbyterian Church. This time the controversy was both sociopolitical and theological. Two local Presbyterian churches in Savannah, Georgia, had serious grievances against the General Assembly, complaining of its

> . . . ordaining of women as ministers and ruling elders, making pronouncements and recommendations concerning civil, economic, social and political matters, giving support to the removal of Bible reading and prayers by children in the public schools, adopting certain Sunday School literature and

teaching neo-orthodoxy alien to the Confession of Faith and Catechism, as originally adopted by the general church, and causing all members to remain in the National Council of Churches of Christ and willingly accepting its leadership which advocated practices such as the subverting of parental authority, civil disobedience and intermeddling in civil affairs.

If that were not enough, they also charged that the General Assembly "made pronouncements in matters relating to international issues such as the Vietnam conflict and has disseminated publications denying the Holy Trinity and violating the moral and ethical standards of the faith."

Deciding that there was no hope of reconciliation with the general church, the two congregations voted to withdraw from it and to reconstitute the local churches as an autonomous Presbyterian organization. The general church responded by directing the Presbytery of Savannah to take over the local churches' property and administer it until a new local membership loyal to the general church could be established. The local churches' countermove was to bring a lawsuit in a State court to vindicate their right to keep the property as the true representatives of authentic Presbyterianism.

A trial was held in which the jury was called upon to decide whether the actions of the general church amounted to a fundamental or substantial abandonment of the original tenets and doctrines of Presbyterianism. Since jurymen may not be questioned about their religion there is no way of knowing how many if any of them were themselves Presbyterians or even Christians. In any event, they decided that the general church (i.e., the General Assembly up North) had indeed been guilty of a substantial departure from doctrine and accordingly had no right to deprive the local churches of their property.

When the case, known as *Presbyterian Church in the United States* v. *Mary Elizabeth Blue Hull Memorial Presbyterian Church*, reached the Supreme Court, that court held that under the

Establishment and Free Exercise clauses, as interpreted in the earlier Presbyterian Church case and in the Russian Orthodox case, a jury, being an arm of the State government, could not pass judgment regarding the tenets of Presbyterian doctrine and whether the general church has departed from them, substantially or otherwise.

What the three Supreme Court decisions (the two Presbyterian and the Russian Orthodox) indicate is a strong policy of government non-involvement in ecclesiastical controversies. This may well result in abandoning the congregation to the mercies of an arbitrary and despotic priesthood. The Court in the 1969 case seemed to have recognized this and apparently sought to guard against it. It suggested that if the decision of a church tribunal was found to be fraudulent, collusive, or arbitrary, a secular court need not accept it as final. More important, it ruled that States could, if they wished, provide secular ("neutral") criteria by which right to possession and control could be ascertained. A State, for example, could decide by statute or judicial decision that the right to possession and control of church property should be deemed vested in the individual or corporation in whose name the title to the property is recorded in the appropriate county office. Or it could provide that all church organizations must have written constitutions that specifically state where right to possession and control should lie. Finally, it could treat a religious corporation like any other corporation and decide questions of ownership and control according to the laws applicable to secular corporations. The only thing it might not do is decide or allow its courts to decide the question on the basis of contested ecclesiastical law.

These would appear to be quite effective safeguards. Indeed, when the 1969 case was returned to the Georgia courts after the Supreme Court decision, they decided that according to the secular laws of that State, the local congregations were entitled to keep possession and control of the churches. Nevertheless, in most cases these safeguards are likely to be inadequate, and congregations may be faced with the alternative of complying with priestly commands that are no longer acceptable to them or relinquishing to the priesthood the land, building, and other assets which they had built up during the years and starting a new congregation and church from scratch. Difficult as this choice may be, it is far preferable to the conversion of secular courts into ecclesiastical tribunals in which, for example, Protestant, Jewish, and even atheistic judges might overrule a cardinal's, or, conceivably, a pope's, interpretation of Catholic dogma.

The Church in Politics

Power

Politics is the exercise of power, and the men of the church hunger for it often as avidly as do those of the state. From the days of Zadok and Abiathar, David's priests who joined rival factions in the struggle for the royal succession, to the Maccabees who declared themselves kings of Judea and simultaneously High Priests of Israel, to the Holy Fathers who, as monarchs of the Papal States, fought with emperors over disputed claims to territory, to cardinals such as Richelieu and Mazarin and archbishops such as Makarios of Cyprus, the world has witnessed churchmen in the thicket of politics struggling for secular power without relinquishing their claims to spiritual sovereignty.

The generation that fashioned our republic was well aware of this history and wanted no part of it. After our Declaration of Independence, the colonies became States and wrote constitutions for their governance. Common to these were provisions forbidding clergymen to hold public office, often accompanied with a sanctimonious expression of concern that they not be diverted from their higher duties. Typical is the following from the New York constitution of 1777:

> And whereas the ministers of the gospel are by their pro-
> fession, dedicated to the service of God and the care of souls,
> and ought not be delivered from the great duties of their
> function; therefore, no minister of the gospel or priests of
> any denomination whatsoever, shall at any time here-
> after, under any pretence or deception whatever, be eligible
> to, or capable of holding any civil or military office or place
> within this State.

(The reference to "any pretence or deception whatever," was partly a reflection of the anti-clericalism of the
generation and partly a recognition that when God's men
compete for power in Caesar's domain they are likely to
follow the standards or lack of standards applicable to that
arena.)

Jefferson, in drafting the constitution for Virginia,
sought to include a similar prohibition but was dissuaded
from doing so on the ground that it would violate the principle of religious freedom and the nonrecognition of religion
by civil government. In time, most of the other States came
around to the same conclusion and dropped the provision
from their constitutions, although Maryland and Tennessee
still bar "ministers of the gospel" from serving in their
legislatures.

The constitutionality of such provisions is highly
doubtful. If enacted by Congress, they would clearly violate
Article VI of the Constitution, which forbids religious tests
for Federal office, as well as the Free Exercise and Establishment clauses of the First Amendment; if enacted by a
State, they would violate those clauses and the Equal Protection Clause of the Fourteenth Amendment. In 1961 the
Supreme Court ruled in the case of *Torcaso* v. *Watkins* that
Maryland could not constitutionally disqualify atheists from
eligibility to serve in public office; the reasoning of that case
would seem equally applicable to disqualification of clergymen.

Notwithstanding the absence of exclusionary provisions in the Federal and all but two of the State constitu-

tions (assuming these two are still enforced, which is highly doubtful), until recently comparatively few clergymen have held either Federal or State office. Clergymen have frequently served on special or temporary governmental citizens' committees, usually without compensation; Father Theodore Hesburgh, president of Notre Dame University, served for many years as chairman of the United States Civil Rights Commission. Rarely, however, did they make governmental service a full-time career.

Recently we have been witnessing a significant change, one which has come from what would have been considered, but a short time ago, a highly unlikely source. One aspect of the ferment within Catholicism that was an aftermath of Vatican II has been a growing dissatisfaction among priests and nuns with the limited scope of their permissible functions, and an urge to expend their energies outside the parish church or its parochial school. Thus we find, as a not uncommon example, a nun resigning from her order and from her position as head of a Catholic college to become president of a municipal college in New York City or some other secular school. The next step appears to be to accept the civic or political office without resigning from the priesthood or religious order. This requires approval of the appropriate ecclesiastical superior, but priests and nuns are in such short supply and the Church's need for them so great that the superiors often fear risking resignations and therefore grant approval. Thus we see one Jesuit priest becoming dean of the graduate school in New York City University, and another being elected to Congress, and neither of them finding it necessary to resign from their priesthood or their order.

It is really not surprising that Father Groppi and the Berrigans should take radical positions and resort to unconventional and even unlawful measures to express them. Nor is it really surprising that Hesburgh should take an activist position on civil rights, an area in which the Church has not traditionally been particularly active, nor that Robert Drinan has become an articulate spokesman for the dove position on Vietnam and against restrictions on the civil liberties of radicals and communists, areas in which the Church has been opposed. Dissent on the political positions taken by the Church has always existed within it, but it is only after Vatican II that it could be openly expressed and even vigorously acted on in the public and governmental arena without prompting resignation or expulsion from the priesthood.

Self-Interest

Until recently, emulation of the historic Old-World practice of priests entering into the political arena has been rare in this country. Even rarer has been our adoption of the similar European practice of organizing political parties for the advancement of ecclesiastical interests. Catholic or Christian Center Parties are a familiar element in European parliamentary politics, a pattern which has been adopted in Israel where the Religious bloc, a coalition of several religious parties, occupies a strategic position in the nation's multiparty system. In all these cases the religious party is an arm of the church (or, in Israel, the rabbinate), controlled by it, and used to protect and advance its position and interests.

Only once in American history was there an attempt to establish a religious party. In New York in 1841 there appeared on the ballot a "Catholic Party," consisting of candidates pledged to support the position of the Church in its efforts to obtain public funds for its parochial schools. In comparative figures, the Catholic Party received a small number of votes and soon disappeared as a separate party, but from that time on the Catholic Church was in politics to stay. What changed was not substance or objective, but only tactics. The American people would not accept the Church in politics in an open and acknowledged stance, but their legislators, at least, found no difficulty in accepting it as another interest or pressure group, like the National

Association of Manufacturers, the NAACP, or the labor unions, seeking to protect and advance its interests in accordance with the traditional rules of group politics. It is in the light of this that one can fully appreciate the following report appearing in the *New York Times* on August 7, 1972:

> The Nixon Administration and the Democratic party—the latter in the person of Representative Wilbur D. Mills—are vying for the Roman Catholic vote with a plan for a new form of tax assistance to parochial schools.
>
> Less openly, the two sides may also be competing to attract some Southern segregationist votes with the same tax-aid plan, which would apply to all private primary and secondary schools, not just to those with religious affiliations.
>
> The legislation was originally devised by a Catholic member of Congress, Representative Hugh L. Carey, Democrat of Brooklyn. It is being sponsored by Mr. Mills, an Arkansas Democrat, who has a long record of opposition to tax credits on principle. The measure has also been endorsed by the Nixon Administration, though it opposed similar proposals in the previous years.
>
>   * * *
>
> Mr. Carey, in discussing his bill, speaks frankly of the political, as well as the substantive, merits that he sees in it.
>
> He said that he had no trouble in gaining Mr. Mills' support for the measure "once the chairman went national" —that is, once Mr. Mills, the chairman of the House Ways and Means Committee, decided to make a bid for the Democratic presidential or vice-presidential nomination.
>
> With Mr. Mills' hope for a place on the ticket now dashed, his main political aim in scheduling hearings next week on the Carey-Mills bill, Mr. Carey thinks, is to blunt the President's appeal to the Catholic, the elderly and other interest groups.

Congressman Carey found nothing wrong in treating Catholics as just another self-interest interest group, nor do most other legislators. And what is true of the Catholics is no less true of other religious groups; during the same

1972 presidential campaign the two major parties in professing their love for Israel and their loyalty to American Jews outdid Goneril and Regan in ardor and eloquence.

While this turn to what has become fashionably known as ethnicity does not disturb American legislators and others professionally engaged in partisan politics, it does trouble the Supreme Court when religious groups are involved. In its decision in *Lemon* v. *Kurtzman*, declaring unconstitutional governmental subsidies to pay the salaries of parochial school teachers, the Court expressed its concern about the divisiveness resulting from such laws. Speaking for the Court, Chief Justice Burger said:

> A broader base of entanglement of yet a different character is presented by the divisive political potential of these state programs. In a community where such a large number of pupils are served by church-related schools, it can be assumed that state assistance will entail considerable political activity. Partisans of parochial schools, understandably concerned with rising costs and sincerely dedicated to both the religious and secular educational missions of their schools, will inevitably champion this cause and promote political action to achieve their goals. Those who oppose state aid, whether for constitutional, religious, or fiscal reasons, will inevitably respond and employ all of the usual political campaign techniques to prevail. Candidates will be forced to declare and voters to choose. It would be unrealistic to ignore the fact that many people confronted with issues of this kind will find their votes aligned with their faith.
>
> Ordinarily political debate and division, however vigorous or even partisan, are normal and healthy manifestations of our democratic system of government, but political division along religious lines was one of the principal evils against which the First Amendment was intended to protect. The potential divisiveness of such conflict is a threat to the normal political process. To have States or communities divide on the issues presented by state aid to parochial schools would tend to confuse and obscure other issues of great urgency. We have an expanding array of vex-

ing issues, local and national, domestic and international, to
debate and divide on. It conflicts with our whole history and
tradition to permit questions of the Religion Clauses to assume such importance in our legislatures and in our elections
that they could divert attention from the myriad issues and
problems which confront every level of government. The
highways of church and state relationships are not likely to
be one-way streets, and the Constitution's authors sought
to protect religious worship from the pervasive power of
government. The history of many countries attests to the
hazards of religion intruding into the political arena or of
political power intruding into the legitimate and free exercise of religious belief.

Ideology

Catholic spokesmen were of course critical of the
Lemon decision as a whole, but some of them put particular
emphasis upon Chief Justice Burger's justification for it.
What, they claimed, he was saying was that religious groups
have no right to speak on such moral issues as abortion and
birth control because these have also become political issues.
Political debate and division, the Chief Justice said, was
normal and healthy, but it suddenly becomes an evil when
it is engaged in by religious groups. Do not churches, they
asked, enjoy freedom of speech and of petition as do other
institutions in our society? Why should they be silenced
simply because they seek to judge legislative and other
governmental action by moral and spiritual standards?

These spokesmen, however, seem to have misinterpreted the Court's intent. As suggested in the first chapter
of this book and as stated by Justice Douglas in his concurring opinion in the 1961 case of *Times Film Corporation* v. *Chicago*, religious groups seek to translate their own particular
hierarchy of values into categorical imperatives for the community at large and to shape the culture of the community
according to their own concepts of the good life. In this en-
deavor they naturally seek to influence government and
law, and the Court in the *Lemon* case found nothing wrong in

this, as appears from the paragraph of the opinion which follows immediately after the extract quoted above:

> Of course, as the Court noted in *Walz*, adherents of particular faiths and individual churches frequently take strong positions on public issues. We could not expect otherwise, for religious values pervade the fabric of our national life. But in *Walz* we dealt with a status under State tax laws for the benefit of all religious groups. We are here confronted with successive and very likely permanent annual appropriations which benefit relatively few religious groups. Political fragmentation and divisiveness on religious lines is thus likely to be intensified.

What the Court was saying here, and two years later in *Committee for Public Education and Religious Liberty* v. *Nyquist*, is that divisions across religious lines on political issues are inevitable where universal values are concerned; it is the price we pay for a pluralistic democracy. Religious institutions are so pervasive in our society that their immunity from taxation, which was upheld in the *Walz* case, is in the nature of a universal value. Subsidies for parochial schools are on a different footing. Here political fragmentation and divisiveness along religious lines are not normal and healthy and are avoidable by outlawing subsidization of religious schools. In short, the Court rejects the church as a self-interest interest group but accepts it as an ideological interest group.

The church has a long history as an ideological interest group in the United States. During the Revolutionary War, Anglican churches actively defended and promoted the loyalist cause, while the rest of Protestantism was committed to the Revolution. In the 19th century the hotbed of abolition was in the Protestant denominations, and there too would be found the most militant defenders of laws against obscenity, gambling, birth control, divorce, and consumption of alcoholic beverages; the Comstock Law (forbidding interstate or mail distribution of contraceptive materials), the New York Society for the Suppression of Vice, the Watch and Ward Society of New England, the Women's Christian Temperance Union, the Anti-Saloon League—these are all names associated with Protestantism. In the 20th century, Catholicism took over the struggle for the enactment, strengthening, or retention of laws against obscenity, contraception, divorce (but not gambling or consumption of intoxicating liquors), and added to it a militant defense of anti-abortion statutes. In Catholicism, too, were to be found the staunchest advocates of national defense and loyalty, and opponents of communism, both domestic and foreign.

These ideological clashes within the church take place most often in the forums of public opinion and the halls of legislatures (for example, the Unitarian Universalist publication of the Pentagon Papers). In recent years, however, they are also taking place with increasing frequency in courtrooms. This occurs most often when the particular suit before the judges affects the church as a self-interest interest group; it was to be expected that the United States Catholic Conference, the National Council of Churches, and the Synagogue Council of America would file friends-of-the-court briefs when the *Walz* tax exemption case reached the Supreme Court; but the last two organizations also filed briefs when the Court was called upon to decide the constitutionality of the death penalty. Besides these umbrella organizations, individual denominations, too, resort to friend-of-the-court briefs to present their ideological positions to the Supreme Court; the Unitarian Universalists intervened in a court challenge by the Civil Liberties Union against military surveillance of civilians engaged in peace demonstrations. It can reasonably be expected that such church interventions in judicial resolution of ideological controversies will increase in the future.

God, Caesar, and Taxes

According to the Bible, when the Pharisees, seeking to entangle Jesus, asked him whether it was lawful to give tribute to Caesar, he responded: "Render unto Caesar the things which are Caesar's, and unto God the things which are God's." The Bible relates that when the Pharisees heard these words, they marveled and left him and went away. What the Bible does not tell us is what they marveled about, but perhaps it was the ingenious way in which he avoided entanglement by not answering their question while seemingly answering it with profundity. For in truth his answer was no answer; he did not tell them what things were Caesar's and what were God's, nor, in lieu thereof, who was to decide what rightfully belonged to each. Suppose Caesar says to a loyal but God-fearing citizen: "Give me a tithe of your money for I need it to fight a war in Vietnam," and God says, "Give it not to him." The answer given by Jesus to the Pharisees seems hardly helpful in these circumstances.

In the United States it would be the Supreme Court that would be expected to decide between these contradictory commands, but as yet it has not done so. In *Flast* v. *Cohen*, the Court in 1968 upheld the right of a taxpayer to sue for an injunction against the expenditure of Federal funds alleged to be in violation of the Establishment Clause of the First Amendment, but it took great pains to frame its decision in language that clearly excluded a taxpayer's right to sue for an injunction against expenditure of tax-raised funds to finance the Vietnam War on the ground of its unconstitutionality in not having been declared by Congress.

In the *Flast* case, the plaintiffs also claimed that appropriation of public funds to maintain parochial schools violated their rights under the Free Exercise Clause because it constituted a tax for religious purposes. This was not an unreasonable claim; the history of the struggle for religious freedom in America is written in large measure in terms of resistance to compulsory taxation for religion. Since, however, the Court had upheld the plaintiffs' standing to sue under the Establishment Clause, it did not find it necessary to consider their Free Exercise claim. Nevertheless, it intimated that it would not allow standing where only Free Exercise was claimed.

The reasoning for the distinction is not quite clear, but it does indicate that the Court would not be more receptive to a suit by one claiming that the commandment "Thou shalt not kill" means also that you will not allow your money to be used to pay others to kill, and that, accordingly, financing of the Vietnam or any other war violates the taxpayer's free exercise of religion. Nor would the Court recognize standing to sue on the part of a Christian Scientist seeking to prohibit use of tax-raised funds to fluoridate the municipal water supply, or of a Jehovah's Witness objecting to the purchase of flags for public schools, or of a Catholic who does not want his taxes to be used to pay for contraceptive and abortion services in municipal hospitals. Should the Court accept any of these cases, the probabilities are that, for reasons which will appear later in this book, it would hold in all of them that the tribute rightfully belongs to the state and may not be withheld on religious grounds.

Tax Exemption

Church Land

It is somewhat paradoxical that, while in recent years religious organizations have been quite successful in prevailing upon legislatures to appropriate tax-raised funds for the support of church schools, many of the same legislatures are subjecting to serious scrutiny the universal exemption of American churches from various forms of taxation. The explanation is the same in both cases: the sky-rocketing costs faced by state and church in carrying out their respective functions impel each to search for new sources of financing, and each casts a covetous eye on the assumed riches of the other.

In the United States, the church enjoys numerous benefits, including exemption from real-estate taxes on its land and buildings. Neither tax exemption for church-owned property nor opposition to it is particularly new. Scripture relates that when Joseph bought the Egyptians' land for the food he had stored during the seven years of plenty, he turned back to each Egyptian his land and "made it a law over the land of Egypt unto this day that Pharaoh should have the fifth part [of the produce]; except the land of the priests only, which became not Pharaoh's" (Genesis 47:26). Later, when Artaxerxes, king of Persia, authorized Ezra to levy a tax for the rebuilding of the Temple, he specifically directed that "touching any of the priests and Levites, singers, porters, Nethinim, or ministers of the house of God, it shall not be lawful to impose toll, tribute, or custom, upon them" (Ezra 7:24). Exemption enjoyed by Christian churches goes back to the 4th century, when Constantine, in the process of establishing Christianity as the state church of Rome, accorded this privilege to church buildings and to the land about them which was used for church purposes.

Opposition to tax exemption for churches is likewise not a recent development. Two Presidents of the United States, Madison and Grant, were opposed to it. Opposition has been based not merely on the feeling that fairness requires that the church contribute to the cost of the public services it receives, but also on a concern about the accumulation by the church of wealth (and the power that wealth controls). This concern caused the enactment during the Middle Ages of mortmain statutes limiting the amount of property churches could hold, and similar statutes are still in effect today in some States.

The constitutionality under the Establishment Clause of exemption from taxation for land and buildings used for worship and other religious purposes was a matter of controversy for many years. Madison deemed it a violation of the clause and many constitutional lawyers similarly found it difficult to justify. The theory of tax exemption generally was explained on the basis of *quid pro quo*: the exemptee (hospital, library, school, etc.) relieved the state of a financial burden it would otherwise bear, and in return the state relieved it of tax liability for the land and buildings used for the rendering of the public service. This obviously was not applicable to land and buildings used for religious worship;

were the church not to provide that service the state would not and could not constitutionally do so; therefore, no *quid* for the *quo*.

In the 1950s and '60s several efforts were made to bring the question to the Supreme Court, but on each occasion it refused to take the case. For some unexplained reason, it finally agreed to do so at the instance of Frederick Walz, a rather eccentric New York City lawyer who bought a small lot of land for the sole purpose of becoming a real estate taxpayer and thus eligible to bring a lawsuit challenging the exemption accorded to realty owned by churches and used for religious purposes.

In 1970, to the surprise of no one, the Court (with the expected dissent of Justice Douglas) upheld the exemption law. Perhaps the only surprising thing about the decision is why the Court took the case in the first place; there certainly was no need to do so, since the Court could have continued its practice of rejecting appeals and leaving the tax exemption situation where it had found and left it when the Court handed down its decision. Candor compels the conclusion that the Court supplied no more satisfactory rationale for exemption than had been offered before it took the case.

Nevertheless, it did supply a different rationale. Only two years earlier in the *Allen* case the Court had applied the purpose-effect test, which had been announced in the *Schempp* decision, to uphold a textbook loan law, but carefully avoided using that test in the *Walz* opinion, and did not of course use the *Everson* no-aid rule either. Instead it held that the purpose of the Establishment Clause was twofold: to prevent government sponsorship of religion and excessive governmental entanglement with religion. Tax exemption for churches does neither. As to the first, it is unlike subsidization of religion which does entail at least some degree of sponsorship. Tax exemption is not sponsorship because the government does not transfer part of its revenue to churches, but simply abstains from demanding that the church support the state. As to the second, exemption involves even less entanglement than non-exemption, for it does not require the government to examine the affairs of the church and audit its books and records. Finally, the Court noted, tax exemption for churches has existed since the founding of the Republic and is the law in every State in the Union; such longevity and universality, the Court said, are strong evidence of constitutionality.

Why the Court decided to take the *Walz* case at all can only be a matter of speculation since it gave no reason for doing so. Yet the fact that the Court avoided employing the purpose-effect test as formulated in the *Schempp* case gives rise to the inference that it was dissatisfied with the widespread assumption among legislators and constitutional lawyers that the *Allen* decision completely nullified the *Everson* no-aid test and gave legislators practically *carte blanche* in granting public funds for the support of parochial schools. This point will be examined further in our chapter on the state and private schools; here we suggest only that the Court took the *Walz* case because it was the first opportunity it had to clarify what it had held in the *Allen* case and to caution the legislatures, interest groups, and the general public that the decision in that case did not mean that subsidies to religious schools would necessarily be upheld.

A number of factors, in addition to the Court's refusal to reaffirm and apply the purpose-effect test without modification, support this inference. In the first place, the Court took pains to differentiate between exemption and subsidization and to point out that the latter, unlike the former, could entail forbidden entanglement. Secondly, in the *Lemon* decision, in which subsidization was held unconstitutional, the Court, in an obvious attempt to set the record straight, stated that the *Walz* decision "tended to *confine* rather than *enlarge* the area of permissible state involvement with religious institutions." In the third place, when the Court in the *Lemon* decision did refer to the purpose-effect test as applied in the *Allen* case, it did so only to make clear that even if a law passes that test it would still be unconstitutional if it failed the entanglement test. Finally, the fact that Justice White (who wrote the majority opinion in the *Allen* case) was the lone dissenter in the *Lemon* case is a clear indication of his unhappiness with what the *Walz* decision had done to the *Allen* ruling.

As has been noted, the major organizations of American Protestantism, Catholicism, and Judaism had filed briefs in the *Walz* case in support of constitutionality. So, too, perhaps surprisingly, did Americans United for Separation of Church and State, as well as a number of denominational groups. Briefs on the other side were presented only by the American Civil Liberties Union and the dauntless Madalyn Murray O'Hair, who had unsuccessfully petitioned the Court to stop astronauts from praying on the moon.

When Americans United and the United States Catholic Conference file briefs on the same side in a church-state case, it is hardly surprising that the Court should decide in their direction rather than in Ms. O'Hair's. But the victory for the church as a self-interest interest group was far from complete. The friends-of-the-court briefs asked for a decision not merely that the States may grant exemption without violating the Establishment Clause, but that they must do so else they would violate the Free Exercise Clause, since, they contended, a tax upon land and buildings used for worship was itself an interference with freedom of worship.

In her brief, Ms. O'Hair noted rather irreverently that while there may be no atheists in foxholes, neither are there any temples, and that the Founder of America's major faith preached and prayed in the open fields. But even if buildings are required for worship, there are those who assert that the use and the exemption are often greatly disproportionate. (In 1970 a group of militant Puerto Ricans in Harlem in New York City took over a Methodist church to use as a place for feeding and caring for children while their mothers were at work, and as a rehabilitation center for drug addicts. They justified the takeover on the ground, among others, that while the church enjoys tax exemption for 365 days a year, actually it is used for worship only three hours a week, remaining closed and idle the rest of the time.) Hence, logically, even if denial of exemption were to be held an interference with freedom of worship, the interference would be limited to the proportionate time the building is used for that purpose. Since church and synagogue buildings are perhaps the most notoriously underused structures in our society, proportionate tax exemption, even if mandatory, would be of very limited benefit to the churches.

In any event, the Supreme Court refused to give the churches even that; it would not hold that they are entitled to exemption as a matter of right, but are given it by the state only as a matter of grace. The unavoidable implication is that what the state gives, the state can take away, and should the state decide to do so or, as is more likely, begin to limit exemption, the First Amendment will not stand in the way.

Caesar's Price for Tax Exemption

It is not to be assumed that all within the ranks of God are happy with the tax-exempt status of His temples. Rumblings of discontent are heard, mostly among Protestant churchmen. Some, and not merely Protestants, question the morality of expending large sums of money in the midst of want and hunger, to build costly edifices often used for only a few hours a week on Sunday mornings. Others are troubled by the ethics of receiving the benefits of community service without contributing to their cost, and a few churches and religious organizations, such as the United Presbyterian Church, have gone so far as to make voluntary contributions to the community in lieu of taxes. In most cases the amount is hardly more than nominal and their value to the community mostly symbolic; nevertheless, it has met with little sympathetic response within the religious world and, in fact, has been expressly opposed by the Guild of St. Ives, an influential group of Episcopal lawyers and clergymen in the New York diocese, on the ground that it might establish a dangerous precedent.

Still others realize that for everything there is a price, and that the price for dependence on the state may be the independence of the church. This is particularly true of churches which deem it part of their mission to speak on what are considered to be political issues. Two cases have reached the Supreme Court questioning whether the government may condition the tax exemption of the church on what it says politically or even on its not saying anything politically. In both, the Court was urged by the churches to hold that such conditions unconstitutionally infringe upon their freedom of religion and speech, but in both cases the Court avoided deciding the question.

The earlier case, *First Unitarian Church* v. *County of Los Angeles*, came to the Court in 1958. It involved a California constitutional provision making non-advocacy of the overthrow of the government by force, violence, or unlawful means a prerequisite for receiving tax exemption and requiring all applicants for exemption to take an oath that they do not engage in such advocacy. The church refused to sign the oath, saying:

> The principles, moral and religious, of the First Unitarian Church of Los Angeles compel it, its members, officers and minister, as a matter of deepest conscience, belief and conviction, to deny power in the state to compel acceptance by it or any other church of this or any other oath of coerced affirmation as to church doctrine, advocacy or belief.

The Court refused to decide that the State could or could not deny tax exemption to a church which advocated overthrow of an unjust government (e.g., the Congregational churches of New England which urged the overthrow of King George's government in 1776). It held, instead, that if the State could do so, it would have to be on proof that the particular church was guilty of the offense, and could not take as adequate proof the fact that the church refused to sign an oath stating that it did not do so.

The second case, *United States* v. *Christian Echoes National Ministry*, involved a church, established and headed by the Reverend Billy James Hargis, a fundamentalist right-wing duly ordained minister. Its "Articles of Faith" declared that "atheistic world forces seek the destruction and overthrow of all the religions of the World and the destruction of all free government." It considered its mission to be to "combat militantly and aggressively, and to expose publicly, any person or organization whose words or actions inculcate leftist, socialist or communist philosophies or aims, intentionally or otherwise, into any phase of American life." It declared itself to be "the largest, fastest growing and most active organization in America solely devoted to combatting Communism."

The Internal Revenue Service revoked the church's tax exemption on two grounds: first, the church had violated a provision in the Internal Service Code forbidding tax-exempt organizations from devoting a substantial part of their activities to propaganda or other efforts to influence legislation; and second, it had violated another provision forbidding them to participate in political campaigns in behalf of any candidate. In respect to the first ground, the Federal court of appeals found that the church had expressed itself on such issues as prayer in the public schools (it favored prayer), the McCarran-Walter Immigration Law (it opposed immigration), freedom of speech in the United States (too much was dangerous), the responsibility of the press (the press was irresponsible), the continuance of the House Committee on Un-American Activities (yes), Federal aid to education (no), socialized medicine (no), public housing (no), the Federal income tax (no), and the United Nations (absolutely not). In respect to the second ground, the court found that the church had endorsed the candidacy of Senator Goldwater in the 1964 presidential campaign.

Since the court of appeals upheld the revocation on both grounds and the Supreme Court, in rejecting the appeal of the church in 1973, did not state the reason for its action, we do not know on what ground the rejection was based. If it was on the second ground, the decision was quite narrow and easily defensible. If, however, it was on the first ground, the consequences may be quite grave.

Religion has a long history of expressing itself on what are generally considered political matters. Isaiah preached against the monopolists of Judah, "Woe unto them that join house to house and lay field to field till there be no place for others" (Isaiah 5:8). The established priesthood of Israel charged the prophet Amos with conspiracy because of his condemnation of tyranny and injustice in the Northern Kingdom (Amos 7:10). Jeremiah suffered imprisonment and risked his life for his public opposition of the war policies of the king of Judah (Jeremiah 37:11-38:28). Jesus, Luther, Savonarola, Muenzer, Martin Luther King, and many other Christian prophets inveighed against the political evils of their times.

In the United States, the political arenas in which religion has intervened are manifold. Slavery, prohibition, birth control, abortion, capital punishment, war and peace, child labor, civil rights and race relations, civil liberties, communism, national security—these are some of the more prominent examples.

The court of appeals rejected the contention by the church that just as a direct prohibition against church expression of positions on political matters would clearly violate the Free Exercise and Freedom of Speech clauses of the First Amendment, so too would an indirect prohibition achieved through forfeiture of tax exemption. The court of appeals refused to accept this argument on the ground that tax exemption was not a right granted by the Constitution but a privilege conferred by Congress, and what Congress gives, it can give conditionally. The Internal Revenue Code does not impose forfeiture of exemption for any occasional or incidental expression on political issues, but only for substantial activities in the political arena. But Congress could just as well impose forfeiture for any political expression by a church. And even under the present law, it is up to the Internal Revenue Service to decide in each case whether a particular church transgressed into the realm of substantiality.

Therein lies the grave danger in the court of appeals' ruling should it be adopted by the Supreme Court. As a matter of economic reality in contemporary America, tax exemption (and with it the deductibility from taxable income of gifts to religious institutions) means survival or death to many churches and synagogues. The inevitable result would be a reign of self-censorship. It would take a particularly courageous congregation and pastor to risk suffering the fate of the Christian Echoes Ministry by expressing what they deem the conscience of the community where controversial public issues are involved. Spiritual leaders, either by command of their congregations or by their own dictates of caution, are likely in a great many cases to restrict their sermons and other public expressions to bland pieties and platitudinous generalities.

Sooner or later the Court will have to decide definitively whether the state can demand political silence of the church in exchange for the privilege of tax exemption. If it should answer affirmatively, a church which believes that its sacred mission compels it to pass judgment on a secular world will have to face the painful alternative of rendering to Caesar what is Caesar's *or* to God what is God's.

(An analogous case, involving freedom to act rather than to believe or express, is now in the Federal courts. It concerns Bob Jones University, a fundamentalist Protestant institution among whose religious tenets is the separation of the races. Accordingly, it denies admission to black students and expels whites who date members of another race. On learning that the Internal Revenue Service was about to revoke its exemption, it brought suit in Federal courts to establish its right to retain both its exempt status and its racial restrictive practices. At the present writing the case is a long way from a decision by the Supreme Court, but it is reasonable to predict that if and when the Court decides the constitutional issues in the case, it will rule against the university, even if it should hold earlier that tax exemption may not be revoked for political beliefs or expressions.)

The Uncertain Future of Exemption

Recently the churches have experienced serious declines in contributions and this, accompanied by inflationary trends in the economy, has caused considerable belt-tightening within some of the major denominations. Naturally, therefore, discontent regarding the wisdom or ethics of accepting tax exemption has been muted within the church. Conversely, however, the same factors have aggravated discontent elsewhere. The church as a self-interest interest group is coming into conflict with its own constituency, which in large measure is middle-income America.

Tax exemption for city churches does not visibly affect urban middle-income Americans, but more and more of them are moving to the suburbs and becoming owners of heavily mortgaged homes. In the suburbs, large estates are often bought up and converted to churches, thus taking them off the tax rolls while at the same time requiring the community to provide additional costly services. Since, in the suburbs, real estate taxes are almost the sole source of local finances, the increased burden on the homeowner can become quite heavy. The resulting unhappiness has manifested itself not only by a growing feeling among suburban homeowners that churches should pay taxes on the property they own, as indicated by public opinion polls, but also by the action of many town authorities in refusing zoning permits for the establishment or the expansion of churches.

Even in the cities, where most people live in rented apartments and therefore do not directly pay real estate taxes, discontent with the present situation is widespread. The more sophisticated citizens recognize that increased taxes result in increased rents, so that indirectly, but realistically, they are bearing the burden of church exemption. City councils, faced by the alarming threats of commercial institutions to follow residents out of the cities if taxes upon their properties continue their upward course, look hungrily to the tax-free land of the churches in the most valuable districts (such as St. Paul's Episcopal Church on Wall Street and St. Patrick's Cathedral on Fifth Avenue, both in New York City).

Because of these and other factors, we can understand why the churches sought to obtain from the Supreme Court a decision that exemption is constitutionally protected. The Court's refusal to make such a decision leaves the state legally free to limit and even abolish exemption. The church is still a powerful interest group and so it is unrealistic to expect abolition to come shortly, but it is fairly predictable that the years, if not the days, of unlimited exemption are numbered. A possible development may be a change in the tax laws which would allow each congregation a specified exemption measured by the value of a modest church structure situated reasonably close to where the congregational members live and adequate in size to accommodate them. The congregation could, if it wished, build a more costly church structure on a larger or higher priced parcel of land, but the value above the specified exemption would be subject to taxation as non-exempt property. Whether this or some other alternative to unlimited exemption is adopted, churches would be wise to plan for a future in which they will no longer enjoy unlimited exemption.

Church Business

A second major tax benefit enjoyed by churches is exemption from taxation (Federal and State) of the income from businesses and other commercial enterprises owned by them or in which they have made investments, most often by purchase of stock. The ownership exemption has but a short lifespan remaining, at least at the Federal level, but it is worth noting as an illustration of the church's effectiveness as a self-interest interest group.

In the 1940s a professor of law at New York University advised the institution that under the Federal tax law, as it then read, it could acquire the stock of the Mueller Spaghetti Company and pay no tax on the profits earned by the sale of spaghetti so long as these profits were all used for educational purposes. The university accepted the advice and found itself in the spaghetti business and in a position to undersell its non–tax-exempt competitors. It was not long before other tax-exempt organizations followed suit.

The ensuing hue and cry raised by non–tax-exempt corporations forced Congress in 1950 to change the law so as to limit the exemption to income earned from enterprises directly related to the purpose of the exempt organization. The change would, for example, continue the exemption on profits of university presses (if university presses make profits) but not of spaghetti factories, for there is no visible direct relation between spaghetti and scholarship. The church lobbies, however, proved more powerful than educational and charitable lobbies and the Treasury Department; at the last moment the bill was amended to continue the exemption on unrelated business activities of churches.

Parenthetically, it may be noted that an analogous situation occurred in 1964. In that year Congress passed the historic Civil Rights Law, one section of which provided that no Federal funds were to be paid to any institution which discriminates on grounds of race, color, religion, or national origin. At the last moment, the bill was amended to eliminate the word "religion," thus permitting sectarian welfare institutions such as homes for the aged, the infirm, or the orphaned to receive Federal grants even though they bar admission to all but members of a particular denomination.

The result of the tax amendment was that a church could operate a girdle business (which one did) or an apartment house or a department store without paying a Federal income tax on the profits, but nobody else could. Even the religious groups could not long accept this. In its brief in the *Walz* case, the United States Catholic Conference informed the Court that it did not defend exemption from taxation accorded church properties used or operated for commercial purposes, and that it had so advised Congress in a joint statement with the National Council of Churches presented to a Senate committee holding hearings on tax-reform bills.

In view of the position adopted by the major American religious organizations, and the widespread protest of non-religious groups, Congress had no choice, and in the Tax Reform Act of 1969 it put the word "religion" back into the law. Churches were thus placed in the same category as other tax-exempt institutions, except that they received a five-year grace period during which they continued to be exempt on the unrelated businesses they owned when the amendment was passed.

This change in the law aborted a lawsuit brought in New York by Americans United, but the question whether income from unrelated business activities of churches may constitutionally be exempted from taxation remained undecided. However, the Tax Reform Act affected only Federal taxation, and some States retained the exemption in respect to their own income tax laws, thus affording the Supreme Court an opportunity to pass upon the constitutional issue in the case of *Diffenderfer* v. *Central Baptist Church of Miami.*

This church owned nearly a square block of land in downtown Miami which was occupied by a church building and an offstreet parking lot. On Sunday, parking was supplied without charge to persons attending the church for worship, but during the rest of the week the lot was operated as any other commercial parking lot in a city business district. Under Florida law, the parking lot was completely exempt from real estate taxation inasmuch as all of its income was used to support the church. Two taxpayers sued in the Florida Federal court challenging the exemption and, when they lost there, appealed to the Supreme Court.

In February 1971 the Supreme Court agreed to take the case and put it on its calendar, but, within a few months thereafter, the Florida legislature changed the law so as to limit the exemption proportionately to the extent that the church property was used for religious purposes. In respect to the church's parking lot, this meant that the exemption amounted to roughly one-seventh of the tax which would have been imposed had the owner been an ordinary business corporation.

In his reply brief to the Supreme Court, the lawyer for one of the plaintiffs conceded that the new statute was constitutional and he did not contend that if any part of church-owned property was used for commercial purposes the Constitution forbade exemption to that part which was used for worship. He conceded too that to the extent that the lot was used for worshipers' parking it was being used for worship within the purview of the *Walz* decision. The lawyer for the other plaintiff disagreed and argued that if church property is used even partly for commercial purposes the property could not constitutionally be exempt to any extent.

Apparently agreeing with the first lawyer's position, the Court held that the case was moot since the Florida legislature had by amendment given to his client all to which he was constitutionally entitled. There was, the Court said, no need therefore to pass upon the question whether government may constitutionally exempt from taxation church-owned property used for commercial purposes. Accordingly, when the case reached the Court for decision in 1972, the appeal was dismissed.

It is probable that those States which still exempt from taxation property used only partly for religious purposes will follow the lead of Florida and amend their statutes accordingly. Hence, it is unlikely that this aspect of exemption will reach the Supreme Court for resolution of the constitutional question. Yet the matter may not rest there. The

Federal government and all the States that have income tax laws exempt from them passive income received by churches, that is, income from corporate stocks and bonds owned by them. Such laws clearly do not affect state sponsorship of religion any more than the real estate tax exemption upheld in the *Walz* decision. However, unlike the latter type of taxation, there is no significant entanglement involved when a church is required to pay an income tax on dividends from corporate stock; no examination of the books of the church nor surveillance of its activities is required. Indeed, by the simple device of withholding (familiar to all wage earners), the state could avoid practically all contact with the church. Finally, the presumption of constitutionality from long usage, which supported the ruling in the *Walz* case, is not present with the same force in respect to income taxation.

The church as stockholder is not always merely a passive investor. Some denominations are now sending their representatives to stockholders' meetings of large corporations to introduce and support resolutions calling for the end of the manufacturing of napalm, for the hiring of more blacks and other racial minorities, and for ending the pollution of air and water. In 1972 the policy-making committee of the World Council of Churches voted overwhelmingly to liquidate its financial stake in all corporations doing business with white-ruled African countries, thus universalizing a policy which had originated in the American churches and had grown increasingly popular in recent years.

We find here internal tensions between the church as self-interest interest group and as ideological interest group. Corporations can make a lot of money in manufacturing napalm and other defense products; ecology protection is expensive, and South Africa and Rhodesia present attractive investment potentialities. In taking the principled positions that it does, the church is sacrificing interest for ideology, but, more relevant to the subject of this section, it may also be endangering its tax-exempt status. We have seen in the *Christian Echoes* case that the Internal Revenue Service takes a dim view of church activism in the political arena even against atheistic communism; it may not be more tolerant of activism in business and industry, particularly where the cause is less popular with the established economic order and the government's nationalist concerns. In the eyes of those responsible for the enforcement of the tax laws, piety and profits may mix very well, but not piety and politics, and particularly not unpopular politics.

Deductions

The most important and least controversial tax benefit enjoyed by churches is the deductibility from reportable gross income of contributions made to them by taxpayers. It is most important because even among churches engaged in profit-making enterprises (in proportion to membership the Mormon Church probably ranks first), the major part of church income comes not from business profits but from voluntary contributions; and the most important nonspiritual incentive to contributions is tax deductibility. It is least controversial because unlike, for example, oil-depletion allowances, it is a game any number can play and of which most taxpayers can take advantage. True enough, it is of no value to the very poor, who pay no taxes, nor to the moderately poor, who do not itemize their deductions but take the flat ten percent allowable under the law. But political power in the United States does not lie in the very poor or the moderately poor, but in the middle income and affluent, and these can and do play the game.

One form of tax benefit akin, if not identical, to deductibility has aroused controversy: the according of tax credits for tuition payments to parochial schools. This, however, is closely related to governmental aid to church schools and is more conveniently treated in the chapter dealing with that subject.

Chapter Three

The Family

Marriage

Marriage, in our legal system, is a civil institution, as it was in biblical times. No particular religious rite, such as the offering of a sacrifice, was associated with it. No priest solemnized it, nor was it required to be entered into at the temple; Cana or any other place would do as well. Catholicism made of it a sacrament, but Protestantism refused to follow suit, and neither it nor Judaism requires that marriage ceremonies be performed by a clergyman, or take place in a church or synagogue.

True enough, religious ceremonial marriages have become traditional and most Americans are married by clergymen. The latter, however, are licensed by the States to solemnize marriages and when they do, they act as State officials and to that extent they are in the same category as justices of the peace and municipal marriage clerks. Because marriage remains a civil institution it is within the constitutional power to require that all marriages be licensed and recorded. Although no State does so, it is probably also constitutional to require (as in many European countries) that the couple appear before a governmental official and enter into a civil solemnization in addition to their religious one, and to refuse to accord legal recognition to a purely religious ceremony.

Clearly, under the Free Exercise Clause a State may

not forbid a couple to participate in a religious marriage ceremony, and under that clause, as well as the Establishment Clause, it may not do the converse; that is, require all marrying couples to participate in a religious ceremony. Lest it be supposed that this suggestion is fanciful, it should be pointed out that until a few years ago this is exactly what at least one State did require. Under Maryland law, no marriage was legal unless it was solemnized by a clergyman of some faith. No couple sought to challenge the constitutionality of the law; the wheels of justice move very slowly, and even the most conscientious anti-religious couple would find it easy to drive across the border to Virginia, Delaware, or the District of Columbia rather than make a Federal case about the matter.

While, due to the influence of Protestantism, a religious marriage ceremony is not required under American law (Maryland was originally a Catholic colony), Protestantism did transmit to secular law biblical concepts of permitted and prohibited marriages. With minor modifications, Mosaic principles of the degrees of consanguinity which disqualify a couple from marrying are to be found in the marriage statutes of every State in the Union; in the United States, Chapter 18 of Leviticus is the law of the land.

The religious origin of the prohibition of marriage between brother and sister or father and daughter does not make it unconstitutional under the Establishment Clause, any more than does the presence of "Thou shalt not kill" in the Ten Commandments invalidate governmental prohibition of homicide. In *McGowan* v. *Maryland*, the Court, in upholding the constitutionality of Sunday closing laws, recognized that their origin was religious; but, the Court held, the test is not what the laws once were but what they are today, and today they are secular welfare laws designed to secure for every person at least one day's rest in seven. Because marriage is now a civil institution, it is subject to governmental regulation in respect to who may and who may not marry whom.

The state's power and judgment in this respect are not unlimited. In *Loving* v. *Virginia* (1967), the Court ruled that under the Equal Protection Clause, a State may not forbid marriage between persons of different races. By reason of that clause and the Establishment and Free Exercise clauses, it even more certainly may not prohibit marriage between persons of different religions. However, where secular concerns are involved its judgment as to marital eligibility is quite broad.

For this reason a State may outlaw bigamous marriages (licit under the laws of both Moses and Jesus), even where commanded by religion. This, as we have seen, is what the Court held in *Reynolds* v. *United States*, where it said:

> Marriage, while from its very nature a sacred obligation, is nevertheless, in most civilized nations a civil contract, and usually regulated by law. Upon it society may be said to be built, and out of its fruits spring social relations and social obligations and duties, with which government is necessarily required to deal.

Since the monogamous family is still at least nominally the basis of Western society, it is not likely that the Court will soon upset the *Reynolds* decision. This is so not because deviations from the monogamous lifestyle are rare. (In 1946, in the case of *Cleveland* v. *United States*, the Court held that a fundamentalist Mormon who traveled across the State border with his wives was guilty of violating the Mann Act —officially known as the White Slave Traffic Act—which makes it a crime to transport in interstate commerce "any woman or girl for the purpose of prostitution or debauchery or for any other immoral purpose.") The kept mistress, the modern counterpart of the biblical concubine, is a well-known institution in our society, and while it is true that few can afford it, this has always been the case in respect to a second wife or a concubine. The functional equivalent of concubinage in middle-America, particularly in suburbia, is adultery and, apparently with increasing frequency, wife-swapping parties. But these operate on the fringes of monogamous family life and do not openly challenge its integrity. America has accepted plural marriages so long as they are consecutive, but we can expect neither repeal of anti-bigamy laws nor decisions holding them unconstitutional in the foreseeable future.

Despite widespread acceptability of divorce, the state still retains strong interest in the permanence of marriage, and may therefore take appropriate measures to avoid hasty and ill-considered marriage. It may prohibit marriage between persons it deems immature or at least require the consent of their parents. It may impose a waiting period between the obtaining of a license and the marriage, and may prohibit clergymen from advertising or otherwise soliciting marriage (just as it may forbid advertising and solicitation by lawyers and physicians), and in each case may disregard the religious convictions of the persons involved. It may require premarital medical examination for venereal disease and perhaps even forbid marriage until remedial measures are taken. Whether it may bar marriage in the case of incurable hereditary disease is a more difficult question which has not yet reached the Supreme Court. The closest the Court has come to the question is in compulsory sterilization cases.

Even more basic in our social structure than the monogamous is the heterosexual marital relationship. It is therefore not surprising that in the 1972 case of *Baker* v. *Nelson*, the Supreme Court rejected an appeal by a male couple who sought to compel a marriage clerk to issue a license to them. Nor should one expect an early modification of our marriage statutes to accommodate the understandable desires of homosexual couples for a legally recognized permanent marital status.

The newspapers do, however, report, often with pictures, what purport to be ceremonial weddings between persons of the same sex, usually males. So far the public response has been more of amusement than indignation and, so long as the peace is not disturbed, the police do not appear to have interfered. What would happen should public tolerance in some community be strained beyond the breaking point and governmental officials take action to punish the participants in a homosexual marital ceremony is more than a merely interesting academic question. If the person performing the ceremony and the couple claim membership in a religious sect which countenances and perhaps even commands homosexual marriages, a real question under the Free Exercise Clause would be presented.

In the *Reynolds* case the Supreme Court upheld laws punishing Mormons who engage in polygamy; in *Davis* v. *Beason*, decided in 1890, it held that members of the Mormon Church could be disenfranchised even if they did not personally practice polygamy, and in the same year it held in the case of *Church of Latter Day Saints* v. *United States* that the Mormon Church itself could be outlawed, its charter revoked, and all its assets declared forfeited to the government, thereby forcing the Church to change its divinely ordained doctrine and renounce polygamy in order to achieve legitimacy.

Since that time the Court has manifested considerably more tolerance of less conventional religious sects. It has spread the mantle of First Amendment protection over such marginal groups as Jehovah's Witnesses, "I Am," and Black Muslims. But none of these groups has presented so grave a threat to our basic social structure as did the Mormons, who at the time of the Court decisions against them were growing alarmingly in membership notwithstanding or perhaps because of the persecution they were suffering. The contemporary gay movement has already begun to channel some of its organizational activities into the religious domain, and we may anticipate a clash between the command of their beliefs and those of the state with a recourse to the Supreme Court for its ultimate resolution. It should be noted that in this clash we will not be dealing with private acts between consenting adults, but with an open challenge to the nation's family system which could be quite alarming if our birth rate should decline below zero population growth and homosexual liaisons multiply with growing acceptability. The Court, in such circumstances, may be no more hospitable to religiously motivated homosexual families than it was to polygamous ones in the last quarter of the 19th century.

Divorce

America's divorce laws, like most family and sex laws, were written by Protestants, defended by Catholics, and ultimately yielded to by deists. Protestantism interpreted the words of Jesus as sanctioning divorce but only for adultery, and this was reflected in many State divorce codes; indeed, it is barely a decade since even so religiously pluralistic a State as New York amended its laws to allow divorce on grounds other than adultery. (Surprisingly, New England Calvinism was to some extent more liberal. In colonial Massachusetts, female adultery, though not male, was a ground for divorce; but so too were cruelty by the husband and abandonment by either.)

Among the major faiths, Judaism permitted husbands to divorce for almost any cause or perhaps even no cause at all; according to the Talmud, a man could divorce his wife if she burned his food in cooking. New York Jews, who make up a substantial percentage of the State's population and are politically influential even beyond their numbers, had no religiously founded difficulty in urging liberalization of the divorce law. Protestants joined Jews and deists in working for reform, but resistance by the even more politically influential Catholic Church delayed it for decades.

Catholic Canon Law is clear on the subject. It goes back at least to the Council of Trent, which decreed:

> If any one saith that the Church has erred in that she has taught and doth teach, in accordance with the evangelical and apostolical doctrine, that the bond of matrimony cannot

be dissolved on account of the adultery of one of the married parties; and that both, or even the innocent one who gave not occasion to the adultery, can not contract another marriage during the lifetime of the other; and that he is guilty of adultery who, having put away the adultress, shall take another wife, as also she who, having put away the adulterer, shall take another husband, let him be anathema.

The Catholic Church, with all its political power, could not turn back the clock and effect complete repeal of the State's divorce law even in cases of adultery. It could, however, for many years effectively overcome efforts at liberalization. Many Catholics felt uncomfortable with this stance of the Church, and found it difficult to justify even within the framework of Catholic dogma and principles. Contraceptive birth control, artificial insemination and abortion, all opposed by the Church, are deemed by it to be violations of the natural law which is binding on all human beings, even the unbaptized. But Catholicism does not deny that divorce is permissible under the laws of Moses and Mohammed; Jesus forbade it only to those who entered into marriage as a holy sacrament. The explanation lies in the urge of religious groups to translate their own concepts and values into imperatives for the entire community.

But even the Rock of Peter cannot withstand forever the winds of change. Within Catholicism itself there is growing discontent with the rigidity of the traditional Church doctrine on divorce and remarriage. Not only laymen but priests too are demanding that some means be found within doctrine whereby marriages of divorced Catholics can be recognized as licit. In any event, New York joined the ranks of the other States and liberalized its laws to make divorce legally possible when the judge is convinced that the marriage is not salvageable. Like many other States, New York imposes upon the divorce court the responsibility of exploring the possibility of reconciliation and of seeking to effect it if the possibility exists. Some of these statutes authorize the judge to enlist the assistance of clergymen of the faith to which the parties belong. Illinois had such a statute, but in 1950 the State supreme court declared it unconstitutional as a violation of the principle of separation of church and state under the First Amendment. The issue has never reached the United States Supreme Court and is not likely to so long as the parties are free to refuse the clergyman's offer of consultation or assistance. Should a court deny a divorce decree because of such refusal by one or both of the parties and the case reach the Supreme Court, it is hard to see how the constitutionality of the statute could be upheld under either the Establishment or Free Exercise Clause.

Today, divorce by consent, with waiting periods of up to three years, is legally feasible in every State in the Union —legally, but not necessarily economically. Divorce can be quite expensive; court fees must be paid and lawyers must be hired. For many poor people, the total cost may be prohibitive. The Supreme Court has attempted to alleviate the situation to some extent. In *Boddie* v. *Connecticut*, it held in 1971 that under the Equal Protection Clause of the Fourteenth Amendment, a State could not deny a poor person a divorce because he or she could not afford to pay the customary court fees. This meets only part of the problem; until the Court rules that under the amendment the States must provide poor people with lawyers in civil cases as they are required to in criminal ones, the only divorce available to many poor people will be the *de facto* one of simply leaving home and setting up an independent establishment elsewhere with or without another helpmeet.

Prevention of Birth

Contraception

Dead-letter laws are to be found in the domains of both God and Caesar, and prohibition of contraception (as of Sabbath desecration) is such a law. God's law came first, going back, according to Catholic doctrine, to the death of

Onan, grandson of the patriarch Jacob, for spilling his seed on the ground rather than impregnate his brother's widow. While this explanation was not shared by Judaism or Protestantism, orthodoxy in both agreed that the practice was sinful, or at least immoral, and it was Protestant influence which wrote the prohibition in Federal and State laws in the United States. Mainstream Protestantism has long since given up its support of such laws and in fact now takes the directly opposite position that governmental failure to encourage and assist in the use of contraception as a means of population control is itself a dereliction of moral and ethical duty. In Judaism, only Orthodoxy, committed as it is to the immutability of Mosaic law as interpreted and applied by later rabbis, still adheres to the sinfulness of contraception (except under special circumstances); but very few Orthodox Jews abide by the doctrine, and contraception among them is almost as universal as among other Jews and Americans generally.

Catholicism's opposition to reform or repeal of birth control laws was the major stumbling block standing in the way of legitimizing a universal practice. Unlike Protestantism and Judaism, there are, theoretically at least, no divisions in Catholicism and the only doctrine is orthodox. In Catholic doctrine, interference with the birth-producing effect of intercourse (except by limiting intercourse to the "safe" periods) violates not merely canon law but natural law, and it is therefore legitimate and indeed obligatory upon secular government to forbid it to all. But the Catholic doctrinal prohibition of contraception, even to Catholics, is almost as much a dead-letter law as secular prohibition is to others. Notwithstanding increasing protests within Catholicism and widespread acquiescence (if not affirmative encouragement) by priests in the prevalent disregard of the prohibition by the faithful, the Church itself has not yet found a way to get this old man of the sea off its back.

In the realm of Caesar, most States had little difficulty in converting from Protestant orthodoxy to deistic libertarianism by the simple device of allowing an exception for

"health" reasons, and who is to say that condoms are purchased at the corner pharmacy for reasons other than
health (they are still euphemistically called prophylactics)?
In Massachusetts and Connecticut, where Congregationalist Calvinism had been replaced by Catholicism as the
dominant religiopolitical force, there was no "health" exception; and efforts to repeal or amend the anti-contraception laws failed because of Church opposition. Deists and
their allies in those States had therefore no recourse but
to appeal to the Supreme Court to achieve their objective.

The Court, however, showed itself quite reluctant to
get involved. In 1943 a physician in New Haven brought a
suit against Connecticut officials alleging that their enforcement of the State's anti-contraception law interfered with
his professional duty to advise three patients whose lives
would be endangered by childbearing. The Court dismissed
the appeal (*Tileston* v. *Ullman*) on the ground that while the
patients whose lives were endangered by enforcement of
the law could have sued, the physician had no "standing" to
do so.

Learning the lesson of this decision, the law and medical faculties of Yale University conspired in 1961 to force the
Supreme Court to pass upon the question. Accordingly, the
plaintiffs' attorney (a professor at the Yale Law School)
brought suit not only on behalf of a physician (head of the
gynecology department of the medical school), but also for
two married couples who alleged that contraceptive treatment was necessary, in the one case to prevent birth of
infants with congenital abnormalities, and in the other to
prevent probable loss of the wife's life should she become
pregnant. This was to no avail. A majority of the Court held
(in *Poe* v. *Ullman*) that since, as a matter of fact, the statute
was not enforced, and contraceptive advice and assistance
were freely available in Connecticut without fear of prosecution, there was no real or substantial controversy for
the Court to adjudicate, and again the appeal was dismissed.

To the Court, Connecticut's anti-contraception statute

was a dead-letter law, but the justices did not deem it their business to issue the death certificate. They were, however, mistaken; the law was dead only as it concerned the middle class and the affluent, who could consult their family doctors and obtain contraceptive materials without fear of prosecution or interference. The poor, however, were not so fortunate; they could afford neither medical help, except perhaps when they were really ill, nor the cost of contraceptive devices. For them, contraception was available only if free or low-cost birth control clinics could lawfully operate in the State, and this was not possible in Connecticut.

So the Yale law and medical faculties went back to the drawing board. Under the auspices of the Connecticut Planned Parenthood League, the gynecology professor opened a birth control center in New Haven and, together with the league's executive director, got himself arrested for violating the anti-contraception law. The law professor having died, another took his place and again brought the case to the Supreme Court.

This time persistence was rewarded. In 1965, the Court not only took the case (*Griswold* v. *Connecticut*), but ruled the law unconstitutional. The first part was easier than the second; all the justices agreed that the appeal should be taken, but two of them dissented from the holding that the law was unconstitutional, and the other seven could not point to any specific provision in the Constitution that the law violated. Justice Douglas, writing for the majority of the Court, asserted that within the spectrum of the Bill of Rights there is a right of marital privacy upon which the state may not infringe. (Earlier decisions had read general rights of privacy and of association into the Bill of Rights.) "Would we," he asked, "allow the police to search the sacred precincts of marital bedrooms for telltale signs of the use of contraceptives? The very idea is repulsive to the notions of privacy surrounding the marriage relationships."

Douglas emphasized in his opinion that, at the clinic,

information, instruction, and advice on contraception were given "to married persons." The right he read into the Constitution was that of "marital privacy." He closed his opinion with a paean of praise for the institution of marriage:

> We deal [he said] with a right of privacy older than the Bill of Rights—older than our political parties, older than our school system. Marriage is a coming together for better or for worse, hopefully enduring, and intimate to the degree of being sacred. It is an association that promotes a way of life, not causes; a harmony in living, not political faiths; a bilateral loyalty, not commercial or social projects. Yet it is an association for as noble a purpose as any involved in our prior decisions.

All this was very fine, and it may have been necessary in order to persuade a majority of the Court to agree to the decision (even though neither the gynecology professor nor the executive director was arrested for practicing contraception in his marital bed). It had, however, one significant drawback: the clear implication of the decision was that the state could forbid contraception by unmarried persons and the supplying of information and materials to them. This raised practical problems. Would a pharmacist have to demand production of a marriage certificate before he sold a package of condoms to a customer, just as a tavern keeper insists upon seeing a birth certificate before he sells a drink to a youngish looking patron? If so, how could he be sure with whom they would be used; had he to insist upon a letter of authorization from the customer's spouse?

What explains the Court's use of the marital-privacy concept to invalidate Connecticut's law is the requirement that the Court determine conflicts between church and state or within the ranks of either in accordance with the rules of the game. This means that if the Court cannot point to specific language in the Constitution, it must justify its decision on the basis of some constitutional principle that it has previously announced, although it may and often does extend it. In the *Griswold* case, as the Court pointed out, previous decisions had recognized a right of privacy; the Court was simply extending it to the marital relationship.

The fact of the matter is that the *Griswold* decision was outdated almost as soon as it was handed down. Nonmarital intercourse on a wide scale was a fact of life and so too was the societal need to limit its progenitive consequences. If the Supreme Court were to cooperate in making this possible, it would have to do so by extending the marital-privacy concept to unmarried persons. This it did in the 1972 case of *Eisenstadt* v. *Baird*.

Following the *Griswold* decision, Massachusetts amended its anti-contraception law to comply with the marital-privacy concept. It allowed physicians and pharmacists to supply drugs or devices for the purpose of preventing pregnancy to married persons but not to the unmarried. Under this law, William Baird, an active proponent of planned parenthood (but neither a physician not a pharmacist), was convicted for handing out contraceptive articles following a lecture on planned parenthood to students at Boston University.

The Supreme Court held the conviction unconstitutional on the ground that the law discriminated against unmarried persons and therefore violated the Equal Protection Clause of the Fourteenth Amendment. True enough, the discrimination seemed to be justified and in fact required by the marital-privacy rationale of the *Griswold* decision, but the Court effectually expanded the concept to encompass sexual privacy (at least in respect to heterosexual relations). The Court's opinion, by Justice Brennan, said:

> If under *Griswold* the distribution of contraceptives to married persons cannot be prohibited, a ban on distribution to unmarried persons would be equally impermissible. It is true that in *Griswold* the right of privacy in question inhered in the marital relationship. Yet the marital couple is not an independent entity with a mind and heart of its own, but an association of two individuals each with a separate intellec-

tual and emotional make-up. If the right of privacy means anything, it is the right of the *individual*, married or single, to be free from unwarranted governmental intrusion into matters so fundamentally affecting a person as the decision whether to bear or beget a child.

Although the Court's opinion seemed to leave open some possibilities for restrictive, though not completely prohibitive, legislation (e.g., under general pure food and drug laws), its practical effect was to wipe out all laws whose purpose was to forbid or restrict contraceptive prevention of births.

As has been noted, Catholicism defends anti-contraception statutes on the ground that artificial contraception is a violation of the natural law which is binding on all persons including the unbaptized. However, it also points to God's punishment of Onan as authority for its position, although neither Protestantism nor Judaism accepts this interpretation of the biblical incident, nor do they necessarily agree that contraception violates the natural law. Catholic spokesmen therefore have found it necessary to offer a broader justification for Catholic opposition to repeal, and have resorted to morality, the reason which Protestants propounded for inducing the legislatures to pass the laws in the first place. Sexual relations between the unmarried, which all agree is immoral (or, at least, did until recently), is deterred by the fear of pregnancy, and if this is eliminated by the availability of contraceptives, widespread promiscuity would result. Since it is impracticable to enforce a law limited to the unmarried, manufacture and sale must be prohibited even though married couples are thereby deprived of their use.

The difficulty with this rationale is that it did not work. Anti-contraception statutes are violated as ubiquitously as traffic laws and there was not the slightest evidence that promiscuity was in any way deterred by their presence in the lawbooks. This does not explain why it was necessary to remove them from the lawbooks. The penal codes in many States still declare it a crime to commit adultery or fornication (the latter defined as sexual relations between unmarried participants). Were these laws enforced there might be more criminals in the United States than innocent jurymen to send them to jail or jailers to keep them there. Why, then, did the Court find it necessary to do in 1965 in the *Griswold* case and in 1972 in the *Eisenstadt* case what it had refused to do earlier in the *Poe* and *Tileston* cases, namely, declare the laws unconstitutional?

Paradoxically, the anti-contraception laws had to be removed from the books because their presence made it impossible for the state to encourage contraception, something it now increasingly deems necessary to do. The middle income and the affluent, married and unmarried, use contraceptives; the poor have babies. When the poor, often racial minorities, are on the welfare rolls, taxpaying Americans rebel and expect the state to do something about it. Depriving the mothers of welfare benefits has been tried in a few States, but most consider it inhumane and the courts have declared it unlawful. Another device that has been tried is to compel the mother to identify the father so that the authorities can proceed against him to force him to support his child. This, too, has not worked, assuming it is constitutional.

The reality of the situation is that welfare recipients are going to sleep together no less than the affluent taxpayers, and the only practical way to keep welfare costs down is to encourage them to practice birth control. The national government already established this policy as part of its program of aid to underdeveloped countries, but the States could hardly follow suit as long as their own laws forbade the practice. After all, how can a city allow or instruct doctors and nurses in municipal hospitals to counsel welfare mothers giving birth in these hospitals regarding birth control or even allow advertisements of planned parenthood groups to appear in municipal buses and subways when contraception is a crime against the State? (In *Eisenstadt* v. *Baird* the Court invalidated not only the ban on providing contraceptive materials to the unmarried but also the provision limiting the source to physicians and pharmacists, a limitation whose obvious purpose was to curtail if not make completely impossible the operation of planned parenthood clinics.)

Yet, Sunday blue laws are as obsolete and universally violated as anti-contraception laws and, only four years before the *Griswold* decision, the Court, in *McGowan* v. *Maryland*, refused to declare them unconstitutional, and left it to the States to repeal them, which the States have still refused to do. Why did it take a more activist approach to anti-contraception laws? The answer may lie in the fact that the justices recognized the need to get the laws off the books to enable the States to take affirmative action toward encouraging and assisting birth control, or at the very least not to prevent private groups from doing so; but they also realized that as a matter of political reality the States were not going to repeal the laws, as the twice-unsuccessful effort in Connecticut evidenced.

In this respect the nine judges on the Supreme Court, being immune to political reprisal since they serve for life, may be performing a significant though quite controversial function; they may be compelling the people to accept what the judges think is good for them but which they would not accept from elected legislators. One example of this is the case of *Reitman* v. *Mulkey*, decided in 1967. There, the Court held unconstitutional a provision written into the California constitution by popular referendum which guaranteed the right of owners not to sell or rent their houses to racial minorities if they did not wish to do so. Another example is the 1972 case of *Furman* v. *Georgia*, in which the Court declared the death penalty to be unconstitutional even though the legislatures in the great majority of States refused to take it off the books by repeal. Birth prevention through contraception may be in the same category, and so too may be abortion.

Abortion

Even more than in the case of contraception, there was until very recently agreement between both church and state that abortion should be forbidden. None of the major (nor any known minor) faiths sanctioned it; the laws of every State in the Union made it a criminal offense. The rationale varied. In Catholic doctrine, life begins with conception and may not be directly destroyed even when necessary to preserve the health or the life of the mother. The Catholic position was set forth in a statement issued by the National Conference of Catholic Bishops in 1970:

> The child in the womb is human. Abortion is an unjust destruction of a human life and morally that is murder. Society has no right to destroy this life. Even the expectant mother has no such right. The law must establish every possible protection for the child before and after birth.

Neither the other faiths nor the state had gone that far. Generally they did not consider abortion to be the destruction of human life until the fetus is quick, which, under most State laws, is placed at 24 weeks after conception. Moreover, they deemed abortion, even after that time, to be justifiable if necessary to preserve the life of the mother and perhaps even her health. But all have agreed that abortion any time after conception, solely to prevent unwanted birth, was sinful, immoral, and punishable.

That is, until recently. The change in public opinion regarding abortion has been rapid and sharp. Polls, if they are to be believed, indicate that even among Catholics, Americans by overwhelming majorities approve abortion where necessary to protect the mother's health or to prevent birth of a possibly defective child; and probably a majority of non-Catholic Americans accept what opponents call abortion on demand. At the Democratic National Convention in 1972 it took the direct intervention of the presidential candidate to head off certain adoption of a plank calling for repeal of anti-abortion laws and asserting that decisions on abortion should be left exclusively to the affected women and their physicians. Although President Nixon had publicly expressed his condemnation of abortion and opposition to repeal, the Republicans followed the Democrats' lead and remained tactfully silent in their national platform. Most remarkable of all, in 1970 the legislature of New York, the State with the largest Catholic population in the nation, made abortion on demand legal at any time up to 24 weeks after conception. A few other States followed suit, and several more liberalized their statutes so as to allow abortion for reasons of mental (rather than merely physical) health. Indeed, by 1972 a Presidential Commission on Population Growth and the American Future, appointed by President Nixon, recommended that abortions should be easily available in all States; and it took White House intervention to prevent distribution to public schools and colleges of a government-sponsored film advocating legalized abortion.

Wherein lies the explanation for this dramatic change? Partly it is to be found in changing standards of morality (manifested, if not to some extent caused, by Supreme Court decisions practically making pornography legal) which now seem to accept premarital sexual relations; partly the women's liberation movement and its claim that a woman has the right to decide what will happen to her own body; partly in the recognition (though hardly new) that realistically the choice is not between legal abortions and no abortions, but between safe legal ones and dangerous, sordid, illegal ones. All this is true, yet it is probable that a major factor here, as in the case of contraceptive birth control, is the taxpayers' revolt against rising welfare rolls and costs. Legalization of contraception not having worked to an acceptable degree, and other measures (such as forfeiture for adoption of all illegitimate children after the second, proposed by a California panel set up by Governor Ronald Reagan to cope with the problem of growing welfare rolls) proving too Draconian for public acceptance, permissible abortion, encouraged by the state, is the next logical step.

This does not mean that voting for abortion repeal is now politically safe. Far from it. The rural New York legislator whose vote contributed to the majority of one for repeal paid for his independence; he was defeated in the next election. The other legislators learned the lesson and at the 1972 session repealed the repealer so as to reinstate the former restrictive law, and it was only the governor's veto which frustrated that effort. In Connecticut, at the urging of the governor, the legislature went further and enacted an even more restrictive law than was previously on the books, and permitted abortion only when necessary to save the mother's life. In Pennsylvania, a similar legislative effort failed only because of the governor's veto, while in most other States the legislatures carefully kept away from the subject.

The reason for this is not merely that politicians are a timid lot—which they are—or are skeptical about public opinion polls—which they may be. It lies in a reality which political scientists learn from studies and statistics and politicians from experience, sometimes bitter. Certain subjects affect particular interest groups so deeply that a legislator's unfavorable position will cause the members to vote against him no matter what his record on other issues may be, while most other voters are not likely to judge him on a single issue. Few Jews, for example, will vote for a candidate whose position is that the government should be less pro-Israel and more pro-Arab or even neutral, no matter what his overall record may be. Most non-Jews, however, will vote for a candidate if they favor the positions he generally espouses even though they do not agree with his position on Israel. Gun control may be in that category in respect to members of the American Rifle Association or even non-members who own rifles. So too is abortion with respect to Catholics. In this case, as in contraception, aid to parochial schools, capital punishment, obscenity legislation, and others, many legislators were probably counting upon the Supreme Court to resolve the issues and thus relieve them of the need to make a painful choice between conscience and prudence.

If so, the first results were inconclusive. In *United States v. Vuitch*, the Court in 1971 refused to declare unconstitutional a Federal statute forbidding abortion in the District of Columbia except where necessary for the mother's life or health. Nevertheless, it so interpreted the law as to make convictions under it difficult. It held that, in order to get a conviction, it was up to the prosecutor to prove to the jury that the abortion was not necessary for the mother's life or health. Since neither the mother nor the physician, nurse, or other participant in the operation could be compelled to testify, it would not be easy for the prosecution to prove that the operation was not necessary. In the second place, the Court interpreted the word "health" to include mental health, and who was to say that a mother's mental health would not be endangered if she were forced to bear an unwanted child?

This was not an adequate resolution of the problem. First, not all States allow an exception for reasons of health; many require that the life of the mother must be endangered by birth, and even where health is allowed as an exception, physical health is what is often meant. Furthermore, and perhaps more important, the decision did not meet the needs of the poor who receive their medical services from municipal and county hospitals and clinics. So long as an anti-abortion law was in the State's criminal code, the physicians and nurses were not likely to perform an abortion or even counsel one where the only reason for it was that the mother was a welfare recipient with seven children and no husband. In 1972 a Federal court in New York held that abortion costs were covered by Medicaid, but such a decision would not seem possible in a State where abortion was a crime.

The *Vuitch* decision, however, was not the Supreme Court's last word on the subject. The Court's opinion said so expressly, and practically invited another all-out attack on the constitutionality of anti-abortion laws. That came in 1973, in the cases of *Roe* v. *Wade* and *Doe* v. *Bolton;* and this time the pro-abortion forces and the legislators who secretly sympathized with them were not disappointed.

The decisions in these cases went further than all but the most optimistic advocates of abortion on demand had any right to expect. Only two of the justices (White and Rehnquist) dissented; the opinions were written by Justice Blackmun, a Nixon appointee, and were concurred in by the other two Nixon appointees, Chief Justice Burger and Justice Powell. (Nixon had often strongly expressed his opposition to liberalized abortion laws.) The importance of the 7-2 vote lies in the fact that it makes an early overruling unlikely.

Moreover, the decisions effected a radical change in existing law; they invalidated anti-abortion statutes in the majority of the States, and substantially weakened them in most of the others.

Finally, while refusing to impose upon the nation the principle of abortion on demand during the entire period of pregnancy, the Court did hold that during the first trimester all women have a constitutional right to abortion on demand, and neither the States nor the Federal government can infringe on it.

The Court refused to hold, as urged by the anti-abortion forces, that a fetus is a "person" within the meaning of the Fifth and Fourteenth amendments to the Constitution, which provide that no person shall be deprived of life, liberty, or property without due process of law; had they so held, all abortions would be unconstitutional, and even laws which permitted them where necessary to save the mother's life would in all probability also have to be declared unconstitutional. (How can the state kill innocent A to save the life of B?) This would have written into the Constitution the most rigid Catholic doctrine, which, polls show, is unacceptable, even to most Catholics.

The Court, too, refused to enter the thicket of medical, theological, and philosophical dispute on when "life" begins. Instead, it approached the problem from the standpoint of the rights of the woman and the powers of the state to restrict them. In the *Griswold* case, the Court had recognized a constitutional right of marital privacy; in the *Eisenstadt* case, it extended the right to encompass bedroom privacy. In the *Roe* and *Doe* decisions, it extended it still further to accord protection to a woman's right to the privacy of her person.

Like all constitutional rights, the right of bodily privacy is not absolute. Though it is a fundamental right, it must nevertheless yield to overriding or compelling contrary interests of the state. Hence, a woman does not have the absolute right to do with her body whatever she wills, any more than a widow has a right to throw herself on her husband's funeral pyre. The state, therefore, may regulate abortion practices to the extent necessary to protect the woman's safety and health. However, the Court continued, statistics show that abortion during the first trimester of pregnancy is at least as safe as allowing pregnancy to continue to term, and that during this period the mortality rate in abortion is lower than in normal childbirth. Because of this, the Court held, during the first trimester of pregnancy, the abortion decision and its effectuation must be left to the will of the woman and the medical judgment of her attending physician. A requirement that all abortions, even those during the first trimester, must be performed in a hospital or only on approval of a medical committee would be unconstitutional.

After the first trimester, the state, in promoting its interest in the health of the mother, may, if it chooses, regulate the abortion procedure in ways that are reasonably related to maternal health; and this might require that all late abortions be conducted in hospitals. However, a requirement of approval by a medical committee has no rational connection with the patient's needs, unduly infringes on her physician's right to practice, and is therefore unconstitutional. So too is a bar on abortions where the woman has not been a resident in the State for a specified period of time, since this too has no relation to the woman's health.

After the fetus becomes viable (i.e., can live outside the mother's body), the state has greater latitude and may regulate or even forbid abortions by reason of its compelling interest in the potentiality, if not actuality, of human life. But even there, it may not forbid abortions which are medically necessary for the preservation of the life or health of the mother.

Such was the reasoning of the Court in *Roe* v. *Wade* and *Doe* v. *Bolton*. Yet it is difficult to escape the conclusion that nonlegal factors significantly influenced the decisions: our socioeconomic situation calls for the availability of abortion as a birth-prevention technique; because of the image of Catholic political power the legislatures cannot be relied upon to effectuate the necessary changes to make birth-preventive abortion available to those who must resort to Medicaid or cannot afford to travel to an abortion-on-demand State; and that for all these reasons the Court had to do what had to be done and did it. (A study made by New York City's Health Services Administration in 1973 indicated that without the State's liberalized abortion law there would have been 24,000 additional children on the city's welfare rolls.)

Sterilization

Sterilization is a third means of preventing birth which, along with contraception and abortion, raises problems for church and state. In the past it has been used primarily for eugenic purposes rather than population control, and it is still rather rarely used in the United States for the latter purpose. Nevertheless, in recent years there has been increased interest in the subject and serious promotion of it as a means of birth control. There have even been suggestions, apparently seriously intended, by some legislators that unwed relief recipients be compulsorily sterilized if they bear more than two or three illegitimate children.

Here, as elsewhere, God seems to speak most clearly through the Catholic.tongue. In Catholicism, sterilization, like contraception and abortion, is a violation of the natural law and therefore should be prohibited by the state to all— non-Catholic and Catholic. Neither Protestantism nor Judaism, theologically fragmented as they are, has a single position on the question, but it is probable that most clergymen in both faiths find no religious obstacle to voluntary sterilization for either eugenic or population control purposes.

The question has reached the Supreme Court in two cases, but both involved compulsory sterilization which was eugenic in purpose. The first case, *Buck* v. *Bell*, was decided in 1927 and in it the Court upheld the sterilization under Virginia law of a feeble-minded eighteen-year-old who, after giving birth to an illegitimate child, was committed to a State institution where her own feeble-minded mother was an inmate. In his opinion for the Court, Justice Holmes said:

> It is better for all the world, if instead of waiting to execute degenerate offspring for crime, or to let them starve for their imbecility, society can prevent those who are manifestly unfit from continuing their kind. The principle that sustains compulsory vaccination is broad enough to cover cutting the Fallopian tubes. Three generations of imbeciles are enough.

Justice Holmes is considered by many to have been the outstanding liberal in the Court's entire history. His opinion was concurred in by Justices Brandeis and Stone, also considered to have been great liberals, and by all but one of the other members of the Court, all generally deemed to have been conservatives. The only dissenter (without opinion) was Pierce Butler, the one Catholic on the Court. The inference appears to be that the ranks of Caesar were united but those of God, divided.

The second case, *Skinner* v. *Oklahoma*, came to the Court in 1942 and resulted in a startlingly different decision. There, the Court unanimously held unconstitutional a statute providing for the sterilization of persons found to be "habitual criminals"; that is, those who had been twice convicted of felonies other than "offenses arising out of the violation of the prohibitory [regulatory] laws, revenue acts, embezzlement, or political offenses." Of the justices who participated in the decision in *Buck* v. *Bell* only Stone was still on the bench, and while he did not call for repudiation of that decision he was clearly concerned about its possible implications. Concern, too, was expressed by Justice Jackson, who said:

> There are limits to the extent to which a legislatively represented majority may conduct biological experiments at the expense of the dignity and personality and natural powers of a minority—even those who have been guilty of what the majority defines as crimes.

The Court, however, did not find it necessary to pass judgment on all compulsory sterilization laws. It declared the Oklahoma statute invalid under the Equal Protection Clause of the Fourteenth Amendment because it found no rational basis for differentiating between persons who commit felonies generally and those who commit felonies which the statute exempts from the consequence of sterilization.

It is appropriate to suggest two possible, though unexpressed, explanations for the difference in results in the *Buck* and *Skinner* decisions. In the interim since the first case, Nazi Germany gave the world an opportunity to see what some governments could do with compulsory sterilization laws based on the same scientific assumptions as the Virginia and Oklahoma laws. While none of the justices expected anything nearly so Draconian to occur in the United States in the foreseeable future, the above quotation from

Justice Jackson's concurring opinion shows that some of them at least were troubled.

The other explanation is somewhat more subtle, but no less real. *Skinner* v. *Oklahoma* may have been the first case in which the Supreme Court implicitly recognized the unfairness and hence unconstitutionality of laws which, whether so intended or not, discriminate against the poor. Skinner's convictions were for stealing chickens and armed robbery; these are poor men's crimes. On the other hand, poor people are not likely to have much opportunity to embezzle trust funds, defraud the revenue bureau, or manufacture impure foods and drugs. The unarticulated premise of *Skinner* v. *Oklahoma* may well be the same that later resulted in decisions invalidating anti-contraception and anti-abortion laws, denials of divorce to persons unable to pay court fees, and imposition of the death penalty (almost invariably against the poor).

Skinner v. *Oklahoma* effectively brought an end to compulsory sterilization, at least of criminal recidivists. Sterilization is not likely to be forced upon persons sleeping under bridges if it must also be forced upon bank presidents. The laws are still on the books in about half the States in the Union, but the operation is performed only with consent— or so it is reported.

Homosexuality

Because God speaks in many tongues, Caesar, even when he wishes to do God's will, may be confused. Leviticus 18:22 commands that "Thou shalt not lie with mankind as with womankind: it is abomination." Through New England Calvinism this was translated into American secular law, as is evidenced by the fact that in the various State statute books it is generally designated "sodomy" (see Genesis 19:4, 5). But consider what happened in Wisconsin in 1972.

There, the minister and congregation of Unitarian Church West decided to include sex education as part of their Sunday School program. No one could really take exception to this; even the Catholic Church, which opposes sex education in the public schools, agrees that it is important and that, to the extent it is beyond the capacity of individual parents, it should be conducted under religious auspices. The trouble was that the proposed course, entitled "About Your Sexuality" and developed by the Unitarian Universalist Association, included some use of still pictures depicting homosexual acts. The local district attorney, hearing about this, threatened to prosecute the minister and members of the congregation for violation of the State's laws against obscenity and impairment of the morals of minors.

The congregation responded by going into the Federal court and suing for an injunction against the district attorney. They presented affidavits to the effect that sex is so intertwined with moral, ethical, and theological values that it is an integral part of Unitarianism and that "About Your Sexuality" was as much a part of their religious practice as the catechism in Catholic and Lutheran churches, and equally entitled to protection under the Free Exercise Clause. The district attorney answered that, as he understood Unitarianism, sex education was *not* intertwined with the basic tenets of the religion, but the judge declined the invitation to enter that theological arena. He assumed that the Unitarian Universalist Association knew what Unitarianism was about, and issued the requested injunction. As far as is known, the district attorney did not appeal the decision, and "About Your Sexuality," including the still pictures of homosexual acts, is proceeding undisturbed in the Unitarian Universalist churches around the country. Had the case been appealed to the Supreme Court it would have been interesting to see how that Court would have decided it in the light of its 1955 decision in the case of *In re Black*, where it refused to disturb the action of State authorities in taking away and institutionalizing children whose Mormon mother persisted in teaching them that polygamy was the will of God.

It should be noted that the congregation of Unitarian Church West did not claim that homosexuality was the command of God; it is not likely that any church claims this now (although, as in the case of contraceptive birth control and therapeutic abortion, it may do so later). It claimed, at most, that Leviticus 18:22 does not accurately reflect the will of God, at least as revealed to Unitarians—a claim increasingly echoed within the ranks of nonfundamentalist Protestantism and Judaism, so infectious has been the virus of deism among God's faithful.

In Catholicism, of course, homosexuality is a violation of natural law. This concept became part of our secular law as is indicated by the fact that in some State criminal codes homosexuality is listed under the category of "Crimes Against Nature" (this term too comes from the Bible: Romans 1:26), along with bestiality and necrophilism. Oral and anal intercourse, even if consensual and between husband and wife, are still crimes under the laws of most States. In a few States, such as New York, the legislatures have had the courage to remove the criminal penalty where the act is consensual and between husband and wife, but in some cases have had to accomplish this not by specific amendment but as part of an overall revision and modernization of the penal code. Under the marital privacy rule established in the *Griswold* case, it is quite clear that the Supreme Court should not allow convictions to stand if the act was consensual and the parties husband and wife. Under the *Eisenstadt* decision, the Court should reach the same result if the parties, though not married to each other, were adults of different sexes and the act was committed consensually and in private. The constitutional problem concerns consenting adults acting in private but of the same sex, in violation of existing laws in every State in the Union.

Until a few years ago there would have been little doubt how the Supreme Court would decide the case. As in the days of Moses, sodomy was abomination. A trusted, high-ranking aide of President Lyndon Johnson had to be dismissed immediately, and his political career ended, when he was arrested for committing sodomy in the men's room of the YMCA in Washington; and even the President's own reelection seemed for a time to be threatened by the incident. The lower courts, Federal and State, uniformly upheld the dismissal of civil service employees or the deportation of aliens known to be homosexuals. As far as is known the claim of unconstitutionality was never raised, much less upheld, in a criminal prosecution for violation of a sodomy law.

All this, however, was before gay liberationists came out of the closet and began marching, demonstrating, and demanding equal rights, and, more importantly, organizing politically to get them. Their claim is a simple one; sexual behavior in private by consenting adults is no business of anyone but themselves. There is no doubt that their appeal to public opinion is making headway. Their marches, first met, at best, with curiosity and amusement and, at the worst, with derision and even violence, now receive pretty much the same response as marches by Negroes, Puerto Ricans, Chicanos, feminists, and other groups protesting for one reason or another against the Establishment. Television programs, perhaps the best test of the nation's level of toleration, increasingly treat the subject frankly and with understanding, and, most significantly, not necessarily as a medical problem, but portraying homosexual characters in sympathetic roles in prime-time entertainment programs.

There is a major advantage that proponents of repeal of anti-homosexual laws have over those urging repeal of anti-abortion statutes, and that is the absence of the most effective appeal of unborn children. Whatever deviate sexual practices can be called, they cannot be condemned as murder. To many Americans, although undoubtedly still a minority, they seem to be part of the perhaps regrettable but nevertheless very real revolution in sexual morality which accepts nonmarital sexual relations as quite normal. Hence, we do not find such passionate opposition to liberalization of law in this area as in the case of abortion, particularly on the part of the Catholic Church.

On the other hand, proponents of liberalization of antihomosexuality laws lack the most potent motivating factor possessed by the abortion reform movement, the economic factor. Homosexuality is not a practical or effective means of curbing the fruitfulness of welfare recipients. Reformers here lack the tacit if not articulate support of irate taxpayers. Moreover, there is not in this area the urgent need for legislative action to effect change, as in abortion reform. Deviate sexual practices do not require intervention by a physician, who risks his career by cooperating. If homosexuals refrain from seducing or molesting minors and restrict their solicitation efforts to gay bars (generally known as such by the police and the community), effective repeal may be achieved through police inaction, which appears to be what is happening now.

For these and other reasons, extensive legislative repeal of consensual sodomy laws appears unlikely in the near future. New York, for example, adopted abortion on demand but refused to repeal its sodomy laws even in respect to private conduct of consenting adults, although it did lower the penalty. Like capital punishment, if these laws are to be removed from the books it will probably have to be by decision of the Supreme Court.

What the prospects of such a decision are is hard to say. The marital-privacy principle as announced in the *Griswold* case is obviously not an adequate basis for declaring unconstitutional sodomy laws as they affect persons of the same sex. In the *Eisenstadt* case, however, the Court extended the principle to sexual relations between the unmarried, but it was obviously speaking in terms of nondeviate heterosexual relations. Yet, the *Griswold* decision would seem to encompass deviate intercourse between husband and wife, and the logic of the *Eisenstadt* decision would extend the right to the unmarried if they are of different sexes. From there it is but a short step to intercourse between persons of the same sex. (As we have noted in the first chapter, the referee makes the rules as he goes along, even though he protests that he is merely interpreting them.)

Another approach might be through the Equal Rights Amendment, should it be ratified by the requisite number of States. This provides that "Equality of rights under the law shall not be denied or abridged by the United States or by any State on account of sex." It is improbable that Congress had homosexuals in mind when it proposed the amendment, but it would not strain the wording too much to read it as encompassing them and immunizing them from prosecution for private sexual conduct or from suffering any other penalty (such as loss of government position) for being homosexuals.

A third approach might well be a recognition that under modern concepts of constitutional democracy the state is no more competent to legislate in the field of morality than in the religious arena. Under the purpose-effect test, the state may not pass laws whose purpose or primary effect is in the field of religion, either for advancement or inhibition. That either may occur as a coincidental byproduct does not render the law invalid. Sunday closing laws may advance normative Christianity, but they are constitutional because their purpose and primary effect is the secular one of assuring to all one day of rest in seven.

Just as the Constitution requires the state to be neutral concerning religion, nonreligion, and anti-religion, it may require it to be neutral concerning morality, amorality, or even immorality. Conduct deemed immoral (and, hence, usually sinful) may be forbidden by the state only if it is also harmful to what would be the equivalent in the field of morality of a secular societal interest in the field of religion.

Under this concept, the state may not outlaw polygamy because it is immoral by American or sinful by Christian standards, but only because it threatens the monogamous family structure of American society. Incest may be prohibited neither because it is forbidden in Leviticus nor because it is considered immoral by most Americans, but only because of the possible harmful genealogical consequences, and abortion because it is the taking of human life. Even the illegality of contraception could be justified under this concept if the nation were faced with what it considered to be an alarming decline in its birth rate, rather than the reverse (at least among poor people).

Were the Court to adopt this concept, it would have little difficulty in justifying its invalidation of sodomy laws. Sinful and immoral as homosexual practices may be to many, there is no evidence that they are harmful by standards which the state may constitutionally accept and seek to protect by prohibitive legislation; some States have already removed all penalties for sodomy within the context of heterosexual marital relations.

This is hardly a new concept. More than a century ago, John Stuart Mill, in his classic work *On Liberty*, stated that the "only purpose for which power can be rightfully exercised over any member of a civilized community, against his will, is to prevent harm to others. His own good, either physical or moral, is not sufficient warrant." Insofar as physical good is concerned, this proposition is at least implicit in the Supreme Court decisions which, during the first third of the 20th century, declared unconstitutional laws for the protection of workers; if, for example, a baker was willing to work 14 hours a day for wages barely reaching the subsistence level, that was his business and not the state's. Because of this the principle has become to a great extent discredited, particularly after the Great Depression of the 1930s showed where an every-man-for-himself political system can lead.

Since Roosevelt's court reorganization struggle in 1937, the Supreme Court has completely discarded this philosophy in respect to physical good. But this fact does not necessarily impair its validity in the area of morality, and should the Court decide to take that approach it would find that it has some judicial precedent to support its decision. In 1969 it held in the case of *Stanley* v. *Georgia* that a State could not constitutionally punish a person for possession in his home of obscene films which he keeps for private enjoyment. Two years later, in *Cohen* v. *California*, the Court went even further and held unconstitutional the conviction of a young protester who wore a jacket bearing the words "Fuck the Draft" on the back. It is true that in both cases the defense was that the convictions violated the Freedom of Speech Clause of the First Amendment, whereas deviant sexual conduct is not generally considered a form of expression. However, the Court has often stated that obscenity is not protected by the First Amendment and has long since rejected the proposition that while freedom to believe or even to speak may be absolute, the state is free to make criminal any conduct it deems undesirable.

The Supreme Court had an opportunity to adopt this approach in the *Eisenstadt* case. The Federal court of appeals had held that in the absence of proof of harm from the use of contraceptives, the state could not forbid it merely because it considered it immoral. The Supreme Court recognized this to be an important question but found it unnecessary to decide it. If contraception *per se* is immoral, the Court held, then it must be made illegal to all and not merely to the unmarried (which, although the Court naturally did not say so, Massachusetts had tried to do until prevented by the *Griswold* decision).

However, the real question here, as in so many other areas of constitutional law, is not how the Court achieves the result it wants, but whether it really wants that result. One of the major factors in determining this is the Court's judgment concerning the general public's acceptability of the particular decision it would like to hand down. In respect to invalidation of anti-homosexual laws, it is a good guess that comparatively few Americans will be very much disturbed about it.

At the present writing, the Court does not seem to be ready to strike down anti-homosexuality laws. In 1972 it refused, in the case of *McConnell* v. *Anderson*, to review the action of the University of Minnesota in rejecting for a position as librarian one of the male couple who, in *Baker* v. *Nelson*, unsuccessfully sought a decision by the Court requiring the State to issue a marriage license to them. The following year, in the case of *Wainwright* v. *Stone*, it upheld on technical grounds a conviction under Florida's criminal sodomy law. It is, however, a reasonable guess that these cases do not represent the Supreme Court's last word on the subject and that in the not-too-distant future it will accord a more sympathetic reception to the constitutional claims of homosexuals.

Illegitimacy

Few chapters in the history of what is called our Judeo-Christian civilization are more sorrowful in chronicling human inhumanity than the chapter on illegitimacy, and it is one which tragically is still far from being concluded. The motif was sounded in Deuteronomy (23:2): "A bastard shall not enter into the congregation of the Lord; even unto his tenth generation shall he not enter into the congregation of the Lord." Christianity took up the theme and expanded on it. In pre-Christian Rome an illegitimate child had the legal right to be supported by his mother and to inherit from her; Constantine, the first Christian emperor, suppressed all rights of illegitimate children against their mother except those born of concubines.

Under the English common law, illegitimate children were *filius nullius*, literally nobody's children. Their situation was vividly described in the following words from Helen L. Clarke's book *Social Legislation* (p. 344):

> The illegitimate child was legally isolated from his parents, for the common law from the Middle Ages recognized no legal relationship between him and his mother, much less

between him and his father. The child was *filius nullius*, or
filius populi, or *heres nullius*. He was kin to no one. Since he was
not even considered the lawful child of his mother, he could
not inherit from her. He could not inherit real property from
his own issue. He had no heirs but those of his own body. If
he died without lawful issue, any real or personal property
he possessed escheated to the crown. He was disqualified
from becoming a member of trade guilds. He could not take
holy orders without special dispensation. Legally, he was
turned adrift. Until the enactment of the poor laws nobody
or no unit of government was responsible for him. *Filius
nullius* was carried to its logical extreme, for even if the child
was born of serf parents, he was free.

With the same eloquence with which Shakespeare protested the inequality suffered by Jews in the famous "Hath
not a Jew eyes?" speech from *The Merchant of Venice*, he protested in *King Lear* (Act I, Sc. 2) the same treatment suffered
by persons born out of wedlock:

> Why bastard? Wherefore base?
> When my dimensions are as well compact,
> My mind as generous, and my shape as true,
> As honest madam's issue? Why brand they us
> With base? with baseness; bastardy? base, base?

In the United States the term "nigger" has long been a
term of obloquy, and, until the Negroes turned it around and
made it a word of pride, so too was the word "black." The
term "bastard" has similarly become a term of obloquy, and
the term "black bastard," characterized its depth. The af-
finity of the two obloquies is symbolized by a Florida statute
(no longer effective by reason of *Loving* v. *Virginia*) which
provided that the child of an attempted marriage between
white and Negro "shall be regarded as a bastard and in-
capable of having or receiving any estate, real, personal or
mixed, by inheritance."

The very word "bastard" evidences that the inequality
suffered by children born out of wedlock begins even before

their birth. Its probable origin is from a Gothic word meaning barn or stable, indicating the place to which the mother was compelled to repair to bring forth her child. The verse from Deuteronomy quoted above evidences that the inequality can endure for as long as ten generations after their death.

But the same book of Deuteronomy also states a directly opposite mandate (24:16): "The fathers shall not be put to death for the children, neither shall the children be put to death for the fathers; every man shall be put to death for his own sin." This principle that the child shall not be punished for the sins of the father, stated as well in other parts of the Bible, found its way into our own Constitution. In empowering Congress to prescribe punishment for treason, the most heinous of political crimes, Article III, Section 3, states that "no attainder of treason shall work corruption of blood, or forfeiture except during the life of the person attainted." By any standard, visiting upon children born out of wedlock the penalty for their parents' violation of the law and moral standards would seem to constitute an instance of "corruption of blood."

While this provision of the Constitution is obviously not available as a means of adjudging unconstitutional all laws imposing inferior legal status on illegitimate children, should the Supreme Court find itself ready and willing to do so, it is not without adequate constitutional ways to achieve this result. One of them is the ban on guilt by association. The Court has ruled in a number of cases that one may not be punished merely for associating, even knowingly and voluntarily, with Communists, criminals, or other socially unacceptable people. How then can a child be punished for unknowingly and unwillingly associating with its unwed parents?

Even more fundamental is the principle that in a constitutional democracy crime is personal and no one may be punished for an offense, no matter how heinous, committed by another. (The rule may, of course, be otherwise in totalitarian states, as the history of Naziism shows.) If fornication, adultery, and incest are crimes, they certainly are not committed by the offspring of the illicit union. To punish them for it would not seem to be consistent with the constitutional guaranty that no person may be deprived of life, liberty, or property without due process of law.

Another approach might be through the Eighth Amendment, which forbids the imposition of cruel and unusual punishment. In 1962, the Court, in the case of *Robinson* v. *California*, ruled that the amendment is violated when a State makes a status, rather than an act, criminally punishable, and that therefore a statute that made the "status" of drug addiction a criminal offense for which the addict could be prosecuted "at any time before he reforms" was as unconstitutional as one which would attempt to make it a criminal offense to be mentally ill or a leper. Six years later the Court, by a 5 to 4 vote in the case of *Powell* v. *Texas*, refused to extend the ruling to chronic alcoholism and upheld a statute making public drunkenness a criminal offense. The decision, however, was based upon the fact that in that particular case the evidence did not show that the defendant was unable to stay off the streets on the occasion of his arrest, and that accordingly he was being punished not for the status of chronic alcoholism but for the act of going into the streets while he was drunk. Obviously, illegitimacy is a status and not an act and hence the *Robinson* rather than the *Powell* rule is applicable.

True enough, unlike the *Robinson* case, no State has declared the status of illegitimacy to be criminal; but this only aggravates unconstitutionality, for no democratic state may impose punishment without crime. It is also true that the inferior status and civil disabilities imposed upon illegitimate persons are not technically punishment, but realistically they are very much so. In any event, neither was the similar treatment accorded Negroes before the Civil War, and it was the purpose of that war and the Thirteenth,

Fourteenth, and Fifteenth amendments which came in its wake forever to abolish the legal status of inferiority by reason of the accident of birth. Most relevant to our discussion is the Fourteenth Amendment and more particularly its Equal Protection Clause, to which we will return shortly.

Throughout the years, as evidenced by the quotation above from *King Lear*, there has been recognition of the harsh injustice visited by society upon the children of unmarried parents. In the United States every State has enacted some legislation ameliorating the situation in varying degrees, the most common examples being legitimation by marriage of the parents and allowing an illegitimate child to inherit from its mother (though not its father) provided she is not survived by legitimate children. Few, however, go so far as to abolish the status entirely as does, for example, North Dakota which, ever since 1917, has had a law on its books that states simply:

> Every child is hereby declared to be the legitimate child of its natural parents and as such is entitled to support and education, to the same extent as if it had been born in lawful wedlock. It shall inherit from its natural parents and from their kindred heir lineal and collateral.

Even so liberal a State as Arizona retains to some degree the Deuteronomic imposition of social ostracism. Its law provides:

> Every child is the legitimate child of its natural parents and is entitled to support and education as if born in lawful wedlock, *except the right to dwelling or a residence with the family of the father if such father be married.*

Because so very few States have adopted North Dakota's stance, it may be suggested that here too it may be the responsibility of the Supreme Court to bring law into harmony with civilized standards. Several cases decided by the Court within the past several years indicate that it may be on its way toward carrying out this responsibility. The first of these, *Levy* v. *Louisiana*, was decided in 1968.

Louise Levy, black and poor, was the unwed mother of five small children who lived with her and were treated by her as a parent would treat any other child. She supported them out of her earnings as a domestic, took them to church every Sunday, and enrolled them, at her own expense, in a parochial school. One day, suffering from tiredness, dizziness, weakness, chest pain, and slowness of breath, she came to the Charity Hospital in New Orleans where she was assigned to a doctor who made a cursory examination and sent her home with a tonic and tranquilizers. A week later she returned with severe symptoms, but the doctor merely looked at her, told her that she was not taking the medicine, and made an appointment for her to see a psychiatrist two months later. She never got to the psychiatrist; within ten days she was dead from hypertension uremia.

Like every other State in the Union, Louisiana has a law which provides that children whose parent's death was caused by the negligence or other wrongful action of another may sue the latter for damages. A suit under this statute was brought in behalf of the Levy children, but the Louisiana courts threw it out on the ground that they were not "children" under the law.

The Supreme Court held this action to be unconstitutional. The Fourteenth Amendment provides that no State shall deny to any person the equal protection of the laws, and the Court, speaking through Justice Douglas, refused to consider an illegitimate child a nonperson and therefore beyond the protection of the Equal Protection Clause. The opinion said:

> The rights asserted here involve the intimate, familial relationship between a child and his own mother. When the child's claim of damage for loss of his mother is in issue, why, in terms of "equal protection," should the tortfeasors go free merely because the child is illegitimate? Why should the illegitimate child be denied rights merely because of his

birth out of wedlock? He certainly is subject to all the responsibilities of a citizen, including the payment of taxes and conscription under the Selective Service Act. How under our constitutional regime can he be denied correlative rights which other citizens enjoy?

The Louisiana court had deemed it necessary to deny rights to illegitimate children in order to "discourage bringing children into the world out of wedlock." (Louisiana is one of the States in which legislation was introduced—though not enacted—providing for the compulsory sterilization of females having more than one illegitimate offspring.) This explanation borders on the incredible. It is hard to imagine a woman about to engage in nonmarital intercourse thinking of her own wrongful death or knowing that in such case any child that might result from the intercourse would not be able to recover legal damages against the person who caused her death.

In any event, the Court rejected the explanation, and in the case of *Glona* v. *American Guaranty Insurance Company* it decided at the same time that it was equally unconstitutional conversely to deny a mother the right to sue for the wrongful death of her child in an automobile accident merely because the child was born out of wedlock.

Three years later, in the case of *Labine* v. *Vincent*, the Court could have taken another step forward but, by a 5 to 4 decision, refused to do so. In rural Louisiana, a 69-year-old man and a 41-year-old woman, both unmarried, began living together and continued to do so until his death seven years later. About a year after they set up home together the woman bore him a daughter. The birth certificate designated him as the father, and two months after the birth both parents appeared before a notary public and in accordance with Louisiana law formally acknowledged their joint parentage of the child. On the father's death, the Louisiana courts ruled that, notwithstanding the acknowledgment, the daughter could not inherit his estate, which was ordered distributed to his brothers and sisters.

The Supreme Court majority held that this did not constitute a violation of the Equal Protection Clause notwithstanding the formal acknowledgment of parentage.

In *Stanley* v. *Illinois* and *Weber* v. *Aetna Casualty and Surety
Company*, both decided in 1972, the Court resumed its forward march. The *Stanley* case involved the custody of three
children born to a couple who had lived together for 18
years without getting married. Upon the death of the mother, the Illinois courts took the children away from the father
and placed them in a State institution for children, holding
in effect that the fact that the father had never married the
mother was legal proof that he was unfit to keep the children. The Supreme Court reversed the decision and ruled
that custody could be taken away if there was proof that the
father was actually unfit, but the fact that he was unwed
could not of itself be held to constitute unfitness.

In the *Weber* case, the father of four children, whose
wife had been committed to a mental institution, took up
with an unmarried woman who bore him two children. They
all lived together in one household until he was accidentally killed on his job. In accordance with the State's law, the
workmen's compensation benefits went exclusively to the
four legitimate children with nothing for the two illegitimate
ones. The Supreme Court held this to be unconstitutional
discrimination in violation of the Equal Protection law. Most
significant is the following from Justice Powell's opinion for
the majority of the Court:

> The status of illegitimacy has expressed through the ages
> society's condemnation of irresponsible liaisons beyond the
> bonds of marriage. But visiting this condemnation on the
> head of an infant is illogical and unjust. Moreover, imposing
> disabilities on the illegitimate child is contrary to the basic
> concept of our system that legal burdens should bear some
> relationship to individual responsibility or wrongdoing. Ob-
> viously, no child is responsible for his birth and penalizing
> the illegitimate child is an ineffectual—as well as an unjust—
> way of deterring the parent. Courts are powerless to prevent

the social opprobrium suffered by these hapless children,
but the Equal Protection Clause does enable us to strike
down discriminatory laws relating to status of birth where,
—as in this case—the classification is justified by no legitimate state interest, compelling or otherwise.

Late in 1972, the Court, in *Richardson* v. *Davis*, upheld a
lower court decision invalidating a provision of the Social
Security Act entitling illegitimate children monthly benefit
payments only to the extent, if any, that the benefits to the
widow and legitimate children did not exhaust the maximum
family benefits allowed under the law. And in two cases decided in 1973 it took further steps forward. In *Gomez* v. *Perez*,
it cited the *Levy* and *Weber* decisions for the broad proposition that "a State may not invidiously discriminate against
illegitimate children by denying them substantial benefits
accorded to children generally." The Court therefore held
that where a State requires fathers to support their legitimate children (as all States do), it may not absolve them of
the same obligation to their illegitimate children. The Court
recognized the problems with respect to proof of paternity
but held that they cannot be made an impenetrable barrier
to according the illegitimate children the equal protection
of the laws.

In the second case, *New Jersey Welfare Rights Organizations*
v. *Cahill*, the Court nullified a statute that limited benefits
under the State's program of "Assistance to Families of the
Working Poor" to families with legitimate or adopted children. It rejected the State's defense of the law on the ground
that it was designed "to preserve and strengthen traditional
family life." Instead, it quoted the above paragraph from
the *Weber* decision, and ruled that benefits under the program
were as indispensable to the health and well-being of illegitimate children as to those who are legitimate, and must be
accorded equally to both.

The eloquence and breadth of the language used in
these decisions, notwithstanding the necessarily limited
nature of the actual holdings, and the fact that Justice

Rehnquist is the only present member of the Court who dissented in them, indicate that the day may not be far off when the Court will do what the legislatures should do but have not done, namely, abolish all legal distinctions between children born in and out of wedlock.

Adoption

Over the years there has been a fairly universal understanding among adoption agencies not to place a child with a couple of a religion other than that of the natural mother. This policy was not limited to denominational agencies but was followed by nonsectarian ones as well. The insistence on religious matching often resulted in keeping children in institutions until maturity even though couples fully competent except for not having the right religion yearned to adopt them. Moreover, it had the further effect of excluding from the privilege of adoption couples unaffiliated with any religion, and even in some cases religiously affiliated couples with less piety than the adoption agency thought appropriate. (It was a common practice to require certification by a clergyman that the couple attended religious services regularly, and that, if they already had a child, they were bringing it up religiously.)

To what degree this restrictive policy is extant today is difficult to say. In respect to Catholic agencies it is almost certain that there has been no substantial change and that a child born to a Catholic mother, even if she had not had it baptized, will not be placed for adoption with a non-Catholic couple. Among non-Catholic agencies the practice has in most cases been liberalized in respect to hard-to-place children, meaning in most cases black children. As for white, healthy infants for whom there are long waiting lists, the probabilities are that the religious matching policy is followed by most agencies.

Religious matching requirements bear down harder upon would-be parents today than ever before. Most out-of-family adoptions involve illegitimate children, and this source has become tighter by reason of the wider availability of birth prevention through contraception and abortion. Moreover, our changing moral standards have to a substantial extent lessened the stigma of unmarried motherhood, and it is becoming quite acceptable for a young woman, often with the encouragement and cooperation of her parents, to keep her baby rather than place it out for adoption.

Consequently, white couples are now doing what they would not dream of doing a few years ago—adopting black babies. Interracial adoption, though still infrequent, has evoked concern among many black social workers, who look at it as a form of racial or cultural genocide. Most white couples, however, shy away from interracial adoption and seek to avoid the barrier against interreligious adoption imposed by agencies through the device of private or non-agency adoption, that is, through direct contact with a pregnant unmarried woman, usually arranged by a doctor or lawyer.

But here, too, there are barriers. An adoption to be legal must be approved by a family court or judge, and many States have adopted what are known as religious protection laws, which provide that wherever practicable or wherever possible approval shall be given only where the child and would-be parents are of the same religious faith. How strictly these laws can be interpreted and applied is illustrated by a case which came to the Massachusetts courts in the 1950s.

It involved illegitimate twins born to a divorced Catholic woman. The natural father was also a Roman Catholic. Two weeks after the birth of the children, a Jewish couple, Reuben and Sylvia Goldman of Marblehead, Massachusetts, took them for adoption. Although the natural mother consented in writing to their being raised in the Jewish faith, the family court judge refused to approve the adoption. He noted that while the Goldmans were otherwise suitable adopters, many nearby Catholic couples had appli-

cations for similar children on file with the Catholic Charities Bureau. He ruled therefore that, even though these
Catholic couples had never sought to adopt the twins and
in fact had never seen them, it appeared "practicable" to
give the twins to a Catholic couple. The Goldmans then
appealed to the State's highest court, but the decision was
affirmed. They then sought to appeal to the United States
Supreme Court, claiming that when a State refuses to approve an adoption for no other reason than difference in
religion, it violates both the Establishment and Free Exercise
clauses of the First Amendment, particularly where the
natural mother voluntarily consents that the child be
adopted by a couple of a different faith and be brought up in
that faith. However, the Supreme Court, in *Goldman* v.
Fogarty, refused to accept the appeal, giving no reason for its
refusal.

A word should be said about the aftermath. The Massachusetts courts not only denied the Goldmans' application
for legal approval of the adoption but ordered them to turn
over the twins, not to the natural mother, but to the Catholic Charities Bureau, even though the twins, then almost five
years old, had lived all but the first two weeks of their lives
with the Goldmans and knew no other parents. Upon the
Goldmans' refusal to turn over the twins, the State Department of Public Welfare started proceedings to take them
away and place them in a Catholic institution. The Goldmans thereupon abandoned their home and business, a
clothing store in Boston, and departed with the twins to establish a new home in another State. The Department of
Welfare took the position that this constituted kidnaping,
and made it clear that should the Goldmans return to Massachusetts they would be arrested and tried under that charge.

About the same time the *Goldman* case was in the Massachusetts courts, a very different result was reached in a
religious matching case in the Pennsylvania courts. The
crazed neighbor of a young couple in Michigan entered
their home and shot them both. The husband had been a

Catholic, the wife a Protestant. They had one young child, whom they agreed to raise in the Catholic faith and accordingly had him baptized as a Catholic. On the death of the couple, the child's (Protestant) maternal aunt came from Pennsylvania, took him, and brought him back with her with the intent to adopt him. The child's (Catholic) paternal grandparents followed her to Pennsylvania and brought legal proceedings to recover the child for adoption by them. The Pennsylvania courts ruled in favor of the aunt and her husband on the ground that the welfare of the child dictated that he be brought up away from the scene of the tragedy and by a couple whose age relationship to him was that of the normal relationship between parent and child. While the religious factor, the courts said, was important and had to be given consideration, it would not be allowed to override the demands of the child's welfare.

In 1972 the Supreme Court again had an opportunity to pass upon the constitutionality of religious protection laws. A county department of social services in New York refused to accept an application as adoptive parents by Robert and Ann Dickens because, in the interview with the assigned caseworker, the husband stated that he was an atheist and his wife said that she no longer had any religious affiliation. The practice of the department when interviewing the natural mother placing a child for adoption was to inquire as to her religious preference for her child. She could opt for her own religion, another religion, or no religion at all. The director of the department testified that in her sixteen years of service no mother ever opted for no religion, although some would indicate that they had no preference among the religions (Catholic, Protestant, and Jewish). In the case of children whose parents were unknown (foundlings) and there was no evidence with respect to the child's religion, the department would take "the first good home that comes along, whether Catholic, Protestant or Jewish." In light of this and the State's religious protection law, the department said that there was no point accepting the applications of persons with no religious affiliation.

The Dickenses appealed to the State courts, which ordered the department to process the application. In the first place, they ruled, the department had no authority to limit placement of foundlings to couples of the three major faiths or of any faith, but had to offer them to the first suitable applicants, even if they had no religious affiliation. Moreover, the State's religious protection law did not make religious diversity an absolute bar to adoption; while religion was an important factor to be considered, it was the best interests of the child which determined whether a particular placement should be made, even if it should be contrary to the expressed wishes of the natural mother.

The Dickenses were unsatisfied and sought to appeal to the Supreme Court on the ground that all religious protection laws should be declared unconstitutional, and that under the Establishment Clause religion may not be considered even as one of the many factors in determining where a child should be placed for adoption or whether an adoption should be approved. In the case of *Dickens* v. *Ernesto*, however, the Supreme Court rejected the appeal.

This is the situation today in practically all the States (including Massachusetts, which has liberalized its religious protection law since the *Goldman* case): all things being equal, children should be adopted by couples having the same religion as their natural parents; where, however, the welfare of a child dictates otherwise, the child may be adopted by a couple of a different religion or of no religion.

The practical effect of this is that couples without religion stand a poor chance of obtaining a child from an agency. In view of the great disparity between the number of couples seeking children and the number of children available for adoption, and the reluctance of people (perhaps especially natural mothers) to state that they have no religion, it will be rare that the agency will be unable to find a suitable family whose religion is that of the natural mother. The Supreme Court's refusal (with only Justice Douglas dissenting) to take the Dickenses' appeal indicates that it is not likely soon to interfere with this situation.

Hamlet advised his mother: "Assume a virtue, if you have it not" (Act III, Sc. 4). Atheist or agnostic couples seeking to adopt a child would be well advised to assume a faith. Once the adoption is formally approved, they can raise the child, which has become theirs, in accordance with their own conscience.

The Upbringing of Children

In a democratic society the state avoids as far as possible intervention into the internal affairs of the family and leaves to it the responsibility for resolution of conflicts among its members. In the United States, with its constitutional policy against entanglement in religious affairs, the mandate of non-intervention is particularly applicable where the intrafamily dispute concerns the affairs of God rather than Caesar. It is this policy which explains the position of the law in respect to ante-nuptial agreements regarding the religious upbringing of children.

Under Catholic Canon Law a marriage between a Catholic and a non-Catholic is "most severely" forbidden unless a dispensation is obtained from the appropriate ecclesiastical authority. Until recently, this could be obtained only if both parties entered into a written contract that all children of the union would be baptized and brought up in the Catholic faith. There have been frequent occasions when State courts have been called upon to enforce these contracts, as when the parties have separated and the non-Catholic parent having custody of the child refuses to bring it up as a Catholic. With rare exceptions, the courts have refused to enforce the contracts, taking the position that where the parties are living together the matter must be settled by themselves, and where they are living apart the parent having custody has the right to determine the child's religious (or nonreligious) upbringing unrestrained by any contract, written or unwritten, even if without it the marriage would not have occurred.

The question has never reached the Supreme Court, and the likelihood that it will has been lessened because of the modification of the canon law provision decreed by Pope Paul VI in 1970. The revision no longer requires a contract be written between the parties but only that a "sincere promise" be made by the Catholic to the Church "to do all in his power to have all the children baptized and brought up in the Catholic Church," and that "at an opportune time the non-Catholic party must be informed of these promises." This modification does not forbid the parties from entering into a written agreement or the priest from urging them to do so, and it is probable that in some cases the previous practice will be continued. It is therefore not beyond the realm of possibility that the question may yet reach the Supreme Court. Should this happen, the probabilities are strong that the Court would rule that judicial enforcement of the contract would violate both the Establishment and Free Exercise clauses of the First Amendment.

A somewhat analogous case involving a Jewish couple was brought to the Supreme Court in the early 1950s. Both parents were Orthodox Jews and upon their divorce the mother, to whom custody was given, continued to bring up the children as Orthodox Jews. The father, however, claimed that the upbringing was not sufficiently pious. Specifically, he objected to the mother's enrollment of their son in a Jewish parochial school in which both secular and religious teaching was given. According to his interpretation of Jewish religious doctrine, all knowledge and truth were to be found in the Torah (Hebrew Scriptures) and the Talmud, and it would be sinful to learn anything else. He therefore demanded that his son be enrolled in a small school operated by the group to which he belonged and which taught only Torah and Talmud. Upon the mother's refusal to comply with his demand, he brought suit in the

New York courts, claiming that both his own and his son's religious freedoms were being violated. The State courts ruled against him and he sought to appeal to the Supreme Court, which, in the case of *Auster* v. *Weberman*, rejected his appeal over the dissents of Justices Black and Douglas.

The state's reluctance to interfere in the upbringing of children, particularly where religion is involved, must nevertheless be set aside when their welfare is at stake. This was established by the Supreme Court in the 1944 case of *Prince* v. *Massachusetts*. There the Court held that a member of the Jehovah's Witness sect could be prosecuted for violation of the State's anti–child-labor law by allowing her nine-year-old child to sell religious tracts on the public streets, notwithstanding the claim that the doctrines of the sect required this to be done. Parents, the Court said, may be free to become martyrs themselves, but that does not mean that they can make martyrs of their children.

It is because of this principle that Christian Scientists may constitutionally be compelled to provide medical care for their children and to cause them to be inoculated against communicable diseases. Although it is a doctrine of the Jehovah's Witnesses' faith that blood transfusions violate the Scriptural prohibition against drinking blood, the state may, for the same reason, authorize a hospital to make a transfusion where necessary for the child's recovery, notwithstanding the parents' refusal to consent.

In our quasi–social-welfare society, the concept of what constitutes welfare is ever expanding, particularly where children are concerned. Yet there must be limits, else the First Amendment would lose much of its meaning. A number of decisions by the Supreme Court culminating in the 1972 case of *Wisconsin* v. *Yoder* indicates that the Court recognizes the danger, although it does not always express its recognition.

In *West Virginia State Board of Education* v. *Barnette*, referred to in the first chapter, the Court upheld the right of Jehovah's Witnesses parents to keep their children in public schools without being required to participate in the daily flag salute ceremony. At that time (1943), Jehovah's Witnesses were the victims of considerable nationalistic persecution because of their refusal to salute the flag, and their nonconforming children suffered isolation, harassment, and even physical violence from their schoolmates and teachers. The Court could easily have held that the welfare of the children dictated compliance with the flag salute regulation for their own benefit, but it refused to do so. Five years later the record in *McCollum* v. *Board of Education* showed that 11-year-old Terry McCollum suffered similar isolation and harassment for his mother's refusal to allow him to participate in the religious instruction being conducted in the public schools of Champaign, Illinois. Although the Court held the entire program unconstitutional, it certainly would not have sanctioned compulsory participation so as to protect Terry from the consequences of his peers' disfavor. This is implicit in the following statement in Justice Jackson's concurring opinion:

> The complaint is that when others join and he does not, it sets him apart as a dissenter, which is humiliating. Even admitting this to be true, it may be doubted whether the Constitution, which, of course protects the right to dissent, can be construed also to protect one from the embarrassment that always attends nonconformity, whether in religion, politics, behavior or dress.

It is, however, not in cases of compulsory participation in patriotic or religious exercises that the clash between the state's interest in children's temporal welfare and the church's interest in their spiritual welfare is most clearly and vividly presented. It is rather in cases concerning forced attendance at and participation in secular instruction, a number of which have reached the Supreme Court. The earliest of these cases was *Pierce* v. *Society of Sisters*, decided in 1925. There, an order of nuns operating parochial schools in Oregon challenged the constitutionality of a law, adopted by popular referendum, which required all children between the ages of 8 and 15 to attend public schools, thus effectively outlawing parochial schools. One of the grounds on which the statute was defended was that it was necessary in order to protect the welfare of children. In arguing before the Supreme Court, the attorneys for Oregon stated:

> The voters of Oregon who adopted this law had the right to act on the belief that the fact that the great increase in juvenile crime in the United States followed so closely after the great increase in the number of children in the United States who were not attending public schools, was more than a coincidence. The voters in Oregon might also have based their action in adopting this law upon the alarm which they felt at the rising tide of religious suspicions in this country, and upon their belief that the basic cause of such religious feelings was the separation of children along religious lines during the most susceptible years of their lives, with the inevitable awakening of a consciousness of separation, and a distrust and suspicion of those from whom they were so carefully guarded. The voters of Oregon might have felt that the mingling together, during a portion of their education, of the children of all races and sects, might be the best safeguard against future internal dissensions and consequent weakening of the community against foreign dangers. . . .

It is rather ironic, and somewhat amusing, that the suggestion should seriously be made on behalf of a State in the Union that attendance at parochial school might lead to juvenile crime, rather than the exact opposite, which has been so often asserted by defenders of the system. However, within the context of our concern, what is relevant is the Court's refusal to allow Caesar's fears to override God's right as exercised by His faithful. The Court said:

> The fundamental theory of liberty upon which all governments in this Union repose excludes any general power of the State to standardize its children by forcing them to accept instruction from public teachers only. The child is not

the mere creature of the State; those who nurture him and direct his destiny have the right, coupled with the high duty, to recognize and prepare him for additional obligations.

On the basis of the *Pierce* decision, the ultra-Orthodox Jews referred to in *Auster* v. *Weberman* sought to defend their violation of New York's compulsory attendance law by claiming that it would violate their freedom of religion to compel them to send their children to schools, public or private, in which secular subjects were taught. The New York courts rejected this defense and quoted the following from the *Pierce* decision:

> No question is raised concerning the power of the State reasonably to regulate all schools, to inspect, supervise and examine them, their teachers and pupils; to require that all children of proper age attend some school, that teachers shall be of good moral character and patriotic disposition, that certain studies plainly essential to good citizenship must be taught, and that nothing be taught which is manifestly inimical to the public welfare.

The parents' rights to control the upbringing of their children, it was held, must yield to the State's right and duty to protect the latters' welfare. The parents sought to appeal to the Supreme Court, but, in *Donner* v. *New York*, the Court rejected the appeal. The upshot of these decisions is that in our society the welfare of children requires that they receive a basic secular education, and, while the state may not dictate where they receive it, it may compel parents to allow their children to receive it notwithstanding the contrary religious convictions of either parents or children.

But for how long? Initially it was deemed sufficient if children received instruction in the rudiments of reading, writing, and arithmetic. As our standards advanced and our world became more complex, required school attendance was extended to eight years of elementary education and then to an additional four years of secondary education. It may not end there; our standards continue to advance and the world to become more complex. Perhaps the state, deciding that without at least two years of college our youth will not be able to cope with the demands of society, will extend the years of compulsory schooling to two years after high school graduation. At what point, if any, does the Free Exercise Clause secure the right of the parent or his child to say, "In the name of God, so far and no further?" That is the question which the Supreme Court had to face squarely in *Wisconsin* v. *Yoder*.

The Yoders and the other defendants in the case were members of the Old Order Amish, an extremely conservative Mennonite group which engages exclusively in farming for its livelihood, wears beards and 18th century–type clothing (as do the Hassidic Jews of Brooklyn involved in the *Auster* and *Donner* cases), refuses to use motor cars, electricity, or other technological equipment, and forbids marriage with non-Amish. Their communities are characterized by a fundamental belief that salvation requires life in a church community separate and apart from the world and worldly influence.

The Amish accept formal education through the eighth grade, but object to it beyond that point because the values taught in secondary schools are in marked variance with their own values and ways of life. The high school tends to emphasize intellectual and scientific accomplishments, self-distinction, competitiveness, worldly success, and social life with other students. Amish society, on the other hand, emphasizes informal learning-through-doing and a life of "goodness," rather than integration with contemporary worldly society. The Amish take literally the injunction of Paul in his Epistle to the Romans (12:2), "Be not conformed to this world."

These facts show that the conflict between the Yoders and the State of Wisconsin, which prosecuted them for violation of the law requiring education until the age of sixteen, was not merely one between the state and a particular religion but also between the state and a particular culture. The arguments presented on behalf of the defendants stressed the claim that compulsory high school attendance would ultimately result in the destruction of the Old Order Amish community as it exists in the United States today.

The Court, however, refused to view the case as anything but a conflict between God and Caesar. It expressly stated in its opinion that if the motivations for the separate community lifestyle of the Amish were philosophical or otherwise secular, their claim could not be upheld against the State's law. A claim based upon the Free Exercise Clause, however, stood in a different and higher position; only interests of the highest order could overbalance such a claim.

Wisconsin asserted that it had a twofold interest in requiring that all children receive a secular education up to the age of sixteen. The first was to assure the community of a citizenry prepared and able to carry out its political responsibilities in a democratic society and economically able to support itself without being a burden on the rest of the community. The second was to protect the welfare of children even against their own parents. The State argued that while Amish children might be adequately prepared for a life within the community, those who left it to join the secular world could well suffer by reason of their lack of educational preparation for its lifestyle.

The Court rejected both claims and ruled the conviction to be unconstitutional. Since the defendants' claim was based upon the Free Exercise Clause, it could be overridden only by convincing proof that to uphold it would gravely and clearly endanger the State's overriding and compelling interests, and such proof was not presented in the case. The Court summed up its conclusion as follows:

> The record strongly indicates that accommodating the religious objections of the Amish by foregoing one, or at most two, additional years of compulsory education will not impair the physical or mental health of the child, nor result in an inability to be self-supporting, or to discharge the duties

and responsibilities of citizenship, or in any other way detract from the welfare of society.

The Court left one important question unanswered. Three children were involved in the case, one aged 14 and the other two 15. Only one of these children was called as a witness at the trial, and she testified that because of her religious convictions she did not wish to go to high school. Neither of the other two children testified, so it was not known whether they shared this wish. Suppose they did not; suppose they wanted to go to high school but were forbidden to do so by their parents. These children were financially dependent upon their parents; they lived at home and were part of the family. Did they nevertheless have a freedom of choice of their own, and a religious liberty entitled to state protection as against their own parents? Douglas, the only justice who dissented in part from the decision, was of the view that if these two children did not agree with their parents' religious views, the latter could constitutionally be prosecuted for withholding a high school education from them. The other justices refused to go into the question, since there was no evidence of this in the trial record and a criminal conviction could not be based upon evidence not presented or proved. Someday, however, the triangular confrontation among God, Caesar, and mature but in-family children may come to the Court in this or an analogous situation. Religious freedom and parental rights generally come to the Court on the same side against the state as the adversary of both, as with respect to the Yoder child who did not want to go to high school. How the Court would resolve a conflict between the parents' rights and the children's religious freedom is impossible of reasonable prediction at this writing.

Chapter Four

The Military

The Constitution in War and Peace

Two competing themes are implicit in all, and explicit in most, of the cases in which the courts are called upon to pass on claims that constitutional rights have been infringed upon by the military. First, with nations as with individuals nothing is more important than self-preservation. It would little profit a citizen that the court forbid the military to impair a particular constitutional right if, as a consequence, the nation is unable to defend itself against a foreign enemy who would destroy not merely that constitutional right but the entire Constitution as well. As was said in one case, the Constitution is not a suicide pact; those who wrote it never intended to tie the hands of the government and render it unable to defend the nation against foreign enemies.

A corollary to this proposition is the assumption that it is the military which is best able to judge what measures are necessary for the nation's defense against foreign aggressors. If a check on the military is needed, there is the President, a civilian who is its commander-in-chief; and if a further check is necessary, there is the Congress, which can always cut off the military's funds if it feels the military is out of bounds, as it ultimately did in respect to Cambodia. Certain it is that those least competent to make the awesome decision upon which the survival of the nation may depend are the nine elderly lawyers who sit in a marble hall far from the battlefield and the falling bombs.

138

It was this approach that led the Supreme Court to uphold the action of the military during World War II in forcibly removing American citizens of Japanese descent from their homes in the Pacific coastal States and confining them to detention centers (called by one of the dissenting justices "concentration camps"), even though there was no evidence or even any charge that they were disloyal to the United States.

The competing and contrary premise was stated in the following words by the Supreme Court in the case of *Ex parte Milligan*, in which it held unconstitutional the trial of a civilian by a military court during the Civil War:

> The Constitution of the United States is a law for rulers and for people, equally in war and in peace, and covers with the shield of its protection all classes of men, at all times, and under all circumstances. No doctrine involving more pernicious consequences was ever invented by the wit of man than that any of its provisions can be suspended during any of the great exigencies of government. Such a doctrine leads directly to anarchy or despotism, but the theory of necessity on which it is based is false; for the government, within the Constitution, has all the powers granted to it which are necessary to preserve its existence.

It is no more necessary, the Court said, to sacrifice the Constitution in order to preserve the nation than it is to sacrifice the nation to preserve the Constitution; the survival of both after the terrible Civil War proves this. The military has all the power needed to defend the nation without going beyond the Constitution.

Since, on this premise, the military can and must wage war within the limitations of the Constitution, and since under our political system it is the courts' responsibility to interpret that document, it follows that it is the courts, and ultimately the Supreme Court, that must pass judgment on the actions of the military and decide whether they are within or beyond constitutional limitations.

The cases considered in this chapter present the conflict or competition between these two approaches in the specific context of religious freedom and the separation of church and state.

Conflict of Loyalties

Over the centuries, both church and state have recognized implicitly that the alternative to their co-existence may be non-existence, for one or for both. Their co-existence, however, has not always been peaceful, not even in the United States; and the tensions between them have been greatest when the forces of either have been at war within themselves, as in the religious wars of the 16th and 17th centuries and the later nationalist wars. We have had none of the former in the United States, but we have had at least our fair share of the latter, and it is to this aspect we address ourselves.

A nation at war or on the verge of war demands the undivided loyalty of its citizens and is not tolerant of dissidents, even those religiously motivated. During the Revolutionary War period, the Anglican clergy shared the violence and persecution visited upon the Tories (Loyalists) by the Patriots (Rebels), and religious pacifists were in Federal prisons alongside socialistic ones in World War I. The church has learned through bitter experience that prudence dictates muting any doubts it may have whether a particular war is moral or whether it is really what God wants.

The state, however, has not had to resort often to force or threats of force to win the silence of the church. Since the faithful of both church and state are in large measure the same people, they have no doubts regarding either the political or religious rightness of the particular war the nation happens to be engaged in at the time. In the 1940s, both church and state (in the United States) agreed that it was right to war alongside the Communists in Europe, and in the 1950s and '60s to war against them in Asia. Besides, as we will see later in this chapter, the state has enough goodies to offer the church, even that division of it established by the Prince of Peace, to buy not only its silence but its active cooperation.

But there are dissidents within the church and they can prove troublesome to the state. Moreover, the state is not satisfied with neutral silence; it often demands articulated loyalty, even from those who are not called upon to serve in the armed forces, and sometimes even from little children. When the God of these children or of their parents says no, the conflict of loyalties can become cruel and bloody, unless the respected referee intervenes to resolve it peacefully. This was the experience of the Jehovah's Witnesses in the World War II period.

In 1898, the day after the United States declared war on Spain, the legislature in New York enacted a law prescribing a daily school opening program with a salute to the flag. Since then, the practice has become universal throughout the nation. In the 1930s the Jehovah's Witnesses issued a pamphlet setting forth the reasons for their refusal to salute the flag or to allow their children to do so.

FIRST: TO SALUTE THE FLAG WOULD BE A VIOLATION OF DIVINE COMMANDMENT STATED IN EXODUS 20:3-5, TO WIT

"Thou shalt have no other Gods before me. Thou shalt not make unto thee any graven image or any likeness of anything that is in heaven above, or that is in the earth beneath, or that is in the water under the earth. Thou shalt not bow down thyself to them nor serve them. . . ."

The flag is the country's emblem. An emblem is an image or representation of something. The flag is the image or representation of the American nation.

The salute to the flag is the rendering of respect, reverence and devotion to the image of the United States government.

SECOND: THE SALUTE TO THE FLAG MEANS IN EFFECT THAT THE PERSON SALUTING THE FLAG ASCRIBES SALVATION TO IT. WHEREAS SALVATION IS OF JEHOVAH GOD. . . .

THIRD: FLAG SALUTING IS PART OF A CREED OF A SECT OF
SO-CALLED PATRIOTS, TEACHING A RITUAL OF PATRIO-
TISM AND FROM SUCH ALL TRUE CHRISTIANS ARE COM-
MANDED TO TURN ASIDE. . . .

The conflict of loyalties between church and state inherent in the flag salute ceremony was starkly expressed by
Judge Rutherford, the leader of the Witnesses at that time.
"The law of the nation or government," he said, "that compels the child of God to salute the national flag compels that
person to salute the Devil as the invisible god of the nation.
The Christian, therefore, must choose to yield to God's
enemy or to remain true to Almighty God."

It is not to be supposed that the Judge was singling out
the United States as the kingdom of the Devil; according to
the beliefs of the sect, the entire worldly kingdom and all
its governments are possessed by him. Nor were the Witnesses the first to equate saluting the flag of a nation as
idolatry entailing loss of salvation. Two thousand years
earlier Jews refused to salute the Roman flag, and some
suffered martyrdom for it, because the flag bore an image
of the emperor to whom the Romans paid divine worship
and to whose banners they offered sacrifices. Even in the
United States, the Witnesses were not the first to refuse to
salute the flag; they were preceded by Mennonites and other
small sects. It was the Witnesses, however, who became the
chief victims of persecution and bloodshed for their refusal,
and ironically this came about in the wake of their insistence
upon invoking the jurisdiction of the Supreme Court to
resolve peacefully their conflict with the state.

The refusal of the Jehovah's Witnesses children to participate in the flag salute ceremony in the public schools resulted in the expulsion of many of them from the schools
they attended. During the late 1930s, the Witnesses tried
several times to appeal to the Supreme Court claiming that
the expulsions violated their religious freedom, but in each
case the Court simply rejected their appeal. Finally, in 1940,

the Court, in the case of *Minersville School District* v. *Gobitis*, decided that it had to hear their grievance because the lower court had decided in their favor and ruled the expulsion of the Gobitis children to be unconstitutional.

The Supreme Court reversed the decision and, as we have seen in the first chapter, held that the Free Exercise Clause does not exempt persons because of their particular religious beliefs from the operation of a general secular law applying equally to all. As for the validity of the law in general and the power of the state to compel all children to participate in a flag salute exercise, Justice Frankfurter, speaking for the Court, said, "National unity is the basis of national security." We live by symbols, he continued, and the flag is the symbol of our national unity. Only Justice Stone dissented.

The *Gobitis* decision elicited two completely opposite reactions. One was shown by the pungent comment of *The Christian Century* that "[it] is bitterly ironical that a free government should inflict a penalty for refusal to salute a symbol of freedom"; by the comment of Dean Christian Gauss of Princeton Theological Seminary that "[when] liberal democratic nationalists, like Felix Frankfurter, write these decisions, we may well ask whether Americanism has not already progressed to an ungodly stage"; and by many other similar comments in law reviews, liberal periodicals, and organs of religious groups—not excluding organs of the Catholic Church, the chief target of Jehovah's Witnesses' diatribes.

The opposite reactions were less intellectual but more emphatic. The Court's decision was announced on June 3, 1940. Between June 12 and June 20 hundreds of physical attacks upon the Jehovah's Witnesses were reported to the United States Department of Justice. At Kennebunk, Maine, their Kingdom Hall was burned. At Rockville, Maryland, the police assisted a mob in dispersing a Bible meeting. At Litchfield, Illinois, practically the entire town mobbed a company of some sixty Witnesses who were canvassing it. At Connersville, Indiana, several Witnesses were charged with riotous conspiracy, their attorney beaten, and all driven out of town. At Jackson, Mississippi, members of a veterans' organization forcibly removed a number of Witnesses and their trailer homes from the town. In Nebraska, a Witness was lured from his house, abducted, and castrated. In Richwood, West Virginia, the chief of police and deputy sheriff forced a group of Witnesses to drink large doses of castor oil, and paraded the victims through the streets, tied together with police department rope. In the two years following the *Gobitis* decision there was an uninterrupted record of violence and persecution of the Witnesses. Almost without exception, the flag and flag salute were the causes.

No student of martyrology would have expected these acts of persecution to weaken the steadfastness of the Witnesses, and in fact they did not. What did weaken, however, was the American people's hate and fear of the Witnesses. After the initial wave of irrationality, Americans found it difficult to identify the few elementary school children who refused to salute the flag with the totalitarian Nazis and Japanese with whom we were engaged in military combat. The clearest evidence of the turn of the tide was the action of Congress in 1942 in enacting a measure, sponsored by the American Legion, which, after describing the flag salute, stated that "civilians will show full respect to the flag when the pledge is given by merely standing at attention, men removing the headdress."

Since pupils do not wear hats in school and the Witnesses did not object to having their children stand while the pledge and salute exercise was conducted, the act of the national legislature vindicated the Witnesses' stand and marked the beginning of the end of this sad but fortunately brief chapter in American history.

When, then, the following year the Court ruled in *West Virginia State Board of Education* v. *Barnette* that children of

Jehovah's Witnesses could not constitutionally be expelled from public schools for refusing to salute the flag, it appeared to be doing nothing more than putting its stamp of approval upon a judgment already made by the American people through their elected representatives in Congress. The Court could have held that the act of Congress protected the right of the children not to salute the flag, but it refused to content itself with this, lest a future Congress change the law and reimpose the requirement. Instead, the Court held in the *Barnette* case that it was the Constitution rather than Congress alone that protected the children.

The Court did this in an eloquent opinion written by Justice Jackson which merits inclusion in any documentary history of freedom:

> Struggles to coerce uniformity of sentiment in support of some end thought essential to their time and country have been waged by many good as well as evil men. Nationalism is a relatively recent phenomenon but at other times and places the ends have been racial or territorial security, support of a dynasty or regime, and particular plans for saving souls. As first and moderate methods to attain unity have failed, those bent on its accomplishment must resort to an ever-increasing severity.
>
> As governmental pressure toward unity becomes greater, so strife becomes more bitter as to whose unity it shall be. Probably no deeper division of our people could proceed from any provocation than from finding it necessary to choose what doctrine and whose program public educational officials shall compel youth to unite in embracing. Ultimate futility of such attempts to compel coherence is the lesson of every such effort from the Roman drive to stamp out Christianity as a disturber of its pagan unity, the Inquisition, as a means to religious and dynastic unity, the Siberian exiles as a means to Russian unity, down to the fast failing efforts of our present totalitarian enemies. Those who begin coercive elimination of dissent soon find themselves exterminating dissenters. Compulsory unification of opinion achieves only the unanimity of the graveyard.

It seems trite but necessary to say that the First
Amendment to our Constitution was designed to avoid
these ends by avoiding these beginnings. . . .

[Justice Jackson concluded:] If there is any fixed star in
our constitutional constellation, it is that no official, high or
petty, can prescribe what shall be orthodox in politics, nationalism, religion, or other matters of opinion, or force
citizens to confess by word or act their faith therein. . . .

The Court did not deal with the *Barnette* case as one
involving freedom of religion, but rather freedom of speech.
It held that saluting the flag was a form of speech, following
its 1931 decision in *Stromberg* v. *California* which struck down
a State law forbidding the public display of red flags. People,
the Court held, speak through symbols as well as through
words, and symbolic speech is no less entitled to the protection of the First Amendment.

The necessary implication of this holding is that nobody can be compelled to salute the flag or pledge allegiance
to it or be punished for refusal to do either. This became
apparent when, in 1973, the Court in the case of *Central
School District* v. *Russo* refused to upset a Federal court's decision ordering the reinstatement of a public school teacher
who had been dismissed for refusing to join her pupils in
the daily Pledge of Allegiance because she did not believe that
our nation provided "justice for all." The previous year, the
Supreme Court let stand another Federal court decision
which ordered the reinstatement of a public school teacher
who had been dismissed for wearing a black arm band as a
symbol of protest against our participation in the Vietnam
War. That ruling followed the Supreme Court's 1969 decision in *Tinker* v. *Des Moines School District* where, on the basis
of the *Barnette* decision, it held that students could not be
suspended for wearing black arm bands in protest against
the war. The following paragraph from the *Tinker* decision, though dealing with freedom of speech rather than
religion, merits quoting here:

In our system, state-operated schools may not be enclaves of totalitarianism. School officials do not possess absolute authority over their students. Students in school as well as out of school are "persons" under our Constitution. They are possessed of fundamental rights which the State must respect, just as they themselves must respect their obligations to the State. In our system, students may not be regarded as closed-circuit recipients of only that which the State chooses to communicate. They may not be confined to the expression of those sentiments that are officially approved. In the absence of a specific showing of constitutionally valid reasons to regulate their speech, students are entitled to freedom of expression of their views. As Judge Gewin, speaking for the Fifth Circuit, said, school officials cannot suppress "expressions of feelings with which they do not wish to contend."

Thou Shalt Not Kill Unless Caesar So Commands

Idolatry may be defined as the sacrifice to a symbol of that which the symbol represents. Under this definition the persecution visited on Jehovah's Witnesses constituted idolatry for it denied them justice because they exercised their liberty not to salute a flag which symbolized liberty and justice for all. In an analogous and larger sense, idolatry may also be defined as the sacrifice of ends for the promotion or preservation of means. In both senses the history of Western civilization for the past two thousand years can in large measure be characterized as idolatry. For roughly half of that period the symbol has been religion, and under its banner untold millions were (and to some extent continue to be) killed for the greater glory of Him who commanded that "thou shalt not kill" and whose prophets foresaw a time when people "would not learn war" anymore. During the other half the symbol has been nationalism and many more untold millions were and continue to be killed to spread and preserve the *pax Romana* or *pax Americana* or to end all wars or bring peace in our generation.

According to the document which declared America independent and established it as a nation, all men are created equal and governments are instituted by them as a means to secure their inalienable rights, most specifically the right to life, liberty, and the pursuit of happiness. Yet, just short of four score and seven years later the President of the United States stated that his paramount object in the most bloody war in American history was "to save the Union" and not "either to save or destroy slavery," and that if he "could save the Union without freeing any slave," he "would do it."

As indicated at the beginning of this chapter, this allocation of values between means and ends is in the view of many just what the Constitution mandates. No value is higher than the preservation of the Union and no liberty is immune from sacrifice where necessary for the defense of that means-become-end. Thus, no individual right, whether inalienable or created by the Constitution or law, can stand in the way of national defense. The Thirteenth Amendment forbids involuntary servitude and contains no exceptions other than "as a punishment for a crime whereof the party shall have been duly convicted." Nevertheless, in the Selective Draft Law cases of 1918 the Supreme Court found itself

> unable to conceive upon what theory the exaction by government from the citizen of the performance of his supreme and noble duty of contributing to the defense of the rights and honor of the nation, as a result of a war declared by the great representative body of the people, can be said to be the imposition of involuntary servitude in violation of the prohibitions of the Thirteenth Amendment.

The Court felt itself "constrained to the conclusion that the contention to that effect is refuted by its mere statement."

Thirteen years later, in *United States* v. *Macintosh*, the Court was no more charitable to a similar contention asserted under the First Amendment's guaranty of religious freedom. It rejected as "astonishing" the assertion that it is a "fixed principle of our Constitution, zealously guarded by our laws, that a citizen cannot be forced and need not bear arms in a war if he has conscientious scruples against doing so." The Court said:

> Of course, there is no such principle of the Constitution, fixed or otherwise. The conscientious objector is relieved from the obligation to bear arms in obedience to no constitutional provision, express or implied; but because, and only because, it has accorded with the policy of Congress thus to relieve him. . . . The privilege of the . . . conscientious objector to avoid bearing arms comes not from the Constitution but from the acts of Congress.

In the *Macintosh* case, as in *United States* v. *Schwimmer* and *Bland* v. *United States*, the Court interpreted the Immigration and Nationality Act as barring religious pacifists from acquiring American citizenship. In the 1946 case of *Girouard* v. *United States*, however, the Court reversed itself and said that it had misinterpreted the Act which, it now held, did not bar naturalization of religious pacifists. Six years later, during the Korean War and the darkest period of McCarthyism, Congress revised the Act to tighten its provisions aimed at protecting America against communism from within and without. Nevertheless, it adopted the *Girouard* rather than the *Macintosh* decision and explicitly provided that religious pacifists were eligible for citizenship and would not be required to take the usual oath to bear arms when necessary to the nation's defense.

This change in the Act, however, did not in any way affect the Court's assertion in the *Macintosh* case that the exemption from military service enjoyed by conscientious objectors was not a matter of right but of grace; it came not from the Constitution but from Congress, and, like tax exemption of churches, what Congress gave Congress could take away. This meant that should Congress decide to change the law and disqualify religious pacifists born abroad from becoming American citizens, nothing in the Constitution would prevent its doing so. It also meant that the right of religious pacifists to escape the legal consequences of their refusal to perform the "supreme and noble duty" of participating in the armed defense of the nation was limited to what Congress gave them.

It was on the basis of this principle that three years after the *Macintosh* decision, the Court in the case of *Hamilton* v. *Regents of the University of California* upheld the right of a State university to expel religious pacifists who refused to enroll in the compulsory military training courses. For the same reason, in the case of *In re Summers*, decided in 1945, it held that a State could refuse to grant a license to practice law to persons who for religious reasons would not bear arms in defense of the nation. In both cases the Court held that while Congress relieved conscientious objectors of the penalty of imprisonment it did not forbid the States from conditioning the grant of such privileges as a free higher education or the license to practice law upon a willingness to fight for our country when called upon to do so.

Conscientious Objection to All Wars

Exemption of specific classes—the newly betrothed, the newly married, the fainthearted, and others—goes back as far as Mosaic times (Deuteronomy 20:1–8). Since all biblical wars were theocratic, there was, of course, no such thing as religious exemption, although it might be noted that according to the Talmud the term "fainthearted" referred to those who were too compassionate to take human life, which may therefore be the earliest instance of exemption from military service for conscientious objection—and nonreligious objection at that. In any event, Oliver Cromwell felt that those whose religious doctrine forbade participation in armed conflict should constitute an exempt class. So too did the legislatures in some of the American colonies, the Continental Congress, and a number of the members of the Congress established under the Constitution. As early as 1789 a resolution was introduced in Congress to amend the Constitution to exempt religious objectors from compulsory militia service, but it failed of passage. The first national exemption of conscientious objectors was adopted by Congress during the Civil War, and like its colonial and State precedents, it was limited to members of well-recognized religious denominations whose articles of faith forbade the bearing of arms.

So, too, was the exemption accorded by the conscription law enacted at the time of our entry into World War I. Exemption was allowed only to those who were affiliated with well-recognized religious sects, the creed or principles of which forbade their members to participate "in war in any form." Lest new sects arise to provide a shelter for unwilling draftees, the law limited the exemption to sects already existing at the time it was enacted, and, to prevent existing sects from altering their doctrine for the same purpose, the law also required that the creed or principle against military service be in existence when the law was passed.

The intended beneficiaries of these exemption laws were the long-established peace denominations, such as the Friends and Mennonites. But the genius of American freedoms is individualistic rather than corporate; the opening words of the Bill of Rights reflect a suspicion of, if not antipathy to, religious establishments. The 1940 selective service law, enacted upon the eve of our entry into World War II, liberalized the exemption to make it more consistent with the American genius. It no longer required membership in a particular sect, but granted the exemption to anyone who by "reason of religious training and belief" possessed conscientious scruples against "participation in war in any form."

Congress, however, had no intention of extending

the mantle of protection to political, intellectual, humanist, or other nonreligious objectors to war. To make this clear, it again amended the law in 1948 to state explicitly that

> religious training and belief in this connection means an individual's belief in a relation to a Supreme Being involving duties superior to those arising from any human relation, but does not include essentially political, sociological, or philosophical views or a merely personal moral code.

So amended, the law gave rise to some difficult constitutional questions. In the first place, religion and belief in God are not necessarily synonymous. As the Court was later to point out in *Torcaso* v. *Watkins*, there are ancient, well-recognized religions that are not theistic, such as Buddhism, Taoism, and Confucianism. A military exemption law limited to adherents of the Christian faith would obviously be unconstitutional; so too would be one which specifically excluded Buddhists, Taoists, and Confucianists. Yet this was what was effected by requiring a belief in God as a condition to exemption. The concept of God as generally understood in this country is basically Judeo-Christian (and Islamic), and, under the Establishment Clause of the First Amendment, Congress could no more prefer these religions over nontheistic faiths than it could prefer Christianity over Judaism or Protestantism over Catholicism.

A second constitutional difficulty arose from the fact that the law imposes upon civil officials the duty of making theological determinations and, moreover, gives them no standards or guidelines by which to make them. How is a draft board to decide whether that in which a particular applicant for exemption believes is a "Supreme Being"? Does he have to believe in the God of the Old Testament or the New Testament or the Koran or all three? Does his belief have to be fundamentalist in essence or may it be liberal and modernist?

Finally, even if the draft boards were to take a liberal position as to what constitutes God and were also to accept as religious training and belief, within the meaning of the exemption, training and belief in nontheistic religions, a constitutional problem would still remain. The Establishment Clause, the Court has held on numerous occasions, does not impose a mandate of neutrality merely as among different religions, but also as between religion and nonreligion. The government may not prefer all religions over nonreligions any more than it may prefer one or some religions over others.

These were some of the difficulties facing the Court in 1965 in three cases decided under the name of *United States* v. *Seeger*. It met them by first taking God out of religion and then taking religion out of religion. Seeger, in applying for exemption, admitted his "skepticism or disbelief in the existence of God," but avowed a "belief in and devotion to goodness and virtue for their own sakes and a religious faith in a purely ethical creed," and cited Plato, Aristotle, and Spinoza in support of such belief. Jakobson, another applicant, stated a belief in "Godness horizontally through Mankind and the World," rather than "vertically, towards Godness directly." The third applicant, Peter, avowed a commitment to religion defined as "the supreme expression of human nature; man thinking his highest, feeling his deepest, living his best."

The Court held that all three applicants were entitled to exemption since all had the requisite "religious training and belief in relation to a Supreme Being." By using the term "Supreme Being" rather than "God," the Court said, Congress intended something much broader than the traditional personal Deity. As for the term "religious belief," that is one which "is sincere and meaningful and occupies a place in the life of its possessor parallel to that filled by the orthodox belief in God of one who clearly qualifies for the exemption.

What this meant is that depth and sincerity can be substituted for dogma and creedal affiliation. The decision assumed the importance of being earnest, but not necessarily of being religious, at least as that word would be understood by the man in the street. By holding that the three applicants all qualified under the exemption, the Court was able to avoid deciding whether the exemption itself was constitutional. Yet it is doubtful that Congress really meant what the Court said it did. The terms "God" and "Supreme Being" are generally considered synonymous. The Declaration of Independence uses the terms "Nature's God," "Creator," "Supreme Judge of the World," and "divine Providence," and certainly did not mean different things in each case.

As for "religious training and belief," it should be noted that Congress went out of its way to exclude from exemption persons motivated by "essentially political, sociological, or philosophical views or a merely personal moral code." This would seem to indicate that Congress used the term "religious training and belief" in the conventional or traditional sense.

Seeger had sent a letter to his draft board in which he wrote:

> My decision arises from what I believe to be considerations of validity from the standpoint of the welfare of humanity and the preservation of the democratic values which we in the United States are struggling to maintain. I have concluded that war, from the practical standpoint, is futile and self-defeating, and that from the more important moral standpoint, it is unethical.

Very few people, including Congressmen, would characterize as "religious" the motivations of the writer of such a letter. Nor would they do so in respect to another applicant who, in responding affirmatively to the question on his application form asking whether his objection to participation in war was based on "religious training and belief," first struck out the word "religious," and later stated that his beliefs had been formed "by readings in the fields of history and sociology." Yet in *Welsh* v. *United States*, the Court, in

1970, held that he too qualified for an exemption under the statute.

The decisions, nevertheless, evoked little articulated protest from Congress or politicians. One can only speculate why, but it should be noted that in providing for college deferments Congress had already opened an escape hatch for many middle- and upper-class men; the *Seeger* and *Welsh* decisions opened another which was likewise not available to the poor, few of whom, it may be presumed, could cite Plato, Aristotle, Spinoza, and their own "readings in the fields of history and sociology" as the sources of their sincere and meaningful opposition to war in all forms.

Wars Immoral

There was the rub—war in all forms. Many applicants were sincere and could not answer negatively the inevitable question put by draft boards: "If you had been alive and of mature age in 1941–45 would you have opposed participation in World War II?" For the applicant who took his sincerity seriously the inevitable answer was: "That was a moral war; the Vietnam War is immoral."

What does "participation in war in any form" mean? Does it mean in any form of war, such as war with one's arms and hands alone, slingshots, bows and arrows, guns, nuclear weapons? Does it mean in all wars? Or does it mean any form of participation in any or all wars? The question came to the Supreme Court in a rather extreme way in the 1955 case of *Sicurella* v. *United States*. Sicurella was a member of the Jehovah's Witnesses sect. He claimed to be "in the Army of Christ Jesus serving as a soldier of Jehovah's appointed Commander Jesus Christ." Inasmuch as the war weapons of the soldier of Jesus Christ were not carnal he was not authorized by his Commander to engage in the carnal warfare of this world. However, the literature of the Jehovah's Witnesses extolled the ancient wars of the Israelites, asserted that Witnesses would engage in a "theocratic war" if Jehovah so commanded them, and declared that they would fight at Armageddon.

On the basis of this evidence the draft board ruled that Sicurella was not entitled to exemption, but the Supreme Court felt otherwise. As to theocratic war, the Court stated that his willingness to fight on the orders of Jehovah was tempered by the fact that, as far as is known, the Witnesses' history records no such command since biblical times and their theology does not contemplate one in the future. And while the Witnesses expected to fight at Armageddon they would do so without carnal weapons, and Congress had in mind real shooting wars—"actual military conflicts between nations of the earth in our time—wars with bombs and bullets, tanks, planes and rockets."

Had the Department of Justice prevailed in its efforts to put Sicurella in prison, the Witnesses would have been deprived of the privilege granted to the more traditional peace faiths, only because of possible differences in eschatological theology. One can only speculate as to the department's motivation, but it is difficult to dismiss the possibility that vestiges of the earlier hostility to the sect were part of it.

Willingness to fight at Armageddon but not in Korea could be tolerated by the Court, but a more difficult question was presented where the acceptable battlefield was Nazi Germany and the unacceptable one Vietnam. In *Gillette* v. *United States*, decided in 1971, the Court held that such selective conscientious objection went beyond the limits of judicial acceptability.

Involved in this case were two applicants for exemption. One of them stated that his refusal to serve in Vietnam was "based on a humanist approach to religion." Under the decisions in the *Seeger* and *Welsh* cases this would not have disqualified him, but he admitted that he would be willing to participate in a war of national defense or one sponsored by the United Nations as a peace-keeping measure. The other applicant was a devout Catholic who believed it his religious duty to discriminate between "just" and "unjust" wars and to refuse to serve in the latter, in which category he placed the Vietnam conflict.

The Court upheld the denial of exemption to both applicants. It ruled first that the term "opposition to participation in war in any form" meant nonparticipation in all wars and that Congress had no intention of letting even religiously motivated draftees choose in which wars they would fight and in which they would not. Nor, said the Court, does the exemption so limited violate either the Establishment or the Free Exercise Clause of the First Amendment. In respect to the former, limiting the exemption to opposition to all wars minimizes governmental entanglement in religion and theology, just as does granting tax exemption to all churches. While the clause also forbids discrimination as between sects or beliefs, pragmatic considerations may justify limiting an exemption to those who hold a particular type of religious belief. Thus, if selective conscientious objection were allowed, fairness could be threatened and objectors who are more articulate, better educated, or better counseled might succeed in avoiding military service, while those less fortunate but no less sincere would not. The resultant feelings that the draft law was unfairly administered could bring on a mood of cynicism and bitterness that might seriously impair the national effort.

As for the Free Exercise Clause, the Court noted that it had long been held that there was no constitutional right to conscientious exception and that compulsory military service was not forbidden by the First Amendment. Congress could have allowed selective objection had it wished, but the Constitution no more required it than it required exemption for objection to participation in all wars.

Priestly Exemption

As noted earlier in this chapter, according to the Book of Deuteronomy, before the Children of Israel went to war the priests announced the exempt classes and sent their members home. No mention of priests was made in the announcement itself, but it is quite clear that, throughout the history of Israel, priests were not required to serve as combatants in the armed forces; Levites, the priestly tribe, were not numbered in the census of those "able to go forth to war" (Numbers 1:3, 47). It may be assumed that immunity of the priestly class from obligatory combatant service was not limited to the Levites of Israel. In most countries it is and probably always has been a concomitant of compulsory military service. In the United States exemption of "duly ordained ministers of religion" has been included in every conscription law.

Exemption of clergymen (and theological students) is not the only privilege accorded them by government in the United States. On the one hand they are empowered, along with justices of the peace and municipal clerks, to place the required legal sanction upon marital relationships. On the other, they are often exempt from such civic duties as serving on juries, paying full fares on rate-regulated trains or full taxes on their homes, or observing all the automobile parking regulations imposed upon the community at large. These amenities are very much taken for granted, but this does not mean that their constitutionality is beyond question. The exemption from military service, at least, was judicially challenged even before the Supreme Court said in the *Everson* case that under the Establishment Clause neither the States nor the Federal government could pass laws which aid religion.

In the Selective Draft Law Cases of 1918 the claim was made that the exemption violated both the Establishment and Free Exercise clauses of the First Amendment, but the Court dismissed it summarily with the remark that its unsoundness was too apparent to require any discussion. Yet the claim merited more serious treatment. No one would contend that under the Establishment Clause government could pay all or part of the salaries of clergymen. During the Civil War the law allowed draftees to avoid actual service by hiring substitutes. Would it have been constitutional for Congress to omit any exemption of clergymen but provide for payments to them out of Federal funds of the amounts necessary to hire substitutes? If this would not have been constitutional, why should an outright exemption be so?

Jefferson's great Virginia Act for Establishing Religious Freedom, which has long been recognized as the progenitor of the First Amendment's religion clauses, states that "opinion in matters of religion . . . shall in no wise diminish, enlarge or affect . . . civil capacities." Does not exemption of clergymen from military service violate that provision? True enough, so does exemption of religious objectors, but, as we have seen, the Court in the *Seeger* and *Welsh* cases interpreted "religious belief" so broadly as to make it mean little more than sincere belief deeply held. The term "duly ordained ministers of religion" cannot be disposed of so easily.

Nevertheless, in view of the *Walz* decision upholding tax exemption for churches, it is hardly likely that the Supreme Court would today rule unconstitutional military exemption for clergymen. Actually, in one respect the latter exemption is more justifiable than the former. Taxing all church buildings would not close the churches, except perhaps the very poorest. But drafting all clergymen would very seriously prejudice the access of the American people to spiritual guidance and thus hinder the free exercise of their religion.

Military Chaplains

Military chaplaincies in the United States go back as far as priestly exemption from military service and tax exemption for churches. Unlike priestly exemption, however (but like tax exemption for churches), they have from an early period been subject to serious questioning as to their constitutionality. James Madison, who drafted the First Amendment and therefore should have had some idea as to what it meant, was of the opinion that military chaplaincies were inconsistent with the spirit of the Establishment Clause and constituted "a political authority in matters of religion."

Two alternate but related rationales can be offered to justify military chaplaincies under the First Amendment. As we have seen, the Free Exercise Clause does not bar compulsory military service even on the part of religious objectors, because national defense is the highest priority. This, however, is equally true of all the other clauses in the First Amendment, including the Establishment Clause. If, therefore, use of government-paid military chaplains is determined to be necessary for the defense of the nation, the Establishment Clause will not stand in the way.

Again we can refer to Scripture for precedent. Before the Israelite soldiers went into combat the priests exhorted them: "Hear, O Israel, ye approach this day unto battle against your enemies; let not your hearts be faint, fear not and do not tremble, neither be ye terrified because of them; for the Lord your God is he that goeth with you, to fight against your enemies, to save you." (Deuteronomy 20:1-4). Such morale building has long been taken for granted as a proper function of military chaplains and its validity has only recently begun to be seriously reexamined by the chaplains themselves, though not by the military establishment, principally because of the ambivalence of many of them toward the morality of the Vietnam War. Yet, even if that war were deemed morally justifiable or at least defensible, military use of spiritual advisers leads to anomalous results: a Christian chaplain serving in the American army in World War I could assure his troops that "God is with us," while his German counterpart, invoking the same Deity and the same faith, could tell his troops with equal confidence, "*Gott mit uns.*" One is reminded of the statement by Madison, in the Memorial and Remonstrance written by him in

1786 in opposition to a Virginia bill to assess taxes on all citizens for the support of churches: "that [the state] may employ religion as an engine of civil policy [is] an unhallowed perversion of the means of salvation."

Unhallowed perversion or not, when Caesar invokes Mars, God can be a useful partner if He is willing. This is illustrated by the following report in the March 1, 1967, issue of the Jewish Telegraphic Agency *Daily News Bulletins*:

> A U.S. Army private who embarked on a "death fast" because he claimed his religious conviction as an Orthodox Jew prevented him from serving "an army practicing violence" in Viet Nam has been taken into custody and confined in a mental ward at Madigan General Hospital, Tacoma, Wash., military authorities revealed today.
>
> The soldier, Pvt. Robert Levy, 22, of Kansas City, Mo., started a hunger strike two weeks ago at Fort Lewis, Wash. For 14 days he ate only milk and honey. Yesterday, he stopped eating altogether stating that "as an expression of my religious conviction as an Orthodox Jew, I break the law of the United States and refuse to remain a soldier."
>
> Defense Department officials disclosed that the Army is trying to get rabbis to convince Levy that the war is righteous and his fast unjustified.

For the government to pay the salaries of priests would in ordinary circumstances be wholly inconsistent with the mandate of separation of church and state embodied in the First Amendment, but war and preparation for war are not ordinary circumstances. Since defense of the nation—and what war is not in defense of the nation?—is paramount over all other concerns, separation of church and state may not stand in the way.

A second constitutional justification might perhaps be found under the Free Exercise Clause. Madison, in his expression of opposition to military chaplains, recognized, although he rejected, a possible exception in the "case of navies with insulated crews." Today, soldiers serving away from their hometowns may be practically as "insulated" as navies. A soldier drafted into the armed forces and sent to camp far from home is deprived of the opportunity to exercise his religion by attending the church of his choice. But only to the extent that the deprivation is necessary to the overriding consideration of national defense is it constitutional; if the government can practicably furnish a substitute in the form of a traveling church, the soldier may have a constitutional right thereto, or at the very least it would not be unconstitutional for the government to furnish the substitute.

Opponents of military chaplaincies recognize the need many soldiers have for spiritual help, particularly in periods of stress and crisis. They argue, however, that the churches could provide this even more effectively and certainly more honestly if the chaplains were not part of the military establishment, if they were paid by the churches rather than the government, if they did not wear military uniforms and did not hold military rank. Godly men are human too, and, in the military, if you want good efficiency reports, promotions in rank, and decorations, you don't go around making waves. A commanding officer who thinks all conscientious objectors are cowardly frauds, and in any event should be made to do their duty as everybody else, is not likely to recommend for promotion a chaplain who seems to be much too trusting in attesting to the sincerity of soldiers who newly discover a conscientious objection to war that they did not previously know they possessed.

There is, however, another side to the matter. Military chaplains, besides building morale, fill a need which civilian chaplains without official rank, status, and pay could not fill, or could not fill so effectively. A young man of eighteen or nineteen, away from home and family perhaps for the first time, who finds himself in some kind of trouble with the overwhelmingly large, disciplined, and impersonal institution known as the army, may need a trusted ombudsman and need him desperately. In such a situation, a chaplain who has the same military rank and wears the same uniform as the commanders, who eats with them and calls them by first name, can be far more valuable than either of the Berrigan brothers with all their idealism and self-sacrifice.

Compulsory Chapel

As noted in the first chapter, in 1963 the Supreme Court declared that a law does not violate the principle of church-state separation if its purpose and primary effect are secular. Since then practically every effort to introduce religion in the public schools or to get public funds for church schools has been accompanied by a recitation of "purpose and primary effect" as if it were a verbal talisman whose mere incantation was sufficient to exorcise the ghost of unconstitutionality. The *reductio ad absurdum* of the purpose-effect test is to be found in the 1972 case of *Laird* v. *Anderson.*

One would assume that in the United States no one could be forced to go to church. At least four times within the past 25 years the Supreme Court has said so. Nor is this tradition of recent vintage; it is more than three centuries old, dating back to a letter, written in 1654 by Roger Williams to the people of the Town of Providence, in which he said:

> There goes many a ship to sea, with many hundred souls in one ship, whose weal and woe is common, and is a true picture of a commonwealth, or a human combination or society. It hath fallen out sometimes, that both papists and protestants, Jews and Turks, may be embarked in one ship; upon which supposal I affirm, that all the liberty of conscience, that ever I pleaded for, turns upon these two hinges —that none of the papists, protestants, Jews, or Turks be forced to come to the ship's prayers or worship, if they practice any. I further add, that I never denied, that notwithstanding this liberty, the commander of this ship ought to command the ship's course, yea, and also com-

mand that justice, peace and sobriety, be kept and practiced, both among the seamen and all the passengers.

The military, however, have a tradition of their own. As early as 1821 the United States Military Academy of West Point promulgated a regulation requiring all cadets to attend religious service at the academy chapel. Later the regulation was ecumenicized; in addition to the Protestant chapel, Catholic and Jewish chapels were built so that the cadet could worship in the church of his faith so long as it was Protestant, Catholic, or Jewish. The regulations of the Naval Academy at Annapolis and the Air Force Academy at Colorado Springs were even more liberal; they allowed midshipmen and cadets to attend religious services at an appropriate town church or synagogue approved by the Senior Chaplain.

The regulations were strictly enforced; "no cadet is exempt," the West Point regulation said. Unexcused absence from attendance was punished in the same manner as violation of other regulations, i.e., by reprimands, demerits, punishment marching tours, confinement to quarters, and for repeated violations, expulsion.

Neither permissiveness nor dissidence is encouraged at these academies and it is therefore not surprising that there does not appear to have been any expressed protest to the practice over the years. In 1970, however, a few cadets and midshipmen braved the displeasure of the authorities and called upon the American Civil Liberties Union to bring suit in their behalf challenging the constitutionality of the practice.

At the trial of the case, Assistant Secretary of Defense Roger Kelley and Admiral Thomas Moorer (later Chairman of the Joint Chiefs of Staff) testified that the regulations did not require the cadets and midshipmen to *worship* but only to *attend*, and the purpose and primary effect were to make better and more effective combat officers of them. How? Because if a cadet observed young men at prayer and worship he would learn how they responded to religion, and when the cadet became a combat officer he would be able to put this knowledge to use on the battlefield. Secretary Kelley testified:

> The opportunity to observe others at worship is clear manifestation of the manner and extent to which they draw upon God or a supernatural being in the conduct of their lives.

Attendance at religious services, Admiral Moorer said, "is a vital part of the leadership package" and it would be "as inconsistent with the responsibility the Academies have to train complete combat officers to ignore this necessity as it would be to ignore the more obvious physical and tactical education."

The purpose and effect of the regulations, the Department of Defense argued, were secular; they were not to inculcate faith but to make better military officers, and therefore they were constitutional. Nevertheless, the testimony raised a number of other questions, among them the following:

1. What could a cadet learn by watching the behavior of other men in the peace, quiet, and solemnity of a church service that would be helpful to him in a combat situation on the battlefield, or for that matter anywhere else but in a church during religious services?

2. If anything relevant and useful is thus learned, could it not be learned in one or two visits to the church? What additional knowledge would be gained by repeating the process Sunday after Sunday, month after month, year after year, during the cadet's entire four-year stay at the academy?

3. If there was militarily valuable knowledge that could be gained by watching other men at worship, why was the cadet required to attend services of his own faith? Would it, in fact, not have been wiser to forbid this, for it

was quite likely that he had attended such services all his life and could hardly gain additional knowledge from continued attendance?

4. Why was he limited by the regulations to attendance at the services of one faith rather than to require him to attend worship of many faiths, for was it not unlikely that in a religiously pluralistic society such as the United States he would ever have soldiers of only one faith under his command?

5. At West Point the cadet could not attend services in town but only at one of the three denominational chapels at the academy. In these circumstances how would he observe potential soldiers under his command? Moreover, since the cadets were required only to observe but not themselves to participate in worship and prayer (indeed, should they not have been forbidden to do so since it would have diverted them from the serious business for which they were there?), was it not possible that a cadet might find himself observing other cadets engaged not in worship or prayer but in observing him observing them, in a sort of never-ending multifaceted mirror?

Many other questions might also be asked, but these are enough to suggest that the explanation of the military authorities for the regulations bordered on the incredible— except for the fact that the district judge believed it. He accepted the testimony and ruled that the regulations were constitutional since their purpose and primary effect were not religious but militarily secular.

The American Civil Liberties lawyers appealed the decision to the court of appeals, claiming that the regulations violated not only the Establishment but also the Free Exercise Clause. The three judges split three ways: one accepted in full both the testimony and the legal arguments of the Department of Defense; a second was of the view that the regulations violated the Establishment Clause but did not prohibit the cadets' free exercise of their religion; and the third found them inconsistent with both clauses of the First Amendment. Since the upshot was that, for whatever reason, the regulations were unconstitutional, the Department of Defense appealed to the Supreme Court; that Court rejected the appeal. Shortly thereafter, in 1973, Secretary of Defense Melvin Laird issued an order annulling the regulations for compulsory attendance of religious services in military academies and elsewhere in the armed services, thus bringing to an end a tradition and practice that had been unquestioned and unchallenged for a century and a half.

Chapter Five

The Schools Public

Origins of American Public Education

The American public school system is the child of New England Calvinism. A major factor in the Protestant Reformation was the Church's arrogation to itself of exclusive competence and authority to understand the Bible and communicate its message to the faithful. The Church did more than discourage the reading of the Bible by the laity; it did all it could to make it impossible, on occasion going so far as to put to death some who dared to translate it into the common tongues. The dedication in the Authorized King James translation of the Bible refers to the "Popish persons at home and abroad" who malign the translators because the latter "are poor instruments to make God's holy truth to be yet more and more known unto the people, whom they desire still to be kept in ignorance and darkness."

If the common people were to read the Bible they had to learn to read, and as a practical matter this could be achieved only through schooling. Quite naturally, therefore, the Calvinists in theocratic Massachusetts adopted a compulsory educational law in 1647 and stated as its purpose and preamble:

> It being the chief project of that old deluder, Satan, to keep men from the knowledge of the Scriptures, as in former times by keeping them in an unknown tongue, so in these later times by persuading from the use of tongues, that so at least the true sense and meaning of the original might be

clouded by false glosses of saint-seeming deceivers, that
learning may not be buried in the graves of our fathers in
the church and commonwealth. . . .

The law required all towns to establish schools in
which children could be taught to read. However, since the
Protestant ethic required the faithful to be thrifty, diligent,
and economically self-supporting, the schools were also to
teach writing and arithmetic so that the people would be able
to cope with and prosper in an anticipated mercantile society
on the eastern shores of the new world.

Anglican Virginia was considerably more tardy in establishing public schools, partly because Anglicanism was less
Bible-centered and less egalitarian than Calvinist Congregationalism, and partly because Virginia anticipated a plantation and agrarian society wherein universal mastery of the
three R's was not a necessity. Jefferson, egalitarian and
humanist, early espoused the cause of universal education.
"If," he wrote, "the condition of man is to be progressively
ameliorated, as we fondly hope and believe, education is to
be the chief instrument in effecting it." The optimism of
deist humanism and its faith in the potency of reason and
education is indicated by his dictum: "Enlighten the people
generally, and tyranny and oppression of body and mind will
vanish like evil spirits at the dawn of day." Great as his influence was, nevertheless some time passed before it proved
sufficient to overcome Southern apathy to schooling for any
but upper-class children.

In the middle colonies, characterized by multiple
establishments rather than a unitary one as in New England
and Virginia, each denomination established its own schools,
usually associated with the separate parishes—the pattern
later adopted by the Catholics. In all the States there were,
to a greater or lesser degree, charity schools maintained
through church or private philanthropy for the very poor.

The coming of Jacksonian democracy brought fruition
to Jefferson's dream. Under the leadership of such far-think-

ing men as Thaddeus Stevens, Horace Mann, and Henry Barnard, the States began to recognize their responsibility for assuring universal education; and one by one the legislatures included in their budgets sums to help local communities finance their own schools. So universal did the American consensus become that every State admitted into the Union after the Civil War has been required by Congress to include in its constitution a provision requiring the establishment and perpetual maintenance of a Statewide public school system.

Public education in the United States rests on a number of fundamental assumptions. First, that the legislature has the power to tax all—even the childless and those whose children attend private schools—in order to provide free public education for all; second, that the legislature has the power to require every parent to provide for his children a basic education in secular subjects; third, that the public schools maintained by the State (directly or through local school boards) must be open to all on equal terms; finally, that those schools must be secular. None of these assumptions was accepted without a struggle. Many persons found it difficult to agree with the proposition that education is a function of the state (the Catholic Church still does not fully accept it), and could not understand why they should be taxed to educate other people's children. And it was not until 1954 that the Constitution was interpreted by the Supreme Court as requiring the public schools to admit black and white children on equal terms. It is, however, the last of these assumptions—that public education must be secular—with which we are concerned in this chapter.

The Secularization of American Education

When the States resolved to assume responsibility for public education it was quite natural that they should simply take over the existing church school systems, including the charity schools. The buildings were available; the teachers—

mostly ministers—were available; and so too was the basic curriculum, consisting of the four R's: reading, 'riting, 'rithmetic, and religion. The last caused some trouble for a time since the schools, while all Protestant, were controlled and conducted by different denominations with varying theological doctrines. Fortunately, all the denominations shared a common denominator—the Holy Scriptures in the Authorized Version sponsored by King James. Under the leadership of Horace Mann in Massachusetts, a compromise *modus vivendi* was arrived at in the 1840s which can be characterized succinctly as Bible yes, sectarianism no.

What this meant was that it was perfectly permissible —and in fact commendable—to read to the children and, as they progressed, to have them read from the King James Bible, but that sectarian interpretation or theological instruction was forbidden since the student body in each common school (so called for that reason) was made up of children from a variety of sects and denominations. In theory this was fine; all Protestants agreed that God's Word was clear and needed no ecclesiastical intermediary to make it understandable to the ordinary layman. In practice it was not quite that simple. Children do not understand all the long words adults use, and the difficulty is compounded when many of those words are in Elizabethan English rather than 19th century American English. Moreover, children are naturally curious and many of them congenitally disputatious—the lifelong conflict between Esau and Jacob began before they left their mother's womb. Questions, simple or contentious, were therefore inevitable in the classroom, and with them the danger of overreaching by evangelical teachers and of verbal if not physical religious wars among the children.

The solution was to permit nonsectarian exposition and forbid sectarian indoctrination. Some States began to put in their constitutions or laws provisions which either banned sectarian instruction or books in the public schools, with or without an express exception for the Bible, or required or authorized Bible reading without sectarian comment. In other States, where the constitutions and laws were silent, either the same *modus operandi* was arrived at by general consent at the local or community level, or the minister-teachers did what came naturally to them and continued to teach as they had been doing when their employer was the synod or congregation.

The one universal Protestant prayer, the Lord's Prayer, is found in the Bible so that its recitation in the public school was obviously justifiable under law or custom permitting Bible reading. Other prayers too are found in the Bible, and their use is similarly acceptable. From this it was but a short step to allow prayers which, while not taken verbatim from Holy Scripture, reflected its spirit and were not inconsistent with it. The same was true of religious hymns, and they too could be found in general use in public schools east of the Mississippi in the 19th century. Finally, the curricula in all public schools included history, and subjects such as the rise of Christianity and the Reformation were of course part of history and were therefore taught by instructors brought up in the Protestant tradition.

All in all, well into the 20th century a pan-Protestantism in varying degrees of intensity characterized American public education, strongest in the South (Bible belt) and most attenuated in the Pacific and Rocky Mountain regions. Yet all together, the Scriptural reading, prayer recitation, hymn singing, and the occasional Protestant-biased teaching of Old World history (most of the history taught in the elementary schools was American), constituted a small fraction of the public school program; unlike the Catholic parochial school system, secularity and not religion was the pervading influence.

Two major factors contributed to this development: the deist-humanist influence of Jeffersonian-Jacksonian democracy, and the influx of Roman Catholics, first from Ireland and later from southern and eastern Europe. The humanist influence dominated not only the State colleges and normal schools where the public school teachers received their training, but also the originally Protestant denominational universities such as Harvard, Yale, Princeton, and Columbia (formerly Kings), whose education faculties trained public school administrators and teachers for colleges and normal schools. Marginal religious incursions which took but a few minutes of the school day could be tolerated, but the school day was too short and the work to be done too great to allow any significant amount of time to be expended on such subjects as the relative claims to truth on the part of the adherents of adult as against infant baptism or *vice versa*.

In this respect the colleges and universities reflected the general American consensus. Post-Revolutionary America was a secular nation; its Constitution did not mention God. In the 17th century, Quakers were executed as heretics and Anne Hutchinson was exiled to her death because she preached a "covenant of grace" as opposed to a "covenant of works." After the Revolution, Americans were ignorant of, apathetic to, and occasionally amused by intra-Protestant theological disputations. (One of the longest running plays in the history of the American stage, *Life with Father*, was a comedy based upon a woman's efforts to induce her husband to be baptized.)

The second factor, the influx of the Roman Catholics, was not so amusing. We will return to it in the next chapter in connection with the development of the Catholic parochial school system, but here our concern is with the trials and tribulations of the half of the Catholic school-age population who attended public schools.

Catholic Children in Unfriendly Schools

The first major influx of immigrants into the United States came from impoverished Ireland in the 1830s and increased substantially with the potato famine of the 1840s. The Catholic bishops, fearing that dispersion would result in assimilation and disappearance in a sea of Protestantism, encouraged the immigrants to settle in the large eastern-seaboard cities and urged them to send their children to the growing parish or parochial schools which were placed adjacent to every parish church. Many Catholic parents were not overly receptive to these urgings, preferring to have their children receive instruction with their native American peers in the common schools. Had these schools accepted the Irish children as cordially as American-born children and accorded them equal treatment, it is quite possible that there never would have developed the nationwide Catholic parochial school system which has become so familiar.

This, however, was not to be. The reception to the alien children was on the whole one of unfriendliness, if not outright hostility. The explanation may well lie more in the fact that they were immigrants, who came in large numbers and concentrated on the east coast, than that they were Catholic; German Catholic immigrants, who came in smaller numbers and dispersed themselves more widely, did not on the whole experience corresponding hostility. The Nativist movement which arose during the '40s was just that, primarily a xenophobic rather than a religious force.

If religious difference was more the symptom than the cause, the pan-Protestantism of the public school system made it a salient one. Moreover, the French and English humanist rationalism which had infected the United States had left Ireland untouched. As a result, the Irish immigrants to this country took their religion much more seriously than did the cross section of American parents and teachers.

Canon law still forbids Catholics to read or even possess copies of the Protestant version of the Bible. This is quite understandable in view of the fact that until the 20th century the King James translation was the only Protestant version in English (even today it is by far the most popular one available), and the dedicatory preface to it refers to the pope as the "man of sin." The ecumenicism spawned by the Second Vatican Council has made this provision of the canon law generally a dead letter, and it undoubtedly will be eliminated or greatly modified in the revision now in progress. But in the 19th century it was quite alive, as many thousands of Catholic public school children and their parents could attest.

It would have been no difficult task to excuse Catholic children in the public schools from participating in the Bible reading and prayer recitation exercises. Undoubtedly, in many schools this was done. In many others, however, the refusal of these alien children, encouraged and even commanded by their priests, to participate was taken as a rebellious defiance of lawful authority which called for a firm response. The result was one of the most unhappy chapters in American history.

In school after school, nonparticipating Catholic children were punished for their obdurance. On occasions they were beaten, sometimes severely. There were wholesale expulsions and other forms of disciplinary actions. In 1843 the action of the Philadelphia school board in allowing Catholic children either to refrain from participating in Bible exercises or to use their own version of the Bible (it is not clear which) led to bloody riots in which lives were lost and Catholic churches burned to the ground. In New York, the Catholic bishop felt it necessary to place large groups of armed men around each church, with instructions to defend the building by force if necessary. In Ellsworth, Maine, a Catholic priest was tarred, feathered, and otherwise cruelly treated because he had urged a parishioner to go to court when the town school committee adopted a regulation requiring all children to read the King James Bible.

Notwithstanding this incident, the case did go to court and ultimately reached the State's highest court. Its decision (*Donahoe* v. *Richards*), handed down in 1854, appears to be the first by a State supreme court to suggest a legal justification for Bible reading in the public schools. The Maine constitution, as did those of all the other States in the Union, guaranteed freedom of belief; but, the court held, "reading the Bible is no more an interference with religious belief than would reading the mythology of Greece or Rome be regarded as interfering with religious belief or the affirmance of the pagan creeds." The fact, the court said, that the school committee had designated the King James version as the text to be used was immaterial, since the selection of books was exclusively within the discretion of the committee, and its selection of a particular version did not place a sanction of "purity" on the version selected.

It requires no sophisticated mind to recognize that the Maine court was engaged in a legal fiction, for the last thing wanted by the school committee and the Protestant community of Ellsworth was that the Bible should be read "as the mythology of Greece or Rome." Yet, if reality is ignored, the Maine court was legally correct. When, some ninety years later, the United States Supreme Court passed upon the constitutionality of Bible reading in the public schools, it held that there was no legal barrier to reading the Bible as a work of literature just as the works of Homer and Vergil are read.

The Nonsectarian Bible in the Nonsectarian School

While the Maine court decision disposed of general State constitutional provisions guaranteeing religious liberty, it left unanswered the question whether Bible reading, especially when the King James version was specified, was consistent with constitutional and statutory prohibitions of sectarianism in the schools. This was taken care of by a Boston judge who, in 1859, dismissed charges against a teacher who had whipped an 11-year-old Catholic boy named Tom Wall until he agreed to read the Ten Commandments from the King James Bible. In his decision (in the case of *Commonwealth* v. *Cooke*) the judge said:

> The Bible has long been in our common schools. It was placed there by our fathers, not for the purpose of teaching sectarian religion, but a knowledge of God and His will, whose practice is religion. It was placed there as the book best adapted from which to "teach children and youth the principles of piety, justice and a sacred regard for truth, love to their country, humanity, and a universal benevolence, sobriety, moderation and temperance, and those other virtues which are the ornaments of human society, and the basis upon which a republic constitution is founded."
>
> But in doing this, no scholar is requested to believe it, none to receive it as the only true version of the laws of God. The teacher enters into no argument to prove its correctness, and gives no instructions in theology from it. To read the Bible in school for these and like purposes, or to require it to be read without sectarian explanations, is no interference with religious liberty.

Initially, it should be noted that the Boston judge's rationalization does not seem quite consistent with that of the Maine court. The latter justified Bible reading by comparing it to the reading of mythological works of ancient Greece and Rome, which are read for their literary value and hardly to "teach children and youth the principles of piety, justice, and a sacred regard for truth, love to their country, humanity, and a universal benevolence, sobriety, moderation and temperance," as suggested by the Boston judge. There is, nevertheless, a common theme in the two approaches: in both, the underlying rationale is secular (literature in the one, ethical and patriotic virtues in the other), rather than the inculcation of religious belief (expressly disclaimed in both opinions).

What this testifies to is the strength and universal acceptance of that rule of the game which is known broadly as the separation of church and state. Almost habitually every demand for religious teachings or practices in the public schools or tax funds for parochial schools, as we shall see, or other involvements of God in the works of Caesar is pref-

aced by a protestation that the demander believes in the
separation of church and state as much as the next fellow,
but that the specific demand in no way encroaches upon
that great principle. The Boston judge went even further
and in a splash of patriotic purple prose showed that it was
not McLaurin Cooke, the teacher, but Tom Wall, the pupil,
who threatened the principle of church-state separation.
Said the judge:

> That most wonderful specimen of human skill and human
> invention, the Suspension Bridge, that spans the dark, deep
> waters of Niagara, with strength to support the heaviest
> engines with cars laden with their freight, and defying the
> whirlwind and the tempest, is but the perfection of strength
> from the most feeble beginning. A tiny thread was but safely
> secured across the abyss, and final success became certain.
> Thread after thread were interchanged, until iron cables
> bound opposite shores together. May not the innocent
> pleading of a little child for its religion in school, if granted,
> be used like a silken thread, to first pass that heretofore im-
> passable gulf which lies between Church and State, and when
> once secured, may not stronger cords be passed over it, until
> cables, which human hands cannot sever, shall have bound
> Church and State together?

The Boston court disposed of the problem of sectarianism in the schools by declaring the pan-Protestant compromise to be the law of the land. The teacher could not
accompany the reading of the Bible with any "sectarian
explanations," and the Bible itself was not a sectarian book.
Sectarian/nonsectarian became the motif of the many Bible
reading cases that came to the State courts all over the nation in the century following the Maine and Boston decisions. As Tom Wall's judge noted, "The Bible has long been
in our common schools," schools in which he and most other
American judges received their elementary education. In
these schools Bible reading was as much a part of the daily
regimen as arithmetic, spelling, and geography, and was no

more sectarian than the study of any of those subjects. It is, therefore, hardly surprising that in the majority of the State cases, the courts adjudged the Bible to be nonsectarian and its reading permissible.

This resolution of the problem was acceptable to, or at least was accepted without much protest by, all but the Catholics. The descendants of the 18th century deists considered the matter to be insufficiently important to make a fuss about. The Jews and the conscientious atheists were too few and too isolated to take any effective action, although they were undoubtedly quite unhappy with it; not until the mid-20th century did they enter into the fray. It was left to the Catholics to carry the burden of protest and litigation. Until the *McCollum* case in the late 1940s, to which we will come shortly, every suit challenging Bible reading or other religious practices in the public schools was brought by Catholics.

As indicated, in most States they were unsuccessful, but in a few they prevailed. More important, even where the courts ruled against them, their persistence, courage, and undeniable conscientiousness, and, perhaps most important, their ever increasing numbers, could not but have an effect on public school teachers and administrators. The result was the gradual, *de facto* but nevertheless real, secularization of American public education, to the extent that many Protestants became alarmed that our schools, and thus our people, would become Godless. The few minutes of almost *pro forma* reading from the Bible remained; often this was accompanied by an equally *pro forma* recitation of a prayer, usually the Lord's Prayer, but except for the "Bible belt" in the South, that was about all. The pan-Protestant compromise and the courts' decisions, even those upholding Bible reading, forbade sectarian exposition, and to most teachers and administrators the only way to assure this was to forbid all exposition in the public schools, leaving this function to the Sunday or other nonpublic schools.

The Released-Time Plan

If the Sunday schools had the responsibility for providing Protestant children with a Christian education they were not, in the eyes of many Protestant leaders and spokesmen, fulfilling it. To them, however, the fault lay not in the Sunday schools or in Protestantism, but in the public schools and in a misguided assumption of what the principle of church-state separation meant. As Nicholas Murray Butler, the highly respected president of Columbia University, said in his 1934 report:

> The separation of church and state is fundamental in our political order, but so far as religious instruction is concerned, this principle has been so far departed from as to put the whole force and influence of the tax-supported school on the side of one element of the population, namely, that which is pagan and believes in no religion whatsoever.

(This is a variation of the theme in Tom Wall's case; the judge there viewed the exclusion of the Bible as violating the separation of church and state by putting the force and influence of the tax-supported school on the side of another element of the population, namely, the Catholic.)

Wherever the fault, the sad fact remained, according to Protestant leadership, that we were raising a nation of religious illiterates and only the public school system could provide salvation. Sunday school was simply not enough; religious education had again to be made a weekday matter. But, as Justice Frankfurter noted in his opinion in the *McCollum* case,

> children continued to be children; they wanted to play when school was out, particularly when other children were free to do so. Church leaders decided that if the week-day church school was to succeed, a way had to be found to give the child his religious education during what the child conceived to be his "business hours."

Fine denominational differences between Methodists and Episcopalians or Lutherans and Presbyterians no longer had the weight they once had, but as a practical matter we could not go back to the good old days when Christianity according to Protestant vision was an integral part of the common school curriculum. The impediment lay in the fact that in the interim a substantial number of Catholics and a lesser, though still considerable, number of Jews had become part of the American population, and that at least half of the Catholic and almost all of the Jewish schoolchildren had entered the public schools. It was realized by Protestant leadership that Protestantism could return to the public schools only if it was accompanied by Catholicism and Judaism, and out of this realization came the released-time program.

The program started in Gary, Indiana, in 1914, and it was a rather simple one. It provided that, with the consent of the parents and the cooperation of church authorities, children in the public schools could be released for one or more periods during the week to go to a nearby church of their own faith and there participate in religious instruction, returning to the public school at the end of the period, or if the period was the final one of the day, going home at its conclusion.

The idea spread to other communities, but quite slowly. The reason for this was, partly, general Protestant apathy at the local level, partly Catholic opposition, and partly—and perhaps most importantly—the practical difficulties in implementation. As initially conceived, the Gary plan, as it came to be known, assumed that the religious instruction would be given outside the public schools, but this often resulted in many inconveniences. If the weather conditions were unfavorable, and particularly if the church school was located at a distance from the public school, the public school authorities were reluctant to release the children. Even when weather conditions were good, the time taken by transportation impinged upon that available for regular instruction or religious instruction or both. Some school authorities tried to meet or at least minimize this problem by requiring that the released-time instruction be scheduled for the last school period of the day, but this gave rise to problems of its own. In many communities the church school authorities did not have the resources to handle the public school children if they were all released at the same time. And, if the children were not required to return to the public school at the conclusion of the religious instruction period, it often turned out that a goodly number of them somehow fell by the wayside and did not show up at the church school at all. Finally, there was the problem of getting the children home after the religious instruction; the cost of separate buses for the nonreleased children at the public school and the released children at the different church schools was often prohibitive.

The *McCollum* Case

The obvious solution to these problems was to send the teachers to the children rather than the children to the teachers, i.e., to have the religious instruction take place within the public schools rather than in church schools. This was the pattern adopted in many rural and small urban communities, including Champaign, Illinois, seat of the University of Illinois.

There, in 1940, an interfaith council, with Protestant, Catholic, and Jewish representatives, was formed for the purpose of offering religious instruction within the public schools during regular school hours. The program, as approved by the Champaign board of education, provided that the instructors of religion were to be hired and paid by or through the interfaith council, subject to the approval and supervision of the public school superintendent. At the beginning of each term the public school teachers distributed to the children cards on which parents could indicate their consent to the enrollment of their children in the religious instruction classes. Children who obtained such consent were released by the school authorities from the secular work for a period of thirty minutes each week in the elementary schools and forty-five minutes in the junior high school. Only the Protestant instruction was conducted within the regular classroom; where children were released for Catholic or Jewish instruction they left their classroom for other parts of the building. Nonparticipants were also relocated, sometimes accompanied by their regular teachers and sometimes not. At the end of the session, the children who had participated in the Catholic or Jewish instruction or who had not participated in any religious instruction returned to the regular classroom, and regular class work was resumed.

This, at least, is how it was supposed to work; how it actually worked is somewhat different. Theoretically, participation was open to all religious groups, but all had to work through the interfaith council and this requirement eliminated participation not only by Jehovah's Witnesses but by the more orthodox Lutherans as well. Theoretically, enrollment in the program by children was to be entirely voluntary, but both teacher and peer pressures operated to assure 100% enrollment in many classes. Since the Jewish classes were discontinued after a few years, Jewish children thereafter enrolled and participated, either actively or passively, in the Protestant instruction. Theoretically, adequate provision was to be made for children whose parents did not wish them to take religious instruction, but this could not always be achieved, particularly where a class contained but a single nonconformist.

This, in any event, was the experience of Terry McCollum, whose parents refused to consent to his participation in religious instruction. At first the fifth-grader was placed at a desk in the hall outside the classroom, a procedure sometimes employed as a method of punishment. Passing schoolmates teased him, believing he was being punished for being

an atheist and for not taking religious instruction. Terry went home crying as a result of the experience, and his mother protested to the school authorities, thereby bringing an end to the practice. When the music room was unoccupied, the boy was placed there, his teacher making certain that the door was kept closed. This too brought a protest from Terry's mother, and the teacher finally arrived at the happy solution of depositing the boy in the other fifth grade class while religious instruction was being given in his own.

Happy, that is, for all but Terry and his mother. She felt so strongly about the matter that she brought a lawsuit to forbid all religious instruction in the Champaign public schools. Unsuccessful in the State courts, she appealed to the United States Supreme Court, and the resulting case, *McCollum* v. *Board of Education* decided in 1948, became a landmark in the history of both American constitutional law and public education.

In the Supreme Court, counsel for the Champaign school authorities challenged Mrs. McCollum's right to be there in the first place. Her appeal to that court was based on the claim that the released-time program was a law respecting an establishment of religion and prohibiting its free exercise, but, counsel asserted, the First Amendment forbade only Congress from making such laws and the Champaign board of education was not Congress. A year earlier, the Court in the *Everson* case had held that by virtue of the Fourteenth Amendment, the First Amendment's ban on laws respecting an establishment of religion was as applicable to the States as it was to the national government, but counsel asserted that this was an erroneous decision and urged the Court to confess its error, overrule the *Everson* decision, and throw Mrs. McCollum's case out of court. This the Court refused to do; it reasserted the *Everson* holding that the States no less than Congress were forbidden to make any laws respecting an establishment of religion, and, since the *McCollum* decision, that holding has become so firmly established in constitutional law that protagonists of

State aid to religion or religious education have given up challenging it in the courts.

Next, counsel for the board of education argued that historically the Establishment Clause had been intended to forbid only preferential treatment of one faith or sect over others and not to bar nonpreferential aid to all religions. The Champaign program, he claimed, was therefore valid since it was open equally to Protestants, Catholics, and Jews. Mrs. McCollum's counsel disputed this and asserted that the interfaith counsel acted as a censor and excluded such unconventional faiths as Jehovah's Witnesses. The Court held that it did not matter one way or the other; in the *Everson* case it had ruled that the Establishment Clause barred aid not only to one religion but to all religions, and here too the Court found no reason to overrule that holding.

Counsel for the board of education argued that there was no infringement upon the Free Exercise Clause since participation in the religious instruction was entirely voluntary. Again Mrs. McCollum's counsel challenged this, and again the Court held that it did not matter who was right. Coercion or lack of it would be significant if only Free Exercise were involved, but Mrs. McCollum's claim was based on the Establishment Clause as well; and as to this, voluntariness was irrelevant since laws aiding religion, coercively or not, were forbidden by that clause.

The crux of the Court's opinion, written by Justice Black, who had also written the majority opinion in the *Everson* case, is contained in the following paragraphs:

> Pupils compelled by law to go to school for secular education are released in part from their legal duty upon the condition that they attend the religious classes. This is beyond all question a utilization of the tax-established and tax-supported public school system to aid religious groups to spread their faiths. And it falls squarely under the ban of the First Amendment (made applicable to the States by the Fourteenth) as we interpreted in *Everson* v. *Board of Education* . . . Here not only are the State's tax-supported public school buildings

used for the dissemination of religious doctrines. The State also affords sectarian groups an invaluable aid in that it helps to provide pupils for their religious classes through the use of the State's compulsory public school machinery. This is not separation of Church and State.

Six years later, in *Brown* v. *Board of Education*, the Supreme Court was to hold that the Constitution required the public schools to be color blind in the sense that they could not segregate or otherwise discriminate against pupils because of the color of their skin. Segregation according to race, the Court held, imputed inferiority to children of minority races. In the same sense, the Court in the *McCollum* case anticipated its decision in the *Brown* case; it held in effect that the public schools must be religion blind.

Whether so intended or not, when school authorities sponsor or authorize religious instruction within the school, the children are segregated according to religion and the effect is to impute inferiority to those of minority faiths. In the *McCollum* case, Protestant instruction was given in the regular classrooms, usually in the presence of the regular school teacher, the symbol of authority. Catholic and Jewish children were sent to other parts of the building for their instruction, and those, like Terry McCollum, who belonged to no faith were shunted off from place to place while instruction in the religion of the majority was being given. It is hard to escape the conclusion that in the minds of the children those who were affiliated with non-Protestant faiths or with no faith at all were segregated because they were inferior.

The Aftermath of *McCollum*

This imputation of inferiority was what had been suffered by Tom Wall and the thousands of other Catholic children in public schools where Bible reading, prayer recitation, and other religious practices took place. When the

Supreme Court accepted Mrs. McCollum's appeal, it finally provided a forum for the vindication of the claims of Catholics during the preceding century.

Surprisingly, however, the Catholic establishment— the bishops, diocesan publications, and other Catholic leaders and spokesmen—were not happy with Mrs. McCollum's case and were considerably unhappy with the Court's decision, which guaranteed the secularity of American public education. Although it did not deal directly with Bible reading or prayer recitation, its ineluctable logic, as the *Engel* and *Schempp* cases were to show fifteen years later, required a determination that these too were forbidden by the First Amendment. Yet, when the decision was announced, the Catholic reaction was far more intensely hostile than that of the Protestant leadership.

Why? No one can say for certain, but a reasonable explanation is not hard to find. The insecurity experienced by the Catholic community in 19th century America was now a matter of history. Nativism, Know-Nothingism, and the Ku Klux Klan were dead, never to rise again. Twenty years before the *McCollum* decision, a Catholic had been nominated for the highest office in the land by one of the nation's two major political parties, and twelve years after another would be elected to that office. Bible reading probably continued in most of the public schools throughout the nation, and prayers, most often the Lord's Prayer, were recited in many of them, but they no longer posed a serious threat to the faithfulness of Catholic children. With the exception of the New Jersey Gideon Bible case, which will be considered later in this chapter, Catholic parents no longer went to court to challenge the Bible in the schools, nor were they encouraged by their priests and bishops to do so.

No, religion in the public schools was no longer a threat to American Catholicism. What was a threat in the minds of Catholic leadership was the constitutional philosophy employed by the Supreme Court to invalidate it. That philosophy—the absolutist interpretation of the meaning of separation of church and state—had been expressed the previous year in the *Everson* case; but because the decision itself upheld public funding of transportation to parochial schools, the implications of the philosophy were not immediately recognized. The *McCollum* decision brought the matter into clearer focus. If separation of church and state mandated that public education be nonreligious, the conclusion would logically follow that so too must be the public funding of education no matter where the education is given. If the government may not allow public buildings to be used for religious instruction, it could hardly allow public funds to be used for that purpose. If the Establishment Clause forbade aid to all religions it forbade it to the Catholic religion and to the schools which taught it. The fault lay in the Supreme Court and in its misinterpretation of the First Amendment and its enthronement of the absolute "separation of church and state," a phrase which the Catholic bishops, in a statement issued after the *McCollum* decision, called the "shibboleth of doctrinaire secularism."

Protestant reaction to the *McCollum* decision was not so intense, nor was it uniform; indeed, the Joint Baptist Committee on Public Affairs had filed a brief as "friend of the court" in support of Mrs. McCollum's claim. Nevertheless, it was on the whole unfavorable. As Catholic leadership was beginning to look eagerly and hopefully to tax-raised funds for the support of its educational system, so too, though perhaps to a lesser degree, did Protestantism look to the public school system for support of its educational goals. Released-time programs were not spreading as fast and as far as Protestantism would have liked, and the thirty minutes set aside weekly for religious instruction in the Champaign elementary schools weren't very much; but the Sunday schools were obviously not doing their job, and released time did present a tangible hope for salvation. Because the *McCollum* decision threatened, if it did not smash, that hope and foreboded a religionless or godless or secularist America, the major voices in Protestantism were raised against the decision and, somewhat more mutedly, against the Court which announced it. (A common cry was that the Supreme Court had established secularism as the religion of America.)

Zorach v. *Clauson*: Released Time Revisited

During the four years that followed the *McCollum* decision, the Supreme Court had many attackers and few defenders. Moreover, the period was marked by the Cold War, and what later became known as McCarthyism was at its peak (or depth). It was a natural thing then to identify godliness with Americanism and communism with godlessness; he who was not patently religious risked being suspect, and he who was openly anti-religious was easily characterized as being an ally of atheistic communism, knowingly or not. Nor was it easy to distinguish between those who opposed religion and those who opposed religion in the public schools; the difference was too subtle for most Americans.

It was during this period, specifically in 1952, that the Supreme Court was again confronted with the problem of accommodating within the Constitution the relationship of the public school system and religious education. The case was *Zorach* v. *Clauson*, and it concerned the large-city variant of released time. In rural and small city areas, like Champaign, it was a frequent if not usual practice to conduct the religious instruction classes during regular school hours within the public school building. In large cities, such as New York and Los Angeles, the instruction was also conducted during regular school hours, usually in the last period of the day, but in church buildings off the school premises.

The constitutionality of both the Los Angeles and New York practices was challenged in the respective State courts, but only the latter reached the Supreme Court. The regulations of the New York City board of education sought to sanitize the program as far as possible. They restricted public school participation to releasing of children whose parents had signed consent cards and specifically forbade "comment by any principal or teacher on the attendance or non-attendance of any pupil upon religious instruction."

The purpose of this and similar regulations was to avoid the charges of pressures and preferential treatment raised in the *McCollum* lawsuit, but, as is often the case, there was a wide gap between regulations and reality. Esta Gluck, a school parent who along with Tessim Zorach brought the case, presented an affidavit which illustrated the extent to which some zealous teachers would go to further pupil participation in religious instruction. She swore that

Miss Jeffries, a second and third grade teacher at P.S. 130 in Brooklyn, was very active in soliciting student participation in released time for religious instruction. Such activities were carried on by Miss Jeffries both on and off the school premises and both during and after school hours. She visited parents for the purpose of recruiting Catholic students for released time and her activity in this respect is common neighborhood knowledge.

During the Spring 1950 semester I called to the attention of Mr. Lubell (the principal) another incident in which Miss Jeffries had participated. A student in her class became ill and vomited in the classroom. Miss Jeffries said to the sick student that she did not object to looking at the vomit as much as she objected to looking at the student's face because he did not participate in the released time program. Mr. Lubell was shocked and told me he would speak to Miss Jeffries about the incident.

Mr. Lubell told me on several occasions of the pressures to which he had been subjected by a minister in the neighborhood who had complained to the Board of Education because the school planned student field trips during the released time hour. As a result of these complaints, field trips generally have been discontinued in P.S. 130 for the period from 2 to 3 o'clock on Wednesdays. Recently, I met the minister, Rev. Harold Sweezey, in connection with some unrelated neighborhood problem and he complained to me about Mr. Lubell's lack of cooperation in the released time program. He told me that Mr. Lubell was not as cooperative as the prior principal, Miss Doughty, had been.

When the case reached the Supreme Court these and similar facts were not considered. The reason is quite technical, but the effect was that the only question before the Court was the constitutionality of the program as set forth in the State statute and the board of education regulations. As so limited, the Court in a 6 to 3 decision found the program to be constitutional.

The Court's opinion was written by Justice Douglas. The situation here, he said, was entirely different from that presented in the *McCollum* case. There, the classrooms were used for religious instruction and the force of the public school was used to promote that instruction. Here, the public schools did no more than accommodate their schedules to allow children, who so wished, to go elsewhere for religious instruction completely independent of public school operations. The situation, he said, was not different from that presented when a Catholic student asks his teacher to be excused to attend a mass on a Holy Day of Obligation or a Jewish student to attend synagogue on Yom Kippur.

Government, Justice Douglas said further, may not finance religious groups nor undertake religious instruction nor blend secular and sectarian education nor use secular institutions to force one or some religion on any person. Government, however, must be neutral in respect to religion, not hostile. We are a religious people whose institutions presuppose a Supreme Being. When the state encourages religious instruction or cooperates with religious authorities, it follows the best of our traditions. For it then respects the religious nature of our people and accommodates the public service to their spiritual needs.

The decision in the *Zorach* case was not surprising. In view of the four-year assault upon the Court for the *McCollum* decision and the nationalistic anti-communist spirit of the time, it was almost to be expected and most constitutional authorities at the time did expect it. Nor surprising, for the same reasons, was the paean of praise for governmental religiosity which the author of the opinion seemed to go out of his way to include though it was not really necessary for the decision. What was at least somewhat surprising was that the author of the opinion should be Justice Douglas. True enough, he was one of the five-man majority which in the *Everson* case had upheld financing of parochial school transportation, but the author of that opinion was Justice Black, who not only wrote the opinion in the *McCollum* case but was one of the three vigorous dissenters in the *Zorach* decision. Moreover, Douglas was the only member of the Court who consistently joined Black in dissenting from the many decisions during the McCarthy period which restricted the constitutional rights of communists and pro-communists; only a year later, he was to provoke the wrath of the nation by granting a stay of execution to the Rosenbergs who had been condemned to death for passing atomic secrets to Soviet espionage agents.

In any event, Douglas was to become the most absolute separationist on the Court. He later sought to explain, rather lamely, his statement about our being a religious people whose institutions presuppose a Supreme Being. He never did repudiate the *Zorach* decision itself—perhaps because no occasion arose in which to do so—but he did express regret for his vote in the *Everson* case, and stated that if a similar case were to come before the Court he would vote the other way. He was the only member of the Court in *McGowan* v. *Maryland* to vote against the constitutionality of Sunday closing laws, and in the *Walz* case against tax exemption for churches. He dissented too in the college-aid cases which will be discussed in the next chapter. It seems almost as if he had decided to devote the rest of his life to making atonement for his aberration in *Zorach* v. *Clauson*.

It seems difficult to reconcile *Zorach* v. *Clauson* with later decisions which interpreted the Establishment Clause as barring laws whose purpose is to advance religion, for releasing children to enroll for religious instruction and not other children would seem to serve no purpose other than to advance religion. Nevertheless, although *Zorach* v. *Clauson* has never been overruled, neither has *McCollum* v. *Board of Education.* On the basis of these two decisions, the present law is that released-time programs are constitutional so long as the religious instruction is given off the public school premises and the public school teachers and authorities are involved in it no more than to the extent of excusing willing and uncoerced children to participate in it.

A Decade of Abstention

During the five-year period from 1947 to 1952 the Court handed down three major decisions on the relations between government and religious education: the *Everson* case on transportation, and the *McCollum* and *Zorach* cases on released-time religious instruction. In the ensuing ten years, the Court deliberately refrained from passing on the question although it had at least three opportunities for doing so, all involving the Bible.

The first of these, *Doremus* v. *Board of Education*, came to the Court about the same time as *Zorach* v. *Clauson*. It was a suit by two New Jersey residents challenging Bible reading in the public schools, one (Doremus) suing as a taxpayer and the other (Klein) as parent of a pupil in a public high school. The New Jersey courts ruled in favor of the practice and the plantiffs appealed to the Supreme Court on the basis of the *McCollum* decision. The Court, however, refused to rule on their claim and threw out their appeal on the technical ground that the plaintiffs had no standing to present the appeal; Doremus was only a taxpayer, and by the time Mrs. Klein's case reached the Supreme Court, her child had graduated and no longer was a pupil in the public school system.

The Court did not have to throw out the appeal. Indeed, it seemed to have gone out of its way to do so. Counsel for the school authorities did not challenge the plaintiffs' standing to sue; he was as eager as they were for a Supreme Court decision on the merits. If Doremus was only a taxpayer, so was Arch Everson and the Supreme Court had accepted his appeal from the decision of the New Jersey courts upholding public financing of bus transportation to parochial schools. In 1968, the Court, in the case of *Flast* v. *Cohen*, was to uphold the right of taxpayers to sue for violation of the Establishment Clause, and at the same time, in the case of *Board of Education* v. *Allen*, it accepted a challenge to a law permitting use in parochial schools of publicly owned textbooks, brought not by parents, nor even by taxpayers, but by members of a local public school board. The Supreme Court had in the past accepted lawsuits by taxpayers even where the question of standing to sue had been raised, and there was no apparent reason why it could not do so in the *Doremus* case.

As speculation is the only resource available for an explanation of the Court's decision in the *Zorach* case, so is it in respect to its refusal to give a decision in the *Doremus* case. The speculated explanation is substantially the same for both. The McCarthy *zeitgeist* made it impossible for the Court to outlaw the minimal aid to religion involved in the New York City released-time program, and, notwithstanding the contrary view strongly expressed by the three dissenting justices, it could uphold that program without overruling either the *McCollum* decision or the principles announced in the *Everson* case. Bible reading was a different matter; there was no way in which its constitutionality could be upheld without repudiating all that had been said and held in the *Everson* and *McCollum* decisions. The majority of the Court was not prepared to do this any more than to give its high and unappealable sanction to Bible reading in the public schools. So it did what it had done so often in the past and would do so often in the future (the birth control cases provide one example): it invoked a technicality to avoid a decision until the times were more propitious for the decision it wished to give.

The second Bible case, *Tudor* v. *Board of Education*, reached the Supreme Court during the same McCarthy period, specifically 1954. There was an interesting aspect to the *Tudor* case. As indicated, all the pre-*McCollum* lawsuits challenging religion in the public schools had been brought by Catholics. With *McCollum*, the burden of litigation shifted to atheists (McCollum, Doremus), humanists (Schempp), Jews (Engel, Gluck), and occasionally liberal Protestants (Zorach). Catholics remained neutrally silent or hostilely articulate. The *Tudor* case was an exception, a vestige of times past. There were two plaintiffs in the case; one was a Jew, but the other was a Catholic, and the latter acted with the encouragement of his parish priest who had the approval of the diocesan bishop. What the reaction was to this on the part of higher Catholic authority or of the general Catholic establishment is not known. It is known, however, that the experience has not been repeated anywhere else in the United States.

The *Tudor* case did not deal directly with Bible reading in the public schools. It involved rather the distribution of an abbreviated version of the Bible among public school students by an organization known as the Gideons Society, an association of missionary-minded Protestant businessmen who, according to their charter, seek to win men and women for the Lord Jesus Christ through placing the Bible in hotels, hospitals, and other institutions.

For the schools, the Gideons prepared a smaller (King James) Bible, consisting only of the book of Psalms and the New Testament. Representatives of the association visited schools and, with the consent of the authorities, addressed the pupils at assembly, offering them copies of the Bible as a gift if they signed a pledge to read it. In a number of communities, Catholics, priests and laymen, as well as Jews objected to the practice, but only in Rutherford, New Jersey, a middle-class suburb of New York City, was a lawsuit brought to halt it.

The trial judge ruled against the plaintiffs, holding in line with earlier decisions that the Bible is a nonsectarian book and, in any event, acceptance by the pupils was entirely voluntary. The State's highest court, however, reversed the decision, holding that at least to the Jews the New Testament could not be deemed nonsectarian, and that because of fear of school and peer disapproval it could not be said that acceptance by the pupils was truly voluntary. The school authorities accepted the ruling and halted all further distribution within the schools. The Gideons, however, sought to appeal to the Supreme Court, but the Court, without giving any reason for its action, refused to accept the appeal.

The third case came from Pennsylvania. In the *Doremus* case the Court had dismissed the appeal from the decision upholding Bible reading on the ground that the plaintiff's child had graduated by the time the appeal reached the Court. In *Abington School District* v. *Schempp*, the plaintiff, having learned the lesson, brought his suit while his children were in the lower grades in school, so that, notwithstanding the law's delays, they were still in school when the case reached the Supreme Court in 1961. But the Court found another way to put off the confrontation.

Actually the plaintiff, Schempp, was successful in the lower court, a Federal district court. That court held that the statute authorizing Bible reading was unconstitutional because it violated both the Establishment and Free Exercise clauses of the First Amendment. After the decision was handed down but before the appeal by the State of Pennsylvania reached the Supreme Court, the State legislature amended the statute so as to provide that any child bringing a written request from his parent was to be excused from participating in the Bible reading exercise. On the basis of this amendment, the Supreme Court decided that it would not hear the appeal but would send the case back to the district court for reconsideration in the light of the amendment.

The Supreme Court did not have to do this, any more than it had to throw out the appeal in the *Doremus* case. In the *McCollum* case, it will be remembered, the Court had ruled that it is immaterial whether or not pupils are compelled to participate in religious instruction, since the Establishment Clause is violated if the State confers any benefit upon religion irrespective of compulsion. Hence, had the Court wished to do so, it could have accepted the appeal in the *Schempp* case and decided the question of constitutionality under the Establishment Clause. But the Court did not wish to do so. Instead it sent the case back and for two years put off biting the bullet on Bible reading.

Prayer in the Public Schools

Ten years after the *Zorach* decision, the Supreme Court resumed accepting appeals involving religion in public education. By 1962 the McCarthy era had passed into history and the passions ignited by the *Brown* school segregation decision had subsided. The nation appeared ready for another "anti-religion" decision, or at least so the justices may have thought. In any event, they agreed to hear an appeal from a New York court decision upholding the recitation in public schools of what most Americans undoubtedly deemed an innocuous and inoffensive short prayer.

In the pre-*McCollum* era, most of the cases involving religion in the public school concerned Bible reading, but in a few the complaints were based upon prayer recitation, usually the Lord's Prayer, either accompanying or independent of Bible reading. The courts in these cases upheld the practice on the same rationale that Bible reading was justified, namely that the Lord's Prayer was nonsectarian and in any event the purpose of the recitation was secular rather than religious. Thus, in one case a Massachusetts court found justifiable the expulsion of a pupil who refused to bow her head during the prayer recitation, because, it said, the purpose of the requirement of bowed heads was merely to insure quiet and decorum rather than to express reverence; and in a Kansas case, the court accepted a teacher's explanation that she caused the class to recite the Lord's Prayer every morning not as a religious exercise but merely to quiet the pupils and prepare them for their regular duties.

So, too, it was primarily secular motivations that impelled the New York board of regents, the State's highest educational authority, to recommend daily prayer in the schools. The board was greatly concerned about the twin evils of communism and juvenile delinquency and felt these evils could best be overcome by encouraging the prayer habit. In a "policy statement," which made up in its equal treatment of the sexes what it may have lacked in elegance, the board asserted that the American people have always been religious, that a program of religious inspiration in the schools would assure that the children would acquire

> respect for lawful authority and obedience to law [and that] each of them will be properly prepared to follow the faith of his or her father, as he or she receives the same at mother's knee or father's side and as such faith is expounded and strengthened by his or her religious leaders.

Joining God to Caesar, the regents recommended that at the commencement of each school day the pledge of allegiance to the flag be accompanied by an act of reverence to God. But being aware that New York had a religiously pluralistic population, they had to assure that the act of reverence would be truly nonsectarian. Apparently unable to find one that was suitable, they composed their own and submitted it to selected clergymen of the three major faiths, who duly approved it or at least did not object to it. The prayer was short, 22 words in all: "Almighty God, we acknowledge our dependence upon Thee, and beg Thy blessings upon us, our parents, our teachers and our country."

The regents' recommendation met a mixed response. In general, the Jews and humanists expressed strong opposition, the Protestants were divided, and the Catholics strongly favored it; a Catholic member of the board of regents, speaking before the Friendly Sons of St. Patrick, went so far as to charge that "the only criticism came from those who do not believe in God."

The regents' recommendation was adopted in perhaps ten percent of the school districts in the State, including the Long Island community of New Hyde Park. There, a number of parents, with the aid of the New York Civil Liberties Union, brought suit in a State court for an injunction, and, meeting no success there, appealed ultimately to the United States Supreme Court. Thus, in June 1962 the Court in the case of *Engel* v. *Vitale* took up where it had left off fourteen years earlier in *McCollum* v. *Board of Education*.

The opinion in the *Engel* case was written by Justice Black, the author of the *McCollum* opinion. Neither that decision nor any other was cited in his opinion, perhaps because he felt the underlying constitutional principles were too well established to require resource to cited precedents. In any event, though not mentioned by name, the principles announced and applied in the *McCollum* case were the ones upon which the opinion in the *Engel* case were based.

Thus, as in the *McCollum* case, the challenged practices were defended in the State courts and upheld there on the grounds that no particular religion was favored in that the regents' prayer was denominationally neutral, and that observance on the part of students was entirely voluntary (nonparticipating students were not even required to be present in the classroom or assembly hall while the prayer was recited). Neither of these facts, said Justice Black, was constitutionally significant. Under the Establishment Clause, aid to all religions was as impermissible as aid to one or more religions, and under that clause, unlike the Free Exercise Clause, it was of no matter that the aid was noncoercive. The only issue before the Court, he said, was whether the invocation of God's blessings as prescribed in the regents' prayer was a religious activity. As to this there could be no question; it was a solemn avowal of divine faith and supplication for the blessings of the Almighty. Caesar may not involve himself in God's affairs; "the constitutional prohibition against laws respecting an establishment of religion must at least mean that in this country it is no part of the business of government to compose official prayers for any group of the American people to recite as part of a religious program carried on by the government."

In the *McCollum* case, Justice Black, probably in anticipation of adverse reaction to the decision on the part of religious groups, concluded his opinion with a protestation that forbidding sectarian instruction in the public schools did not manifest hostility to religion. The effort, as we have seen, was in vain, but in the *Engel* opinion he tried it again. Nothing, he said, could be more wrong than the argument that to apply the Constitution in such a way as to prohibit laws respecting an establishment of religious services in public schools is to indicate a hostility to religion or to prayer. Men who had faith in the power of prayer were the leaders of the fight for the adoption of our Constitution and the Bill of Rights. (It may be noted that the critics of the *Engel* decision hardly denied this. On the contrary, they asserted that because these leaders had faith in the power of prayer they did not forbid it in the Constitution or the Bill of Rights; it was not they but the members of the 1962 Court who were responsible for the exclusion.)

> It is [concluded Justice Black] neither sacrilegious nor antireligious to say that each separate government in this country should stay out of the business of writing or sanctioning official prayers and leave that purely religious function to the people themselves and to those the people choose to look to for religious guidance.

Prayer After *Engel*

Alas, Justice Black was no more successful in seeking to ward off adverse reaction in the *Engel* case than he had been in the *McCollum* case. In fact, the response to the latter was mild compared to that experienced by the *Engel* decision. Southern Senators and Congressmen, still embittered by the decisions outlawing racial segregation in the public schools, were particularly emphatic in their reaction. Representative George W. Andrews of Alabama found a connection; "They put the Negroes in the schools," he said, "and now they've driven God out."

Senator Robert C. Byrd of West Virginia found a conspiracy; although he did not name the co-conspirator (the principal, was, of course, the "they" of Representative Andrews' statement), it did not require the resurrection of Senator Joe McCarthy to find out whom he had in mind. "Can it be," Senator Byrd asked, "that we, too, are ready to embrace the foul concept of atheism? . . . Somebody is tampering with America's soul. I leave it to you who that somebody is." Representative L. Mendel Rivers of South Carolina declared that the "Court has now officially stated its disbelief in God Almighty." And North Carolina Senator Sam Ervin, he of later Watergate fame, asserted that the "Supreme Court has made God unconstitutional." (Senator Ervin later changed his mind and came around to the view that the Court's decision was a wise one.)

Catholic reaction was of course quite forceful.

> I am shocked, and frightened, [Cardinal Spellman of New York stated] that the Supreme Court has declared unconstitutional a simple and voluntary declaration of belief in God by public school children. The decision strikes at the very heart of the Godly tradition in which America's children have for so long been raised.

The Jesuit weekly *America*, on the other hand, appeared to exonerate the Supreme Court for at least willful responsibility for the decision. Responsibility, it said, belongs to

that well-publicized Jewish spokesman, Leo Pfeffer, and such
organizations as the American Jewish Congress, . . . the
American Civil Liberties Union, the Ethical Culture Society,
the Humanist associations, some Unitarians, many atheists
and certain other groups with doctrinaire views on the
meaning and application of the principle of separation of
Church and State.

Protestant voices, lay and cleric, joined the chorus.
Former President Herbert Hoover called the decision "a
disintegration of one of the most sacred of American heri-
tages." The Reverend Dr. Billy Graham, the nation's leading evangelist, asserted: "This is another step towards the
secularization of the United States. . . . The framers of our
Constitution meant we were to have freedom of religion, not
freedom from religion."

Others thought it better to light a candle than curse the
darkness. They found hope in Justice Black's statement in
the opinion that under the Establishment Clause "it is no
part of the business of government to compose official
prayers." Could it not be, they asked, that the fatal flaw
in the *Engel* case was the fact that the prayer in use had been
an official prayer composed by a governmental agency? If
so, use of non-official, non-government–composed prayer,
particularly one of ancient heritage such as the Lord's
Prayer, would not be vulnerable to constitutional challenge.

To most constitutional lawyers, even those unsympathetic to the *Engel* decision, this seemed to be a rather
unrealistic hope. After all, the regents formulated their
prayer because they recognized that Protestants and Catholics could not agree on a single formulation of the Lord's
Prayer and that to the Jews no formulation would be acceptable. If a nondenominational prayer—the regents'
prayer, it will be remembered, was approved by clergymen
of all three faiths—could not pass muster, it did not seem
likely that the Court would accept one whose matrix was
Christianity.

In any event, the hope was short lived. A year after the

Engel decision, the Supreme Court in the *Schempp* case ruled that school-sponsored recitation of the Lord's Prayer was no more constitutional than recitation of governmentally formulated prayer; none of the justices could find any constitutional difference between a prayer prescribed by God and one formulated by Caesar.

Nor did prayer which was neither church-formulated nor government-formulated fare any better. In *DeKalb School District* v. *DeSpain*, a Federal court in 1967 frowned upon what was known as the "cookie prayer," so called because it was recited by the kindergarten children before their morning snack. The work of an anonymous poet of unknown religious affiliation, its simple words were:

> We thank you for the flowers so sweet;
> We thank you for the food we eat;
> We thank you for the birds that sing;
> We thank you, God, for everything.

The kindergarten teacher in Elwood Public School in DeKalb County, Illinois, was no lawyer, but she must have had some inkling of the *Engel* and *Schempp* decisions, for she sought to secularize the prayer and thus make it constitutionally permissible by making it godless. The words of the prayer which she led her pupils in reciting were:

> We thank you for the flowers so sweet;
> We thank you for the food we eat;
> We thank you for the birds that sing;
> We thank you for everything.

This revision obviously sacrificed the rhythm of the original and must have left at least some of the children puzzled as to who was the "you" they addressed. But the sacrifice proved futile; the court issued an injunction against the practice and the Supreme Court refused to upset the decision.

Another approach assumed that the fatal flaw in the *Engel* and *Schempp* cases lay in the school or teacher sponsorship of the prayer programs. If the initiative for the prayer recitation came from the children themselves then, it was felt, the program would be permissible or even required. Thus, in *Stein* v. *Olshinsky*, a group of parents in a New York city school brought a suit in the Federal court in 1965 to enjoin school officials from preventing their children from engaging in self-initiated prayer recitation during school hours. The court was not persuaded; it dismissed their complaint and the Supreme Court refused to review the case.

Stein v. *Olshinsky* held only that parents could not compel schools to permit pupil-initiated prayers; it did not hold that the school authorities may not on their own sanction them. So in 1971 the school committee in Leyden, Massachusetts, adopted a resolution permitting student-initiated religious exercises, in which those students and teachers who wished could participate. The State commissioner of education, believing this to be a violation of the *Engel* decision brought suit against the local school committee to halt the program; and, in *State Commissioner of Education* v. *School Committee*, the State's highest court agreed with him and declared it unconstitutional. The school committee sought to appeal to the Supreme Court, but again the Court rejected the appeal.

Another tack was tried in Netcong, New Jersey. The local school board instituted a program "for the free exercise of religion," which provided for a period prior to the formal opening of classes, during which students who wished to join in the exercise would meditate after listening to the chaplain's opening prayer or "remarks" in the United States Senate or House, read from the Congressional Record. The State board of education ordered the school board to terminate the program and, upon its refusal, went into the State courts and obtained an injunction. The school board appealed to the Supreme Court which, in *Board of Education of Netcong* v. *State Board of Education*, rejected the appeal.

In a last-ditch effort to maintain some vestige of prayer

in the public schools, a number of bills providing for silent prayer or meditation have been introduced in State legislatures, and occasionally enacted. Typical was the Massachusetts law enacted in 1973 over the governor's veto and in disregard of the opinion of unconstitutionality by the State attorney-general. It reads:

> At the commencement of the first class of each day in all grades in all public schools the teacher in charge of the room in which each such class is held shall announce that a period of silence not to exceed one minute in duration shall be observed for meditation and prayer, and during any such period silence shall be maintained and no activities engaged in.

The legislators no doubt offered the children the option of meditation, presumably on some ennobling though not necessarily religious thought, in an effort to assure the constitutionality of the program which might be suspect if limited to prayer. (A New York measure, adopted two years earlier with the governor's approval, expressly provided that the "silent prayer or meditation authorized by . . . the act is not intended to be, and shall not be conducted as a religious service, but shall be considered as an opportunity for silent prayer or meditation on a religious theme by those who are so disposed, or a moment of silent reflection on the anticipated activities of the day.") Whether they have succeeded is at this time not known, since there has not yet been any court challenge to the law or its implementation. But even if both should survive such a challenge, it is improbable that programs of silent meditation and prayer will satisfy those deeply concerned about the godlessness of American public education. The Supreme Court's refusal in the *Schempp* case to retreat from or in any way modify its position in the *Engel* decision made it clear to most proponents of prayer (and Bible reading) in the public school that no remedy existed short of an amendment to the Constitution authorizing what the Supreme Court forbade.

Exodus of the Bible

The Schempps, it will be remembered, had succeeded in Federal court in Pennsylvania in their suit to declare unconstitutional Bible reading and recitation of the Lord's Prayer in the public schools of Abington Township, a Philadelphia suburb. The Supreme Court, however, sent the case back for reconsideration in the light of a newly enacted amendment to the Bible-reading statute which expressly provided that nonconsenting pupils should be excused from participating in the program. To the surprise of no one, the lower court found the amendment irrelevant in view of the express holding in the *McCollum* case that noncoercive aid to religion was no less unconstitutional under the Establishment Clause than coercive aid. Accordingly, the court reaffirmed its original decision, and again the school board appealed to the Supreme Court.

When the Unitarian Schempps reached the Supreme Court they found themselves joined by the nation's most prominent crusader for atheism, Madalyn Murray (later O'Hair). She too had brought suit, in the Maryland courts, challenging Bible reading and Lord's Prayer recitation in the public schools and had appealed to the Supreme Court when the State court dismissed her action.

If the fury which followed the *Engel* decision had any effect upon the Supreme Court it was not apparent, except perhaps in the fact that this time, in the single opinion covering both 1963 cases (*Abington School District* v. *Schempp* and *Murray* v. *Curlett*), the Court spoke through Justice Clark rather than Black, the author of the *Engel* opinion. In the *Schempp* case, Justice Clark noted, opening exercises were broadcast into each room in the school building through an intercom system and were conducted, under the supervision of a teacher, by students attending the school's radio and television workshop. Selected students from this course gathered each morning in the school's workshop studio for the exercises, which included broadcast readings by one of the students of ten verses of the Holy Bible. This was followed by the recitation of the Lord's Prayer, likewise over the intercom system, but also by the students in the various classrooms, who were asked to stand and join in repeating the prayer. The exercises were closed with the flag salute and timely announcements of interest to the students. The student chose the verse he read and could do so from the school-owned King James version or his own Douay (Catholic) or Jewish Publication Society translation.

Schempp testified at the trial that he had considered having his children excused from attendance at the exercises but decided against it for several reasons, including his belief that their relations with their teachers and classmates would be adversely affected. Dr. Solomon Grayzel, editor of the Jewish Publication Society, testified as an expert witness that there were marked differences between the Jewish Holy Scriptures and the Christian Holy Bible; that portions of the New Testament were offensive to the Jewish tradition; that such material could be explained to Jewish children in such a way as to do no harm to them, but if read without explanation they could be psychologically harmful and could cause a divisive force within the social milieu of the school. (Similar testimony had been presented in the Gideons Bible case, discussed earlier in this chapter.)

On the other hand, Dr. Luther A. Weigle, formerly dean of Yale Divinity College, testified as a witness on behalf of the school board that the Bible was nonsectarian, although by this he meant nonsectarian within the Christian faiths.

No trial was held in Mrs. Murray's suit and hence no testimony had been presented, but the Supreme Court reached the same conclusion in both: Bible reading and recitation of the Lord's Prayer as part of public school exercises violated the Establishment Clause of the First Amendment. As in the *Engel* case, the only dissenter was Justice Stewart.

In neither case did counsel for the school boards ask the Court to overrule its rulings in the *Everson* and *McCollum* cases that the Establishment Clause applied to the States as well as to the Federal government and that it barred not only preferential aid to one religion but also aid to all religions. However, the Court went out of its way to reaffirm both holdings and to suggest that further questioning of their history, logic, and efficacy were "of value only as academic exercises."

The test under the Establishment Clause, the Court said, may be stated as follows: what are the purposes and the primary effect of the enactment? If either is the advancement or inhibition of religion then the enactment exceeds the scope of legislative power as circumscribed by the Constitution; to withstand the strictures of the Establishment Clause there must be a secular legislative purpose and a primary effect that neither advances nor inhibits religion.

It was argued that the purpose of the morning programs was not religious but secular, in that they sought to promote moral values, contradict the materialistic trends of our times, perpetuate our institutions, and teach literature. But, Justice Clark said,

> [even if the] purpose is not strictly religious, it is sought to be accomplished through readings, without comment, from the Bible. Surely the place of the Bible as an instrument of religion cannot be gainsaid, and the State's recognition of the pervading religious character of the ceremony is evident from the rule's specific permission of the alternative use of the Catholic Douay version as well as the recent amendment permitting nonattendance at the exercises. None of these factors is consistent with the contention that the Bible is here used either as an instrument for non-religious moral inspiration or as a reference for the teaching of secular subjects.

The banning of religious exercises did not establish a "religion of secularism," nor did it manifest a hostility to religion. Moreover, it might well be said that one's education is not complete without a study of comparative religion or the history of religion and its relationship to the advancement of civilization. It certainly may be said that the Bible is worthy of study for its literary and historic qualities. Nothing in the Court's decision, Justice Clark concluded, should be interpreted to mean that such study of the Bible or of religion, when presented objectively as part of a secular program of education, is not permissible in the public schools. What were banned by the decision were only "religious exercises, required by the States in violation of the command of the First Amendment that the Government maintain strict neutrality, neither aiding nor opposing religion."

The Bible After *Schempp*

The pattern of the response to the *Schempp* decision was the same as that which met the *Engel* decision: the Catholics deplored it, the Jews and humanists hailed it, and the Protestants were split. There were in 1963 only five American cardinals, and all of them were in Rome to participate in the election of a successor to Pope John XXIII. Three responded when asked by reporters to comment on the decision, and they spoke exactly as they would have had the decision been made a decade earlier when McCarthyism reigned supreme. Cardinal McIntyre of Los Angeles stated that the decision could "only mean that our American heritage of philosophy, of religion and of freedom are being abandoned in imitation of Soviet philosophy, of Soviet materialism and of Soviet-regimented liberty." Cardinal Cushing of Boston declared that "the Communists are enjoying this day," and that he deemed it to be "a great tragedy that the greatest book that was ever published cannot be read in the public school system." (He had not apparently read the decision, for it outlawed only *devotional* reading of the Bible.) Cardinal Spellman of New York did not expressly allude to communism but deplored the decision as a victory for "secularism," which in his mind and those of many Catholics was a synonym for communism, and a setback for the national welfare. "No one," he added, "who believes in God can approve such a decision."

Among the Protestant voices, not unexpectedly, was that of the Reverend Dr. Billy Graham who declared himself shocked by the decision, which he called a penalty for the "eighty percent [of Americans who] want Bible reading and prayer in the school." (Dr. Graham was basically correct; every poll of national opinion, both before and after the *Engel-Schempp* decisions, indicated that the great majority of Americans favor, or at least do not oppose, Bible reading or prayer recitation in the public schools.) Episcopal Bishop James A. Pike of California claimed that the decision imposed "secularism by default" on the public school system. Bishop Fred Pierce Corson, president of the World Methodist Council, expressed the belief that the ruling "penalized religious people who are very definitely in the majority in the United States." And Dr. Robert A. Cooke, president of the fundamentalist National Association of Evangelicals, called the decision a "sad departure from the nation's heritage under God [which] opens the door for the full establishment of secularism as a negative form of religion."

These responses were not surprising; what was surprising was that the Catholic reaction was far from unanimous and that the Protestant critics, though influential, represented a minority in Protestant leadership. Among the Catholics, the other two American cardinals, Albert Meyer of Chicago and Joseph Ritter of St. Louis, refused to comment on the decision, while other Catholic spokesmen, though critical of it, spoke perhaps more in resignation than in anger. Indeed, even before the decision was handed down, *America* editorialized forcefully against any effort to amend the Constitution to overrule it should it be adverse.

Among the Protestants, approval of the decision by the Baptist Joint Committee on Public Affairs was expected, in view of its position in the *McCollum* case and generally strong separationist views. More significant was the adoption in May 1963, a month before the *Schempp* decision, of a statement by the General Assembly of the United Presbyterian Church which stated that:

> Religious observances [should] never be held in a public
> school or introduced into the program of the public school.
> Bible reading (except in connection with courses in literature,
> history or related subjects) and public prayers tend toward
> indoctrination or meaningless ritual and should be omitted
> for both reasons.

(This position was later to contribute substantially to tensions and schisms within the United Presbyterian Church.)

Most significant, if not quite as forthright, was the policy statement, "The Churches and the Public Schools," adopted by the General Board of the National Council of Churches of Christ in the United States, the recognized organ of pan-Protestantism, ten days before the decision in the *Schempp* case was handed down. On the use of the Bible in the public schools, the statement had the following to say:

> The full treatment of some regular school subjects requires
> the use of the Bible as a source book. In such studies—
> including those related to character development—the use of
> the Bible has a valid educational purpose. But neither true
> religion nor good education is dependent upon the devo-
> tional use of the Bible in the public school.

When it is remembered that for a century and a half Protestantism had strongly defended devotional Bible reading in the schools, this almost complete turnabout on its part seems quite remarkable, almost as remarkable as the turnabout in the opposite direction by American Catholicism.

There are a number of possible reasons for the substantial difference in the response to the *Schempp* decision from that to the *Engel* decision a year earlier. Many Northern Christians, Protestant and Catholic, and some

Southern as well, though unhappy with the *Engel* decision, undoubtedly felt uncomfortable with the company they had from the segregationist ranks, and suspected that the Southern attack on the Supreme Court was motivated more by its pro-integration than by its anti-prayer stance. Their discomfort must have been aggravated by the fact that the Reverend Dr. Martin Luther King, Jr., who was fast becoming a folk hero and certainly was no anti-religious secularist, had endorsed the *Engel* decision and defended the Court that issued it. There is significance in the fact that the first major effort in Congress toward amending the Constitution to abrogate the *Engel* decision was made by Senator James Eastland of Mississippi and that it was quickly abandoned by him because he could not enlist Catholic cooperation; Episcopal Bishop Pike testified in favor of an amendment at a hearing of the Senate Judiciary Committee, headed by Eastland, but no Catholic ecclesiastical figure of comparative stature was willing to appear.

Among liberal Catholics there must in addition have been considerable discomfort with the McCarthyist tone of much of the attack by Catholic spokesmen upon the *Engel* decision and the Supreme Court. Moreover, the short but dramatic reign of John XXIII and the Second Vatican Council which he convoked gave promise of a new era of liberalism, tolerance, and ecumenicism in which there would be little room for bitter interreligious disputes regarding religion in the public schools.

Whatever the reasons, there was no significant call for defiance of the *Schempp* decision. On the whole there was national compliance with the decision; in the great majority of cases the schools which had the practice of reading the Bible as part of an opening school day program simply discontinued it. There were exceptions: in Florida it was necessary to bring the case of *Chamberlin* v. *Dade County Board of Public Instruction* to the United States Supreme Court three times, in 1963, '64, and '65, before the highest court of the State finally yielded and ordered Bible reading in the public schools terminated. Elsewhere, particularly in the Southern "Bible belt," the practice continued and to some extent continues on a *de facto* basis (i.e., without official sanction) in many rural and small town areas. When the matter is brought to the attention of the State's educational authorities or to a court, the practice is ordered stopped and the order is complied with, however, reluctantly. By and large, it is fair to say that Bible reading and prayer recitation have made their exodus from the American public educational system, subject to reentry should the Constitution be amended to abrogate or modify the *Engel-Schempp* decisions.

Constitutional Amendments

As noted, the first serious effort to overrule the prayer and Bible decisions by constitutional amendment was made by Senator Eastland. He was by no means alone; within a short time after the *Schempp* decision there had been introduced into Congress about 150 separate measures by 111 Congressmen to amend the Constitution so as to permit prayer recitation, Bible reading, or both in the public schools. Many of the measures were introduced for hometown public relations purposes and without expectation or even strong desire that they progress any further than introduction. However, one Congressman, Frank Becker of suburban New York, took the matter seriously and embarked on a one-man crusade to make the effort succeed. His first step was to prevail upon the Congressmen who had introduced separate measures to join on a single bill. His conscientiousness and diligence were rewarded, and in September 1963, less than three months after the *Schempp* decision, H.J. Res. 693, 88th Congress, was introduced. It read:

> Section 1. Nothing in this Constitution shall be deemed to prohibit the offering, reading from or listening to prayers or Biblical Scriptures, if participation therein is on a voluntary basis, in any governmental or public school, institution, or place.

Section 2. Nothing in this Constitution shall be deemed to prohibit making a reference to belief in, reliance upon, or invoking the aid of God or a Supreme Being, in any governmental or public document, coinage, currency, or obligation of the United States.

Section 3. Nothing in this Article shall constitute an establishment of religion.

The bill was referred to the House Judiciary Committee where it received an unfriendly reception from the chairman, Emanuel Celler of Brooklyn, New York. Celler had every intention of burying the bill, but he did not count on Becker's persistence. The latter began rounding up signatures to a petition to discharge the bill so that it could be voted on by the House. Ironically, Becker previously had always refused to sign discharge petitions, including those for civil rights measures aimed at achieving equality for Negroes and other racial minorities. The reason for the difference, he explained, was that all other discharge petitions "dealt with material things and material benefits. This one deals only with spiritual. The urgency of this matter leaves no alternative if we are to prevent the advocates of a godless society to accomplish in the United States that which Communists have accomplished in Soviet Russia."

When Becker succeeded in obtaining some 160 of the needed 218 signatures for his discharge petition, Celler felt it expedient to open public hearings on the Becker and similar proposals; otherwise the Becker proposal would have been taken away from his committee and brought to the floor of the House for a vote when 58 more signatures would be obtained. The hearings, undoubtedly to the surprise and disappointment of Becker, but to the relief of many other Congressmen, turned the tide. Becker learned what Eastland discovered earlier: establishment religion was not interested. Jewish spokesmen, as was to be expected, were practically unanimously opposed. Unexpected, however, was the strong opposition from leading Protestants and the unsympathetic neutrality of American Catholicism. Coupled with this was a statement, entitled "Our Most Precious Heritage," signed and submitted by 223 of the nation's leading constitutional lawyers and professors of constitutional law, expressing opposition to any change in the First Amendment. The result was that the Judiciary Committee took no action on the Becker or other proposals; Becker himself shortly thereafter retired from Congress, and there the matter rested.

But not for long. Early in 1966, Senator Everett Dirksen of Illinois sought to launch a Second Crusade to recover the Holy Grail from the unchristian Supreme Court. Characterizing prayer on one occasion as being "the roadmap to God," and on another as "a pipeline to God," he introduced a proposed amendment to the Constitution which read:

> Nothing contained in this Constitution shall prohibit the authority administering any school, school system, educational institution or other public building supported in whole or in part through the expenditure of public funds from providing for or permitting the voluntary participation by students or others in prayer. Nothing contained in this article shall authorize any such authority to prescribe the form or content of any prayer.

Hearings were held on this proposal and the witnesses and statements for and against it were pretty much the same as on the Becker proposal. The Senate Judiciary Committee, like its counterpart in the House, was decidedly unenthusiastic; but unlike Becker, Dirksen refused to accept as final its unwillingness to report the measure to the floor. By parliamentary strategy he was able to bring it without committee sponsorship to the floor of the Senate for a vote, which took place in September 1966. When the roll-call vote was completed it showed that 49 had voted "yea," 37 "nay" (among them Senator Ervin), and 14 had not voted. The proposal was defeated since a two-thirds affirmative vote was required, but it is a good guess that had a simple majority been all that was necessary, that too would have been unattainable; because there was no chance that the necessary two-thirds would be obtained, a number of the Senators who had no heart for the proposal could afford the luxury of voting in its favor.

Undaunted, Senator Dirksen tried again. In January 1967 he introduced a shorter amendment which read:

> Nothing contained in this Constitution shall abridge the right of persons lawfully assembled, in any public building which is supported in whole or in part through the expenditure of public funds, to participate in non-denominational prayer.

The word "lawfully" was obviously intended to exclude prayer-ins and kneel-ins by peaceniks, civil rights activists, and other assorted anti-establishment protesters. The "non-denominational" limitation was placed in the proposal to meet the criticism that the religious groups whose members were in the majority of a particular school board would otherwise be tempted to exclude other faiths from equal participation in prayer; but the change raised problems of its own, and did not appear to have won over any opponents. Some asked who would decide what is "non-denominational," and what criteria would be used to make the decision; others argued that there could be no such thing as "non-denominational" prayer, and that what was non-denominational to some (e.g., the King James Bible) might be deeply sectarian to others (e.g., Tom Wall and the plaintiffs in the Gideons Bible case). In any case, partly for that reason and partly because of the Senator's declining health and his death in 1969, Dirksen's second effort never got off the ground. Shortly after Dirksen's death, his son-in-law, Howard Baker of Tennessee, another little-known Senator whose name would become a household word by reason of Watergate, announced that he would take up the banner and continue the battle, but quickly forgot all about it.

The next effort, which might be called the Housewives'

Crusade, arose from a most unlikely source, but came closer to success than any of its predecessors, including the Children's Crusade of the Middle Ages. Mrs. Ben Rushlin, a housewife and mother in Cuyahoga Falls, Ohio, was asked one day by her 14-year-old son, Benny, "Why do we park God outside of school?" When she asked him what he meant thereby, he replied that "they have prayers to open sessions of Congress and the United States Supreme Court, but not in school."

So affected was Mrs. Rushlin by this that she determined to do something about it. Representative Chalmers Wylie of Ohio was one of the several Congressmen who introduced Senator Dirksen's proposal in the House but, like his colleagues, did nothing further about it. Mrs. Rushlin prevailed upon him to initiate a discharge petition to remove the measure from Celler's hostile Judiciary Committee. Organizing a cadre of some thirty other housewives she descended with them on Washington, and without fanfare or publicity lobbied for weeks to obtain the requisite 218 signatures. This last intensive drive climaxed her own three-year travels across the country speaking to groups of women and parents' groups urging them to pressure their Congressmen to support the amendment.

Success ultimately crowned her efforts; the 218 signatures were obtained, and on November 8, 1971, the measure reached the floor of the House for a roll-call vote. The session opened with the usual prayer before a practically empty chamber; this time, 20 of the 431 members were present when the House chaplain intoned: "Lord, teach us to pray . . ." When the vote was taken, however, the number present exceeded 400.

By this time, however, Wylie and his co-sponsors had become aware that they lacked the necessary two-third vote for adoption. Recognizing belatedly, as Dirksen to his sorrow had earlier discovered, that the word "non-denominational" was a trap, they amended the proposal to eliminate it and substitute the word "voluntary." Afraid that even this would not be enough, as a last desperate measure they added the words "or meditation," so that the proposed amendment now read:

> Nothing contained in this Constitution shall abridge the right of persons lawfully assembled, in any public building which is supported in whole or in part through the expenditure of public funds, to participate in voluntary prayer or meditation.

Alas, this too was of no avail. Again victory eluded the grasp of the host of the Lord. When the votes were counted, the amendment fell 28 short of the necessary two-thirds; 240 Representatives had voted yea and 162 nay.

Two years later, another effort was made to revive the crusade. Yielding to what can only be described as quite mild pressure, Birch Bayh of Indiana, chairman of the Senate Judiciary subcommittee on constitutional amendments, opened hearings on prayer amendments. At the first session, limited to Congressmen and held on July 30, 1973, testimony was given by six Senators and one Representative who had introduced resolutions for a constitutional amendment. Of the former, Howard Baker and Herman E. Talmadge of Georgia were at that time heavily involved in the Watergate hearings and were too busy, even if they had had the inclination, to participate in another prayer crusade. The Representative, Chalmers Wylie, assured the committee that

> the numerous ad hoc citizen groups around the nation supporting this proposal are again organizing and generating vocal support. The American people, the average law-abiding, constructive citizen, supports a prayer amendment and will continue petitioning their representatives until an effective remedy to the problem is found.

Perhaps so; as indicated earlier, public opinion polls indicate that a substantial majority of Americans favor or at least do not oppose Bible reading or prayer recitation in the public schools. But at the present writing neither the people nor their representatives in Congress are manifesting any strong determination to translate their will into the law of the land by way of an amendment to the United States Constitution.

One interesting postscript should be added. It will be remembered that for the century or more preceding the *McCollum* case, American Catholicism opposed Bible and prayer in the public schools. From *McCollum* to *Schempp*, its position was the opposite; it was the most articulate antagonist of the *McCollum* and *Engel* decisions and strove for the retention of Bible and prayer in the schools. After *Schempp* it turned around again; while it did not affirmatively defend that decision neither did it, after the immediate short-lived denunciations by three of the five American cardinals then in Rome, attack it. On the contrary, to the extent that it did express itself, it manifested opposition to any constitutional amendment to overrule it. The latest, but it may be presumed not the last, chapter showed another turnaround. In September 1973, the Administrative Board of the United States Catholic Conference proposed the following amendment to the Constitution:

> Section 1. Nothing in this constitution shall be construed to (i) forbid prayer in public places or in institutions of the several states or to the United States, including schools; (ii) forbid religious instruction in public places or in institutions of the several states or of the United States, including schools, if such instruction is provided under private auspices, whether or not religious.

> Section 2. The right of the people to participate or not to participate in prayer or religious instruction shall never be infringed by the several states or the United States.

As can be seen, this proposal would overrule not only the *Engel-Schempp* decisions but *McCollum* as well, and would bring religious instruction back into the public schools, so long as it was provided by church rather than by public school teachers. How serious the conference is about this measure is uncertain at the present writing. Now its attention is concentrated on putting through a constitutional amendment to overrule the Supreme Court's pro-abortion decisions. After that is taken care of, it will probably devote its efforts to an amendment to overrule the anti–parochial-school-aid rulings. Only when these campaigns are successfully completed is it likely to push its amendment to bring religion back into the public schools—that is, if it has not by that time again changed its position.

Religious Censorship of Curriculum Content

This chapter has been devoted to an account of efforts to incorporate religious teachings and practices into public school curricula and programs. There is, however, also a converse to this, namely, religiously motivated efforts to keep certain secular teachings and practices out of the schools. To Jehovah's Witnesses, flag saluting was religiously forbidden, but they sought only to have their children excused from participation, not to bar it from the schools. Christian Scientists, who felt similarly about the germ theory of disease and other aspects of hygiene instruction, also limited their efforts to obtaining for their children excused nonparticipation.

Others went further. There have been instances, some of which have reached the courts, involving objections to including social dancing in public school programs. More widespread has been opposition, primarily but by no means exclusively from Catholic sources, to sex education. The subject, however, which received the greatest national attention, and the only one which ultimately reached the Supreme Court, was evolution and the origin of man.

The decade following World War I, like the decade of the 1950s, was one in which there were widespread governmental intrusions on academic freedom. As we shall see in the next chapter, there were in the West and Midwest a number of efforts to outlaw private schools entirely or to forbid the teaching of foreign languages in private or public schools. During the same period, State legislatures turned to religious orthodoxy, particularly in the South and Southwest. In the period between 1921 and 1929, anti-evolution bills were introduced in twenty State legislatures, although in only three of them, Tennessee, Arkansas, and Mississippi, were the bills enacted.

The early Sunday laws, as will be seen in Chapter Seven of this book, made no effort to disguise their religious purpose, since the legislatures saw no constitutional or other objection to the use of governmental compulsory legal machinery to support the doctrines and dogmas of established religion. So, too, the earliest of the anti-evolution statutes, the Tennessee law of 1925, was refreshingly ingenuous. Entitled, "An Act prohibiting the teaching of the Evolution Theory in all the Universities, Normals, and all other Public schools of Tennessee, which are supported in whole or in part by the public school funds of the State, and to provide penalties for the violations thereof," the statute read:

> It shall be unlawful for any teacher in any of the Universities, Normals, and all other Public schools of the State which are supported in whole or in part by the public funds of the State, to teach any theory that denies the story of Divine Creation of man as taught in the Bible, and to teach instead that man has descended from a lower order of animals.

The prosecution of a young schoolteacher named John Scopes and the ensuing trial in which the chief opposing counsel were William Jennings Bryan and Clarence Darrow brought Tennessee's "monkey law" into the eyes of the world, and later into the pages of history, literature, and the arts. Scopes was convicted and the State's highest court upheld the constitutionality of the law, but reversed the conviction on the ground that the jury and not the judge should have assessed the $100 fine. Since Scopes was no longer in the State's employ, the other part of the statutory penalty, namely that a teacher who was convicted for violating the law "shall vacate the position thus held," was now academic. The court therefore saw "nothing to be gained by prolonging this bizarre case," and directed that it be dropped in the interests of "the peace and dignity of the State."

There the matter rested for two score years. Then another young biology teacher, named Susan Epperson, joined by H. H. Blanchard, parent of two boys in the Central High School of Little Rock, Arkansas (the same which had a decade earlier been the object of unwanted national attention when Governor Orville Faubus ordered troopers to bar entrance to black students), decided to test the similar "monkey law" of Arkansas, and pursued their case right up to the United States Supreme Court. Unlike John Scopes, Miss Epperson had not been prosecuted for violating the law nor was anyone threatening to do so, but she took the initiative in suing for an injunction against enforcement of the law should anyone get the idea of doing it.

The ensuing case of *Epperson* v. *Arkansas*, which the Supreme Court decided in 1968, presents almost a casebook illustration of the point, made in part earlier in this chapter, that there is no way to make the Supreme Court take a case when it does not want to, and not much way of stopping it from taking a case when it wants to take it. In 1952 the Court refused to take the *Doremus* Bible-reading appeal because the child of co-plaintiff Klein had graduated from school by the time the case reached the Supreme Court. In 1961, the Court in the case of *Poe* v. *Ullman* dismissed an appeal from a Connecticut decision upholding the State's anti–birth-control statute on the ground that it was a dead-letter law. The Epperson appeal was vulnerable on both grounds. When the case was originally brought, Blanchard's two sons were 15 and 17 years old; the case reached the Supreme Court three years later. It is therefore reasonable to assume that, as Justice Black implied in his concurring opinion, they were either graduated or certainly past the 10th grade in which Miss Epperson taught her godless biology course. As for the law itself, there had never been a single attempt to enforce it since its enactment by popular referendum in 1928, and Justice Black inferred from the "pallid, unenthusiastic, even apologetic defense of the Act presented by [counsel for the State] that the State would make no attempt to enforce the law should it remain on the books for the next century." In fact, the school administration had itself adopted and prescribed a textbook which contained a chapter setting forth "the theory about the origin . . . of man from a lower form of animal."

Nevertheless, the Court accepted the appeal and with no dissent ruled that the law was unconstitutional. Although unlike the Tennessee statute enacted three years earlier, it did not refer to "the story of Divine Creation of man as taught in the Bible," it was in all respects identical to that statute in forbidding the teaching of "the theory or doctrine that mankind ascended or descended from a lower order of animals." The Court concluded from this as well as from other contemporary circumstances that the purpose of the Arkansas, like that of the Tennessee, statute was to protect religious orthodoxy from what the legislature considered dangerous and inconsistent secular teachings. This, the Court said, a State may not do, for as early as 1872 the Court had said: "The law knows no heresy, and is committed to the support of no dogma, the establishment of no sect." Moreover, in the *Everson* case the Court had held that neither a State nor the Federal government could pass laws which aid one religion, aid all religions, or prefer one religion over another. In the *McCollum* case it had ruled that the State could not use tax-supported property for religious purposes, and in the *Schempp* case it had held that while the study of religions and of the Bible from a literary and historic viewpoint presented objectively as part of a secular program of education was constitutionally permissible, the State could not adopt programs or practices in its public schools or colleges which "aid or oppose" any religion. Moreover, the Court had also held in the *Schempp* case that the Establishment Clause was violated by any law whose purpose or primary effect was either the advancement or inhibition of religion, and the purpose of the law was clearly to protect fundamentalist religion.

Finally, the Court said, Arkansas's law could not be defended as an act of religious neutrality. The State did not seek to excise from the curricula of its schools and universities all discussion of the origin of man. The law's effort was confined to an attempt to blot out a particular theory because of its supposed conflict with the biblical account, literally read. Such a law, the opinion concluded, was contrary to the mandate of the First Amendment.

Why did the Supreme Court accept the Epperson appeal at all? Justice Fortas, who wrote the Court's opinion, conceded that it "is possible that the statute is presently more of a curiosity than a vital fact of life" in the three States (Arkansas, Mississippi, and Tennessee) which had enacted it. It is a reasonable guess that the Court was determined to place a seal of finality on a judgment—rendered in the *McCollum* case, deviated from slightly in the *Zorach* case, but reaffirmed in the *Engel* and *Schempp* decisions—that under the American Constitution public education must be secular in determining both what is included and what is excluded from its programs and curricula.

Postscript: In 1972 the Mississippi legislature repealed its anti-evolution statute, thus taking off the back of public education an imaginary monkey which was never there in the first place.

Teaching About Religion

Interestingly enough, another religiously motivated challenge to specific secular content of a public education curriculum occurred which was related to what the Court in the *Schempp* case had deemed permissible. There the Court had stated that the Bible is worthy of study for its literary and historic qualities, that one's education is not complete without a study of comparative religion and its relationship to the advancement of civilization, and that such objective study of the Bible or religion was not forbidden by the First Amendment.

Like most other institutions of higher learning, private and public, the University of Washington offered a course in its English department entitled "The Bible as Literature." In 1966, the Calvary Bible Presbyterian Church and the Tacoma Bible Presbyterian Church, together with their respective pastors, brought suit in a State court for an injunction against the offering of "any course of instruction dealing with the historical, geographical, narrative or literary features of the Bible." The theory of the action was that the choice of texts and the manner of presentation necessarily involved theological and religious considerations, thus violating constitutional prohibitions against the use of public money or property for religious instruction.

It cannot be said that the complaint was unreasonable. In the *Schempp* case, the Court had held that the Bible was an instrument of religion, and that it could not be read devotionally in public educational institutions. But teaching the Bible in a course on literature necessarily implies, even if the instructor does not expressly say so, that it is a work of man, such as the plays of Shakespeare or the poems of Milton; after all, though Job challenged God's justice, neither he nor any other mortal would be so presumptuous as to criticize His literary style. An implication of human authorship can hardly be deemed a manifestation of neutrality; certainly, the millions who ardently believed that the Bible is the sacred and immutable Word of God would not think it so.

Nevertheless, the trial court, in the case of *Calvary Bible Presbyterian Church* v. *Board of Regents of the University of Washington*, dismissed the complaint after trial. The State's highest court affirmed the dismissal, and the United States Supreme Court refused to accept an appeal from that decision.

Courses popularly called "teaching about religion" rather than "teaching of religion" were given at the college level and sometimes at the secondary school level long before the *Schempp* decision. However, the seal of approval there given by the Supreme Court served as an impetus for further promotion, particularly in the secondary or junior high schools. In 1971, under the chairmanship of the Reverend Neil J. McCluskey, S.J., a National Council on Religion and Public Education was formed, containing in it such unlikely partners as Americans United for Separation of Church and State, the Baptist Joint Committee on Public Affairs, the United States Catholic Conference, and the National Conference of Christians and Jews.

At the organization's national convention, held in November 1972, the 300 assembled educators were told by the speakers that teaching about religion in the public schools was not only constitutionally permissible but educationally necessary. An Indiana organization called Religious Instruction Association, Inc., produced a 183-page book written by its executive secretary and associate executive secretary, entitled *Religion Goes to School: A Handbook for Teachers.* Three clergymen, a Protestant, a Catholic, and a Jew, collaborated in producing *The Bible Reader: An Interfaith Interpretation*, a book of some 1,000 pages containing about half of the entire Bible (Old and New Testaments) with appropriate commentary for public school use. A speaker at the 23rd annual awards program of Religious Heritage of America, Inc., held in June 1973, estimated that 1,000 or more public high schools all over the country offered nondevotional religious courses and programs. State attorneys-general were cooperative in issuing advisory opinions that teaching about religion was entirely legal, and a number of State and local public educational boards and commissioners, with varying degrees of enthusiasm, endorsed the programs.

Despite all this, there were many religious leaders and educators who remained unconvinced if not hostile. Fundamentalists, such as those who brought the University of

Washington lawsuit, could not accept any teaching of or about religion even at the college level which did not proceed from an assumption of the literal truth of all contained in the Bible. Jews feared that teachers, because of community pressures, their own biases, or their lack of adequate training, would be less than objective and would slant instruction toward Christianity. Even among educators not committed to any religion, there was considerable skepticism regarding the validity of separate "religion courses," at least below the college level. Recognizing that religion was a fact of life and could hardly be excluded from secondary or even elementary school studies, they were of the view that a better method of dealing with it was to take it up naturally whenever it was relevant to a particular course such as literature, history, music, or art.

Whatever the estimates and optimistic predictions of its supporters and promoters, it cannot be said at this writing that teaching about religion in the public schools has caught fire.

Chapter Six

The Schools Private

Origins of Catholic Private Education

Unwillingly, unlovingly, and unknowingly, American Protestantism cooperated with the Catholic Church in the establishment of the Catholic parochial school system in the United States—so much so that it is probable that without Protestant cooperation, there would have been only a small, religiously elitist system bearing the same proportionate relationship to the whole Catholic community as the Protestant and Jewish private schools bear to their respective communities. Although there are great differences between the public-Catholic dual educational system in the North and the white-black dualism in the South, they are analogous in the sense that both were forced upon unwilling minorities in circumstances that imputed inferiority to those minorities. The motif was racial prejudice in the South, religious bigotry in the North.

When Catholics, particularly from Ireland, began migrating to this country in large numbers during the first half of the 19th century, the bishops and priests were naturally concerned that there be adequate provision for their spiritual needs. They were concerned too about the danger of assimilation and departure from the faith should the small number of Catholic immigrants be dispersed over the wide and continually expanding Protestant country. For these reasons, the immigrants were encouraged to congregate

228

within the large cities on the Atlantic seaboard where priests, churches, and Catholic fellowship would be available.

The bishops and priests were most particularly worried about the assimilation of the Catholic children as a result of their commingling with their Protestant contemporaries in the newly established common schools. The availability of a free, universal, secular education, for girls as well as boys, presented a great temptation to Irish parents coming from a country where no such opportunity existed for them. To meet this threat, as early as 1829 the First Provincial Council of Baltimore declared that it was "absolutely necessary that schools be established, in which the young may be taught the principles of faith and morality, while being instructed in letters."

Succeeding councils, provincial and plenary, reiterated the call. It was made part of the canon law that near every parish church a school—hence, parochial school—be erected, and that all Catholic parents be bound to send their children to these (or other Catholic) schools. Failure on the part of parents to do so, unless they were excused by the local bishop, disqualified them from receiving absolution in the sacrament of Holy Penance. (This is still part of the canon law, although it is likely to be substantially modified if not completely eliminated in the revision now in preparation.)

Despite this serious ecclesiastical sanction and the pressures of the priests, the great majority of Catholic parents elected to send their children to the common schools. In many cases location and convenience dictated the choice. In others, economy was a factor; while tuition in parochial schools was generally nominal or none at all, the expense of maintaining the school rested upon the parents in one way or another. Most important, however, was the fact that most Irish immigrants, like later Jewish immigrants, did not want their children isolated from other American children. They did not share the fears of the bishops and priests that the children would lose their faith if they sat next to non-Catholic children and learned writing and reading and arithmetic with them in the Jacksonian egalitarian, common school.

At this point Protestantism stepped in and saved the day. We have recounted already the suffering inflicted upon Catholic children who refused to participate in Bible reading and prayer recitation in the public schools. But the Protestant orientation of the common school program was not limited to religious exercises; it extended as well to instruction in such supposedly secular and neutral subjects as history and reading, taught by the same teachers who led the children in Bible reading and prayers. In the 1840s Bishop John Hughes of New York protested bitterly against the anti-Catholic bias in the textbooks used in the public schools of the city. In name and in theory the tax-supported schools were common, but in reality many of them were common only to Protestant children.

Finding their children isolated and persecuted, it is hardly surprising, therefore, that many Catholic parents withdrew their children from the public schools and transferred them to parochial schools. The younger siblings of these children were then enrolled in the parochial schools, and so too in time were their children and children's children. For more than a century, these all-Catholic schools, taught by Sisters under the guidance of the parish priest well-known to the parents, constituted cities of refuge and havens of security for Catholic children in Protestant America.

The Catholic child in a Protestant-oriented public school faced two threats: to his faith from evangelism, and to his security from nativism. The parochial school served to meet both threats and therefore took root and flourished. Notwithstanding the ill treatment of the Catholic children and the pressures of the priests and bishops, the Church never came near attaining its goal of every Catholic child in a Catholic school. At their peak, the schools never enrolled more Catholic elementary and secondary school children than did the public schools.

The Changing Catholic Philosophy of Life and Education

Catholicism is undergoing a painful, yet, to many, exciting, process of soul-searching and self-examination, seeking to find its place not only in the 20th but in future centuries. The *sturm und drang* through which it is going cannot help having a great effect on its philosophy of education and upon its parochial school system. Justice Jackson, in his dissenting opinion in the *Everson* case, noted that "the parochial school is a vital, if not the most vital, part of the Roman Catholic Church." He expressed the opinion that, if put to the choice, the Church "would forego its whole service for mature persons before it would give up education of the young"; that "its growth and cohesion, discipline and loyalty, spring from its schools"; and that "Catholic education is the rock on which the whole structure rests."

It is probable that today this view would not be accepted unanimously within Catholicism. Responsible voices in at least that part of American Catholicism represented by *Commonweal* and the *National Catholic Reporter* are beginning to be heard in their questioning of whether maintenance of the enterprise as it is now constituted is worth the effort, even should it be possible without substantial amounts of tax-raised funds. However the case may be today, Jackson's judgment as to the place of the parochial school system in Catholicism's hierarchy of values was certainly valid when it was made in 1947.

The 1929 Encyclical of Pius XI *On the Christian Education of Youth* was then and is still the most authoritative document extant on the nature, purpose, and philosophy of Catholic education. There is hardly a book on the subject which is not based in large measure on that Encyclical. A leading work, the 1956 edition of Redden and Ryan's *A Catholic Philosophy of Education* contains at least 35 direct quotations from or citations to it. Its principles were reaffirmed at

Vatican II, and, at least until the canon law is revised, they are still part of it.

According to this Encyclical, the "only school approved by the Church is one where . . . the Catholic religion permeates the entire atmosphere [and where] all teaching and the whole organization of the school and its teachers, syllabus and textbooks in every branch [are] regulated by the Christian spirit." The "Catholic religion" and "Christian spirit" referred to were the traditional doctrines and dogmas of Catholicism of the pre–John XXIII days; they had to "permeate" the entire atmosphere of education as well as of all life because nothing in this life was of equal importance, or indeed of any importance, except as it contributed to the attainment of salvation and avoidance of damnation in the future eternal life. By reason of original sin and the essential wickedness of man, the only way to salvation was through the one true church and its rites, such as baptism, confession, and communion, all established for that purpose by the Son of God who willingly gave his carnate life so that salvation could be achieved by man.

Permeation: Theory or Fact?

How faithful to the mandate of permeation have the parochial schools been? The evidence is often contradictory and far from conclusive. On the one hand is the following statement from the authoritative *Parochial Schools: A Sociological Study*, written by Joseph H. Fichter, S.J., in 1958 (p. 86):

> It is a commonplace observation that in the parochial school religion permeates the whole curriculum and is not confined to a single half-hour period of the day. Even arithmetic can be used as an instrument of pious thoughts, as in the case of the teacher who gives this problem to her class: "If it takes forty thousand priests and a hundred forty thousand sisters to care for forty million Catholics in the United States, how many more priests and sisters will be needed to convert and care for the hundred million non-Catholics in the United States?"

Another item of evidence is the statement made in April 1969, by Bishop Joseph L. Bernadin, General Secretary of the United States Catholic Conference: "Catholic educators have always maintained that a Catholic school is not one which teaches religion only during one period every day. Rather the whole atmosphere of the school is to be a Christian one, animated by a community of faith— the children, the teachers and the parents."

A third item of evidence is illustrated by the following examples taken from two arithmetic books published in 1957 and 1961 respectively for use in parochial schools:

How much money must I have to buy these four books? *Poems About the Christ Child*, $1.85; *Story of Our Lady*, $2.25; *Saint Joseph*, $1.05; *Saint Theresa*, $2.00?

The children of St. Francis School ransomed 125 pagan babies last year. This year they hope to increase this number by 20%. If they succeed, how many babies will they ransom this year?

David sells subscriptions to the *Catholic Digest* on a commission basis of 20%. If the subscription is $2.50 a year, what is David's commission on each sale?

China has a population of approximately 600,000,000. Through the efforts of missionaries 3,000,000 have been converted to Catholicism. What percentage of the people of China have been converted?

In Africa Father Murray, a Holy Ghost father, was given a triangular piece of ground upon which to build his church. What was the area of this ground if it had a base of 80 feet and an altitude of 120 feet?

* * * *

Jim made the Way of the Cross. He likes the sixth station very much. What Roman numeral was written above it?

In millions of homes Our Lady's challenge has been accepted, but she wants billions throughout the world to join the

Family Rosary for Peace. Do you know how to write in
figures large numbers such as those just mentioned?

Finally, the following from the *Handbook of School Regulations of the Diocese of Providence* (1965):

> Religious formation is not confined to formal courses; nor
> is it restricted to a single subject area. It is achieved through
> the example of the faculty, the tone of the school, the man-
> ner in which the curriculum is taught, and religious activities.

The *Handbook* was part of the evidence at the trial in the
Earley v. *DiCenso* case, which will be examined later in this
chapter. Yet, much of the evidence at that trial supports the
contention, often made by defenders of governmental aid,
that religion does not permeate the curriculum and program
of the parochial schools, and the schools are in reality not
different from public schools except that they teach religion
during one period each day. The *Handbook* was approved by
the Bishop of Providence with a direction that it "have the
force of synodal law in the diocese," but principals and
teachers in a number of the schools, called as witnesses at
the trial, testified that neither the *Handbook* nor the 1929
Encyclical which it quotes was considered binding, that
many of them never read either, and that neither influenced
to any substantial degree the actual operations of the
schools. Take the following from the trial testimony:

> Q. Father, while we are on this one question, do you expect as
>   superintendent of [Catholic] schools that the teachers in
>   your schools, who are teaching secular courses, are to
>   inject religious content into the secular courses?
> A. No, I do not.

John R. Earley, another witness, testified:

> Q. I understand you are the principal in the school?
> A. Yes.
> Q. Do you also teach at the school?
> A. Yes.

Q. What courses?

A. Science, mathematics, social studies.

Q. Do you teach a course in religion?

A. No, sir.

Q. Do you have a copy of the *Handbook* that has been discussed here in court today in your school?

A. Yes, sir.

Q. Do you refer to it in the day-to-day operations of your school?

A. No, sir.

Many other teachers, some non-Catholic, testified to the same effect. Nor did the Encyclical fare any better, as can be seen from the following exchange between counsel for the schools and counsel for the plaintiff-taxpayers:

> *Mr. Wilson:* On page 8 [of the *Handbook*] there is a quote from an encyclical of Pius XI that, I believe, came out in 1925, or '27 or '29. We have informed the other side that that encyclical is not binding and there is no evidence with respect to it. But the fact of the matter is it was never followed in this country, anyway.

> *Mr. Pfeffer:* Your Honor, please, we don't concede to that last qualification. We believe that the encyclical has been in effect in this country, and there is a tremendous amount of literature to show that it has been. We will accept the statement to the effect Father Mullen [Catholic school superintendent] does not consider it binding.

The Secularization of Catholic Education

The foregoing exchange between counsel epitomizes the dichotomy of theory and fact in Catholic education. It is true that there "is a tremendous amount of literature to show" that the 1929 Encyclical has been in effect in this country; the Redden and Ryan book, the Fichter book, and Bishop Bernadin's statement are part of it. But there is often a gap between literature and life, and it is the latter which is evidenced by the testimony in the *DiCenso* case and in almost all the other related court cases.

Counsel for the parochial schools in the *DiCenso* case was in one sense correct in his statement that the 1929 Encyclical "was *never* followed in this country." Notwithstanding its unqualified assertion that the "only school approved by the Church is one where . . . the Catholic religion permeates the entire atmosphere," at the time of the *Everson* decision, half the Catholic school-age population in the United States attended public schools. True enough, while the canon law, which encompassed the Encyclical, decreed that "Catholic children shall not attend non-Catholic, indifferent schools that are mixed, that is to say, schools open to Catholics and non-Catholics alike," it did authorize local bishops "to decide under what circumstances, and with what safeguards to prevent loss of faith, it may be tolerated that Catholic children go to such schools." Nevertheless, it is safe to assume that the great majority of the parents who enrolled their children in public schools never sought nor received ecclesiastical approval.

Inside the Catholic schools, however, the gap between doctrine and reality was not so wide. The Catholic religion did permeate the atmosphere: the schools were adjacent to and bore the name of the parish church; the teachers were practically all garbed nuns, and the few who were not were all devout Catholics; crucifixes, religious pictures, religious statues, and holy fonts abounded throughout the schools; prayers were recited at numerous times throughout the day; the textbooks were either prepared specifically for parochial school use or were standard texts used in public schools but revised and adapted for parochial school use (known as Cathedral Editions); classes were segregated according to sex; discipline was strict if not rigid; obedience to authority was stressed, and individuality was discouraged (the children wore uniform clothes: white shirts and dark trousers for the boys, and white blouses and dark blue jumpers for the girls).

While there were variations, the preceding paragraph

represents a fair depiction of life in the Catholic parochial school system before the ascendancy of John XXIII to the chair of Peter. Then a process of secularization began to set in and progressed with increasing intensity. The testimony or testimonials we have cited must be taken with reservations; they were offered as defense in lawsuits challenging public funding. The picture they present of the parochial as nothing but a public school with a half-hour a day added for vacuumized religious instruction does not quite comport with reality. Nevertheless, secularization is on the march, and at a fairly rapid pace.

In part, the explanation may be found in economics. The 1965 Elementary and Secondary Education Act made Federal funds available for supplying textbooks for parochial school use, and States began following suit. All of these laws required, as the courts interpreted the Constitution to require, that the books be completely secular and approved for use in public schools. The parochial schools thus faced the alternative of paying for their own religion-oriented books or getting public school books without cost. On a broader scale, State legislatures in increasing numbers were experimenting with various means of providing tax-raised funds for the support of parochial schools, and it was generally assumed that these measures would survive constitutional challenge only if they were earmarked for nonsectarian services or supplies; the Rhode Island law that was challenged in the *DiCenso* case, for example, required parochial school teachers seeking salary supplements out of State funds to undertake in writing that they would not teach any religious courses.

Naturally, many schools chose to receive public funds even at the cost of some secularization. Yet it is a fair guess that even if financial considerations and availability of tax-raised funds were in no way involved, the road toward secularization would still have been traveled, although perhaps at a slower pace. Normative Catholicism is far from Unitarianism or even Reform Judaism, but, like Protestantism and Judaism before it, its ethos is finally confronting 18th century deism and is succumbing to its influence. The schools could hardly remain unaffected, and while, as we will shortly see, secularizaton of Catholic education at the college and university level is proceeding at a more rapid and intensive pace, the elementary and secondary schools are not lagging far behind. Protestantism secularized its educational values by turning its precollege school system over to the States; Catholicism is effecting secularization partly by retaining its schools but importing and incorporating the values of the States' educational system, and partly by turning over its children to the State schools, Encyclical or no Encyclical.

Exodus from the Catholic Schools

Parallel to the dramatic strides toward secularization of the Catholic school system in the post–Vatican II decade has been the exodus of Catholics from the parochial schools. Between 1963 and 1973 the number of Catholic schools in the United States decreased from over 13,000 to about 10,500, and the number of enrolled students decreased from more than five and a half million to less than four million. Part of the explanation for the decline in the number of schools is to be found in more efficient management, manifesting itself in consolidation of schools—a process often strenuously resisted by parish priests and congregations. The decrease in the number of enrolled pupils can be attributed to the lower birthrate among the present generation of Catholic parents. Yet, these by themselves are inadequate explanations; the decrease in enrollment, for example, appears not only in raw numbers but no less dramatically in percentages of Catholics of school age, from a high of 50 percent to the present still declining low of 37 percent.

The standard explanation for the decrease is economics. The cost of both public and private education is steadily rising. The public system meets the cost by increased taxation, but the private sector does not have this resource. The Catholic system is particularly hard hit. In any school system the salaries of teachers constitute by far the major item of costs. For more than a century the Catholic system could rely on the services of thousands of dedicated nuns and Sisters who asked nothing in return but their modest subsistence. This resource is fast disappearing. With smaller Catholic families there are fewer daughters to give to the Church and more unwillingness by parents to make the gift. Moreover, among the nuns and Sisters, increasing numbers are unwilling to teach in the schools but elect to fulfill their mission of service by working with the poor, the deprived, and the drug-addicted. What this means is that the schools must hire lay teachers and pay them wages which, though almost uniformly below those paid by the public schools, must nevertheless be high enough, at least in the case of male teachers, to enable them to support a family.

In these circumstances, the parochial schools have no alternatives but either to increase tuition or charge tuition where none was charged before, or to economize on services and equipment, or to do both. Whatever route is chosen, the destination is the same: the decreasing ability of the parochial schools to compete for children with the public schools, particularly in the suburbs to which many Catholics move as they rise on the socioeconomic ladder.

All this is true, yet the factors mentioned represent the symptons rather than the causes of declining Catholic school enrollment. Educational costs are rising, but then so too are the incomes of Catholics whose parents were slum-dwelling unskilled laborers; many are now secure suburban union-organized mechanics, policemen, firemen, and civil service employees whose children are likely to be college-trained professionals and business executives. Parochial schools are inferior to public schools in respect to plant, equipment, and services, but that has always been the case.

Catholic couples have fewer children than did their parents and grandparents, but nobody compels them to practice contraceptive birth control.

The crux of the matter is that the present generation of Catholics is less willing to make the sacrifices necessary to maintain the traditional school system. The reason is two-fold: by virtue of the Supreme Court decisions in the *McCollum-Engel-Schempp* trilogy which sealed the end of Protestant-oriented instruction, Bible reading, and prayer recitation in the public schools, and the election of John Kennedy to the presidency in 1960, the Protestant evangelism and anti-Catholic nativism of the 19th and early 20th centuries have disappeared from the American scene and particularly from the public schools; Catholics, particularly as they move upward economically and socially, are in increasing numbers tasting the fruit of humanistic deism and finding that they like it.

Non-Catholic Schools

Up to this point, we have concerned ourselves exclusively with Catholic schools. The reason for this is that, in terms of the confrontation of God and Caesar in the constitutional arena, the Catholic schools, both quantitatively and qualitatively, occupy the center of the stage. In the struggle for governmental aid, Catholicism has been the chief protagonist, even more so than in the constitutional controversy regarding religion in the public schools, for there, after a brief change of roles, it almost completely withdrew from the arena; in the aid context, however, it still is and will probably continue to be the chief if not sole contender as long as the struggle goes on.

Quantitatively, the comparative stake that Catholicism has in governmental aid to religious schools is indicated by the statistics disclosed in the records of the cases which came to the Supreme Court in the 1971–73 period: in the States involved in those cases (New York, Pennsylvania, Rhode

Island, Connecticut, and Ohio), from 82 to 95 percent of the religious schools were Catholic. These statistics, moreover, do not tell the whole story. Among the non-Catholic schools were Seventh-Day Adventist, Ethical Culture, and Episcopal, whose sponsoring denominations do not favor governmental aid to church schools.

Among the non-Catholic denominations, Seventh-Day Adventists rank first in relation to the percentage of children who attend their schools. Jewish immigrants who came to this country in large numbers during the first quarter of the 20th century and who, like their Irish predecessors, settled mostly in the large cities on the eastern seaboard, did not find it necessary to establish a separate secular-religious school system. In large measure because of the struggles and sacrifices of the Catholics, the public schools in which most of the Jewish children had enrolled had become secularized, and accorded to them the friendliness and equality that had been denied to Catholic children. Enrollment in Jewish schools, however, shows the most dramatic rate of increase in recent years, particularly during the post-1963 decade. (In 1968, there were in the State of New York about as many Jewish schools as all other non-Catholic religious schools combined.) For the Catholics, this decade, as we have seen, has been particularly significant in the context of this book because it followed Vatican II and the *Schempp* decision; for the latter reason the decade has perhaps been even more significant for the Jews, in respect not only to religion in the public schools, but also to government aid to religious schools.

American Judaism, as is well known, has three more or less independent branches with independent but cooperating institutional structures—Orthodox (fundamentalist), Conservative (halfway), and Reform (liberal). With the exception of a small group of the extreme Orthodox, mostly concentrated in New York City, American Judaism, for at least two decades before 1963, had been uniformly committed to the principle of strict separation of church and state. Through their overall coordinating body, the Synagogue Council of America (analogous to the National Council of Churches and the United States Catholic Conference), they submitted briefs as "friend of the court" in many cases involving church-state and religious liberty matters, such as the *McCollum*, *Engel*, and *Schempp* cases, the *Sunday Law Cases*, the Amish case, and others. They opposed, of course, religion in the public schools, but they opposed, too, governmental aid to religious schools.

In 1964, however, the Orthodox branch changed its position on the aid question, and joined Catholicism in the quest for governmental financing of religious schools. It maintained its membership in the Synagogue Council, notwithstanding pressure from its own extreme wing that such association with Conservative and Reform rabbis was forbidden by Talmudic law, but refused to go along with its co-members in opposing aid to parochial schools. On the contrary, it participated actively with Catholics in both the legislative and judicial arenas in the effort to obtain and to defend aid.

There were a number of reasons for this. During the post-1963 period American Catholicism was moving leftward, but American Judaism was moving in the opposite direction. The extreme Orthodox, mostly recent East European immigrants and their children, exerted considerable influence on the more American culture-oriented Orthodox majority, who in turn influenced Conservatism and, through them, Reform Judaism. While *yeshivahs*, the Orthodox Jewish equivalents of the Catholic parochial schools, had been operating in this country since the early part of the century, until World War II there were very few, and almost all were in New York City and limited almost completely to religiously oriented children whose parents expected for them careers as rabbis, religious school teachers, or cantors. The neo-fundamentalist Jews, however, had as their goal every Jewish child in a *yeshivah*, and sparked a campaign to establish *yeshivahs* all over the United States.

Before 1963, Reform Judaism, established in the 19th century by high socioeconomic Jews of German ancestry, was uniformly hostile to Jewish parochial schools. Conservative Judaism, while not hostile, was far from enthusiastic, and conceived of *yeshivahs* primarily as the source for future rabbis, even Conservative ones. But in recent years the position of Jewry on the American scene has changed radically. Anti-Semitism has largely disappeared as a factor in American life. Jews have become not merely an equal but an elitist element in society; they have become presidents of large corporations and of banks; in 1973 the deans of what have traditionally been considered the three most prestigious law schools in the country, Harvard, Yale, and Columbia, were all Jews; most startling of all, the United States Secretary of State was a non-native Jew; (it was not so long ago that Jews, and certainly non–native-born Jews, could not get any position in the State Department above, perhaps, that of stenographer or file clerk).

What American Jewry fears today is not anti-Semitism, but assimilation. The full acceptance of Jews into society has brought with it an alarming increase of intermarriages and the possibility of the complete disappearance of the 2.5 percent of the American population which still identifies itself as Jewish. The Jewish day school, the name Conservative and Reform Jews prefer to *yeshivah*, is viewed by them as a defense against assimilation; and while this fact has not caused them to abandon their opposition to governmental support of parochial schools (urging instead increased financial support by the Jewish community), it has strengthened the present Orthodox position on the issue.

The 1963 *Schempp* decision also played a significant role in the change of position. Before *Schempp*, Jews viewed church-state separation largely in terms of religion in the public schools. Even among the Orthodox, a relatively small percentage attended *yeshivahs*; the overwhelming majority were enrolled in public schools. There, except for predominantly Jewish sections in the large cities and suburbs (and even there by no means completely), Jewish children had succeeded Catholics in being the chief victims of prayers, Bible reading, and other religious practices in the public schools. (The trial record in *Chamberlin* v. *Dade County Board of Public Instruction* presents a graphic but far from the most egregious example.) The only legal defense available to them was the principle of church-state separation.

The *Schempp* decision brought an end to all that. Bible and prayer programs began to disappear from most of the schools attended by Jewish children, and even the always troublesome Christmas programs were becoming increasingly less Christological and theological. As we will see in the next chapter, the principle of church-state separation was also important to Orthodox Jews in their struggle against compulsory Sunday closing laws, and, while they were unsuccessful in the courts, they did succeed in obtaining the relief they sought from the legislatures. Hence, Orthodox Jewry no longer had any strong institutional interest in the principle, which was in any event completely alien to the influential fundamentalists from Eastern Europe.

The net result was a strange coalition of Roman Catholicism and Orthodox Jewry as partners in the struggle for aid to parochial schools, where they had only shortly before been bitter enemies on the subject of religion in the public schools and the enforcement of compulsory Sunday closing laws.

Religion, Racism, and the Private Schools

Another factor helps explain the rise in enrollment in Jewish day schools: the rather startling mushrooming of Protestant parochial schools where they had never before existed (particularly in the South), and the fact that enrollment in Catholic schools declined less precipitously than it otherwise would have. The extent of that factor, called racism by some but aversion to inferior and unsafe schools by others, is subject to considerable dispute; that it exists and is troubling religious leaders, particularly Catholics, is hardly subject to dispute.

In 1954 the Supreme Court handed down its historic decision in *Brown* v. *Board of Education*, declaring that racial segregation in public schools is unconstitutional, and ordering that all segregated schools be integrated "with all deliberate speed." Southern officials, apparently afflicted with limited vision, could see only the word "deliberate" and complied fully and faithfully with the mandate as they were able to see it. After waiting fifteen years and finding no substantial improvement in the officials' eyesight, the Supreme Court decided to change the text. In *Alexander* v. *Holmes County Board of Education* it ruled that fifteen years of deliberation was more than enough and ordered that complete integration be instituted immediately. Two years later, in the case of *Swann* v. *Charlotte–Mecklenberg School District*, the Court ruled that all effective means must be used to achieve integration, including busing, not only of black children into white schools, but also white children into black schools.

These decisions applied only to Southern or *de jure* segregation, that is, segregation decreed by law; they did not directly affect *de facto* segregation, which results from the general requirement that children attend their neighborhood schools, and the fact that black children usually live in black neighborhoods and white children in white neighborhoods. Nevertheless, the *Brown* decision touched the conscience of many Northern liberals. In addition, the steady northward migration of Negroes in the post–World War II era (and their heightened political consciousness) had significant political implications which were not unrecognized by Northern white politicians. Moreover, in the 1973 case of *Keyes* v. *School District No. 1*, involving not a Southern community, but Denver, Colorado, the Supreme Court ruled that the line between *de jure* and *de facto* was quite narrow and indistinct, and what many considered to be the latter was often the former and hence within the scope of the *Brown, Alexander,* and *Swann* decisions.

For these and other reasons, integration programs which involved busing black children into white schools and white children into black schools began to be instituted throughout the North; in most cases they could hardly be effective otherwise. Thus, what followed was an exodus of white children from inner city public schools to white suburbs where feasible, and to white city nonpublic schools where not.

In *Norwood* v. *Harrison,* decided in 1973, the Supreme Court recognized that judicial pressure toward racial integration in the public schools of the South had led to a mushrooming of newly established private schools and "academies." Most of these were nonsectarian, but many were church related, particularly after the Internal Revenue Service ruled that all-white segregated schools were not entitled to tax exemption. In the *Allen* case the Court had upheld the constitutionality of laws providing for free textbooks to parochial schools, but in the *Norwood* case it held that such laws are unconstitutional if the schools exclude children on account of race.

Private schools, especially parochial schools, were comparatively rare in most parts of the South; hence the necessity of establishing new ones. In the North, and in some parts of the South as well (e.g., Louisiana), there already existed a well-established network of nonpublic schools, and the need to create new ones was not so urgent.

The nonpublic school community is a community of white middle- and upper-class children, a fact substantiated by almost every study that has been made. In the urban areas particularly, the private school is often a white oasis surrounded by a nonwhite desert. Few nonwhite children and few children of poor families attend private schools; their universe of education is the public school system. This is shown by the authoritative study made by the United

States Commission on Civil Rights on Racial Isolation in the Public Schools (Vol. 1, pp. 38–39):

NONPUBLIC SCHOOLS

Private and parochial school enrollment also is an important factor in the increasing concentration of Negroes in city school systems. Nonpublic school enrollment constitutes a major segment of the Nation's elementary and secondary school population. Nationally, about one-sixth of the total 1960 school enrollment (Grades 1 to 12) was in private schools. In metropolitan areas the proportion is slightly higher, and divided unevenly between city and suburb. Nearly one-third more elementary school students in the cities attend nonpublic schools than in the suburbs. Almost all of them are white. In the larger metropolitan areas the trend is even more pronounced. A much higher proportion of white city students than white suburban students attend private and parochial elementary schools. Nonwhites in these metropolitan areas, whether in cities or suburbs, attend public schools almost exclusively.

Thus, nonpublic schools absorb a disproportionately large segment of the white school-age population in central cities, particularly in the larger ones. This poses serious problems for city school systems. In St. Louis, for example, 40 percent of the total white elementary school population attended nonpublic schools in 1965; in Boston, 41 percent; in Philadelphia, more than 60 percent.

In Detroit, two-thirds of the children in the public schools are black. In Connecticut, a compilation by the Catholic Archdiocese of Hartford showed that only 2.6 percent of the State's parochial school population is black, and 1.2 percent Spanish-speaking (Puerto Rican). When Catholic parents move from the inner city to the suburbs they are in increasing numbers sending their children to public rather than parochial schools.

This disparity between the percentage of white and nonwhite children in public and nonpublic schools is not merely continuing but is growing steadily. Startling as it may seem, there is today probably more racial segregation in Northern public schools than there was before *Brown* v. *Board of Education* was decided. At least a substantial part of the explanation for this trend is that many parents are withdrawing their children from public schools and sending them to parochial schools, not so that they may better pursue God but more effectively avoid racial integration.

As is well known, leadership in the struggle for racial integration in education is held by the National Association for the Advancement of Colored People. It is also a matter of common knowledge that the NAACP has traditionally kept aloof from controversies which did not directly affect the cause of racial equality. It is therefore significant that in recent years the State branches of the NAACP have not only been participating in the sponsorship of suits challenging governmental financing of parochial schools but have actually joined such suits as parties plaintiffs. Indeed, the NAACP has had a participating role in one form or another in most of the post-1968 cases discussed in this chapter.

Nor has NAACP activity been limited to the litigation front; it has been no less active in opposing legislation seeking to provide public financial aid to nonpublic schools. In Michigan, for example, the NAACP played a leadership role in defeating enactment of a bill providing for purchase of secular services and in the adoption of a constitutional amendment forbidding all financial aid to parochial schools. In Delaware, the State NAACP publicly opposed enactment of a measure for aid to parochial schools expressly on the ground that many white parents send their children to private schools to avoid integrated education. In Maryland, the black community took the same position for the same reason. Blacks all over the nation share these views.

It is not suggested that all or even a majority of parents who enroll their children in parochial schools do so in order to avoid racial integration. Yet, one would have to close his eyes to reality if he did not realize that a substantial number of parents do transfer their children or send them initially to parochial schools when blacks move into their neighborhoods, or are bused to their neighborhood schools, or, even worse, when their own children are bused to black schools.

This situation has been sufficiently serious to cause concern among public officials. In December 1969, Dr. Nathan Brown, Acting Superintendent of Schools in New York City, in an address delivered at a Jewish theological seminary, called it to the attention of Jewish leaders. "I deplore," he said, "any action on the part of Jewish parents who escape the city school system for the sole purpose of avoiding racially integrated schools." He referred to what he called the increasing Jewish enrollment in religious and "pseudo-religious" schools in light of social, ethnic, and class conflicts arising from school reorganization, and expressed the fear that alienation of the Jewish middle class from the system could result in a city of "ghettos surrounded by police protecting one group from another."

In Connecticut, in October 1969, the United States Department of Justice brought suit against the Department of Education of Waterbury, charging in its complaint among other things that

> white children who reside in public school districts where substantial numbers of Negro and Puerto Rican children also reside have been transported by the City of Waterbury from such public school districts to all white or predominantly white independent non-public schools, wherein to a substantial extent, facilities of public schools which commonly are located adjacent to or near the respective independent non-public schools are shared. This practice has resulted in certain public elementary schools becoming and remaining predominantly Negro and Puerto Rican.

Religious leaders, particularly Catholic, are no less concerned. Following the Supreme Court's decision in the *Alexander* case, ordering immediate integration in the public schools in the South, Catholic schools in Louisiana were besieged by new white applicants. The Archdiocese of New Orleans and the Diocese of Baton Rouge promulgated special guidelines to prevent parochial schools from becoming havens for fleeing whites. Similar guidelines or directives were issued by diocesan authorities in other parts of the country. How effective these have been is a matter of speculation. On the one hand, in the *Norwood* suit the NAACP expressly excluded the Catholic schools of Mississippi from its complaint and stated that it did not object to their continued receipt of free textbooks. On the other hand, in Lafayette diocese in Louisiana black parents brought suit to integrate the Academy of the Immaculate Conception which had enjoyed a 22 percent increase in enrollment immediately after the *Alexander* decision.

Many of those who oppose aid to parochial schools argue that the effect may well be serious. They suggest that the preservation of the equalitarian, multiracial, and multireligious public school system envisioned by its founders rests upon the outcome of the struggle for governmental financing of nonpublic schools. To the extent that the public schools, particularly in urban areas, remain multiracial, the explanation, according to them, lies in the fact that most of the white children attending the public schools are members of middle-income families who simply cannot afford to pay the tuition and other expenses for nonpublic schools. These middle-income white children are the flesh and blood of a multiracial public school system. Should the time come when, through increasing governmental support of nonpublic schools, it will be economically feasible for white middle-income parents to send their children to nonpublic schools, the public school system may become the modern equivalent of the pre–public education charity school—an institution for society's rejects, most of whom will be members of racial minorities. We will then, they fear, end up with two school systems—separate and unequal.

The Secularization of Higher Education

As noted in the preceding chapter, Calvinism's stranglehold on education was broken by the secular humanism of the late 18th century reinforced by the Jacksonian democracy of the early 19th. Secularization on the precollege level was achieved when the elementary schools, though retaining a few vestiges of Protestantism such as devotional Bible reading and prayer recitation until the Supreme Court called a halt in 1962–63, were given over bodily to the State and local governments. To some extent, the same pattern was followed on the college level. (What is now Kansas State University, for example, was originally Bluemont Central College, which the Methodist Church gave to the State as the site for a new "Kansas State Agricultural College.") On the whole, however, secularization in higher education came about somewhat differently and more gradually. The institutions remained basically independent of the State governments, which established their own systems from scratch (as they had done on the elementary school level in the West). Progressively, however, the denominational colleges also became independent of church government; the theological seminaries for the training of ministers were legally separated from the rest of the university and were incorporated as separate church-controlled and -operated institutions, and the rest became secular colleges and universities hardly distinguishable from their State counterparts. This was true not only of Calvinist institutions (Harvard, Yale, Princeton), but of Episcopalian (Columbia, formerly Kings), Baptist (Brown, Baylor), Methodist (Wesleyan), Quaker (Swarthmore), and other denominations. As in the case of elementary and secondary schools, some cultural lag was evident; vestiges such as compulsory chapel attendance continued in many institutions until the youth revolt of the mid-20th century, but by now they have practically disappeared.

The experience of the Protestant schools, elementary and college, is now occurring in the Catholic schools. The Catholic metamorphosis started a century and a half after the beginning of the Protestant experience, spurred by the enlightenment of John XXIII and the ecumenicism of Vatican II. While the Catholic elementary schools are not being taken over by the public school system, substantial parts of their population are (except in central city areas where the influx of Negroes triggers migrations in the opposite direction); where they are not being taken over, many Catholic schools are on their way to becoming public schools with a secular curriculum *cum* a half-hour of religion.

At the college level, the development has been even closer to the Protestant model. Elementary schools still remain under the control of the parish priest and the supervision of the diocesan superintendent of schools. Colleges are laicizing their boards of trustees, achieving a *de facto* independence of the dioceses or religious orders which established them, and entering into operational coalitions with secular private and occasionally public colleges. The model for Catholic universities in the United States used to be the pontifically established Catholic University at Washington, D.C.; now many Catholic universities, including Catholic University, are modeling themselves after Harvard and Columbia.

Three items may be presented which, if not evidentiary, are symbolic of the secularization of Catholic higher education that is now taking place: (1) The heads of three Catholic colleges have recently left their posts—one to marry, another to head a campus of a city university, and the third to do both. (2) At the trial in the case of *Tilton* v. *Richardson*, which will be examined later in this chapter, an official of a Catholic college for women was asked if there were holy fonts in the classrooms; her reply was that there were, but they were now used by the students as ashtrays in which to leave their crushed cigarettes as they entered class. (3) At a Jesuit university in Connecticut, student protest in 1972 impelled the trustees to overrule the president and direct him to renew the contract of a teacher of theology who had become an agnostic and left the order.

Not all segments of the Catholic community are happy with what is taking place. The Reverend Charles Whalen, a Jesuit faculty member of Fordham law school, protested proposed changes at the university and stated that the problem was "not how to change it into another Columbia, but how to develop it into a first-rate Catholic university." The defenders, however, assert that there is no alternative; without substantial changes toward secularization there can be no public funds, and without funds there can be no survival. The decision in the *Tilton* case indicates that they are right about the first part of the claim, but the implication that the traditional Catholic college would survive if public funds were made available is questionable. The truth of the matter is that American Catholics, clergy as well as laity, are becoming increasingly unhappy with the normative philosophy of Catholic education as pronounced in the 1929 Encyclical of Pius XI. Humanism is affecting Catholics as it has Protestants. Except for a small elitist group deeply and perhaps professionally committed to institutional religious values, the years of the sectarian colleges are numbered. This would be so even if there were unhindered access to a bottomless purse.

Constitutional Protection of Private Schools

It was not until the 1920s that the States made any serious effort to challenge the right of private schools to exist and operate. On the contrary, pan-Protestantism seemed quite content with the accommodation that the Catholics maintain their own schools out of their own funds and Protestants send their children to public schools maintained out of public funds. World War I, however, brought in its wake a revival of evangelical and fundamentalist Protestant religiosity (evidenced by Prohibition, Aimee

Semple MacPherson, and "monkey laws"), nativist xeno-phobia (evidenced by the nation's first comprehensive anti-immigration law and State anti–foreign language laws), and Know-Nothingist anti-Catholicism (evidenced by the revival of the Ku Klux Klan, with the Pope added to, if not replacing, Negroes as the chief threat to the American republic and its white Protestant purity).

It was in this milieu that the people of Oregon, a State in which the Ku Klux Klan was then influential, adopted by referendum a law whose purpose was to put parochial schools out of business. It did not do so in express words; rather it accentuated the positive and eliminated the nega-tive. It did not mention parochial or private schools, but provided only that all children between the ages of eight and sixteen, with the exception of those who were "ab-normal, subnormal or physically unable to attend school," must attend public schools.

Two suits challenging the constitutionality of the law were brought in the Federal courts, one by an order of nuns who operated parochial schools, the other by a number of retired military officers and private businessmen who owned a military academy. The Supreme Court, in 1925, handed down a single decision (partly discussed in Chapter Three of this book) which became a landmark in constitutional law under the title of *Pierce* v. *Society of Sisters* (also entitled *Pierce* v. *Hill Military Academy*). No question, the Court said in invali-dating the laws, was raised concerning the power of the State reasonably to regulate all schools, to inspect, super-vise, and examine them, their teachers, and pupils, to require that all children of proper age attend some school, that teachers be of good moral character and patriotic disposition, that studies plainly essential to good citizenship be taught, and that nothing be taught which was manifestly inimical to the public welfare.

However, the Court continued, the Oregon law un-reasonably interfered with the liberty of parents to direct the upbringing of their children.

The fundamental theory of liberty upon which all governments in this Union repose excludes any general power of
the State to standardize its children by forcing them to
accept instruction from public teachers only. The child is
not the mere creature of the State; those who nurture
him and direct his destiny have the right coupled with the
high duty, to recognize and prepare him for additional
obligations.

The difficulty with that reasoning was that it was not
the parents who were suing but the operators of nonpublic
schools. (At the time of the suit, the Supreme Court had not
yet held that the Free Exercise Clause of the First Amendment was applicable to the States.) The Court hurdled this
obstacle by noting that the Fourteenth Amendment forbade
the States from depriving any person of his property without due process of law, and that under the Court's previous
decisions the right to engage in business for profit was considered "property" within the meaning of the Due Process
Clause. Even this was not entirely adequate, since the Sisters
who operated the parochial schools had taken oaths of
poverty and certainly were not engaged in a profit-making
business. The Court made no mention of this but simply
brought the Sisters under the umbrella of constitutional protection spread over the owners and operators of the Hill
Military Academy.

Thus the decision in *Pierce* v. *Society of Sisters* became the
magna carta of the American parochial school system. It
meant not only that parochial schools could not be outlawed
but, as extended two years later in the case of *Farrington* v.
Tokushige (which involved a nonreligious private school), that
they could not be so regulated in regard to their operations
as to "deny both owners and patrons reasonable choice and
discretion in respect to teachers, curriculum and textbooks."
(Two years before the *Pierce* decision the Court, in *Meyer* v.
Nebraska, had ruled that States could not prohibit the teaching of foreign languages in private schools.)

Proponents of governmental aid to parochial schools

have sought to extend it further, to make of it not merely a shield but a sword as well. They have argued quite extensively that, under the *Pierce* decision, parents have freedom of choice between secular public and religious private schools, but that this freedom is illusory and meaningless in respect to parents who are unable to pay the tuition necessary to maintain the latter. Moreover, in view of the compulsory school attendance laws requiring attendance at some school, they are deprived of their rights under the Free Exercise Clause, particularly (although this is not usually mentioned) if they adhere to the canon law which forbids attendance of Catholic children at non-Catholic or religiously mixed schools. Finally, it has been argued, to allow free tuition for children whose parents choose to send them to public schools but to refuse it to those who choose parochial schools is to deny the latter the equal protection of the laws guaranteed by the Fourteenth Amendment.

These claims have been presented to the Supreme Court on at least four occasions, and have been rejected each time. In 1962 the Court refused to accept an appeal in the case of *Dickman* v. *Oregon School District*, although the appealing parents of parochial school children claimed that the State court had held that free textbooks could not be provided for children attending parochial schools, but that they could be provided for those attending public schools or private secular schools. In the 1971 case of *Earley* v. *Di-Censo*, the Court simply passed over without mention the claim that the lower Federal court had deprived parents whose children attended parochial schools of their constitutional rights when it invalidated a Rhode Island law providing partial payment of salary to parochial school teachers. In *Brusca* v. *State Board of Education*, the Court, in 1972, affirmed without opinion a decision of a lower Federal court which held that the rights of parochial school parents under the First and Fourteenth amendments were not violated by the provisions in the Missouri constitution requiring State financing of public schools but forbidding it to parochial schools. Finally, in 1973 the Court held, in *Sloan* v. *Lemon*, that Pennsylvania could constitutionally pay the tuition of children attending private secular schools but not those in parochial schools.

State Barriers to Parochial School Aid

The Missouri constitutional provision, upheld in the *Brusca* case, was not unique. Almost every State in the Union, either in express constitutional language or by judicial interpretation, forbids use of tax-raised funds to support parochial schools. Because most of these provisions were placed into State constitutions in the 19th century when anti-Catholic bigotry flourished, and because they were generally applied in the courts against Catholic schools (hardly surprising since most private schools were Catholic), the charge is often heard that they were spawned by anti-Catholic prejudice. Typical of these provisions is Article XI, Section 3, of the New York constitution, and for that reason and the fact that this provision was the first to be the subject of a concerted Catholic Church–led effort toward repeal, it merits individual examination.

Although adopted in 1894, its origins go back to 1840, the year that Bishop Hughes strongly attacked the Protestant orientation and anti-Catholic bias of the New York public schools. Catholic children, he said, could not in good conscience attend these schools, and he therefore demanded that Catholic schools be funded equally with the public schools. Although he had the support of Governor William H. Seward, the State legislature would not go along. It nevertheless recognized the justice of Bishop Hughes' complaint, and accordingly enacted a law in 1844 directing that

> no school shall be entitled to a portion of the school moneys
> in which the religious sectarian doctrine or tenet of any
> particular Christian or other religious sect shall be taught,
> inculcated or practiced, or in which any book or books

> containing compositions favorable or prejudicial to the
> particular doctrine or tenets of any Christian sect shall be
> used, or which shall teach the doctrine or tenets of any
> other religious sect, or which shall refuse to permit the
> visits and examinations provided for in this act.

In 1894, New York engaged in a periodic re-examination and revision of its constitution, and the people adopted a new constitution which contained the following provision (now Article XI, Section 3):

> Neither the state nor any subdivision thereof shall use its
> property or credit or any public money, or authorize or
> permit either to be used, directly or indirectly, in aid or
> maintenance, other than for examination or inspection, of
> any school or institution of learning wholly or in part under
> the control or direction of any religious denomination, or
> in which any denominational tenet or doctrine is taught.

This was by no means the strictest separationist provision in a State constitution; it was limited to schools, whereas Pennsylvania, for example, forbade grants even to denominational welfare institutions such as hospitals and children's homes. Nevertheless, it was quite emphatic, particularly by reason of the word "indirectly." It was the presence of this word that in 1922 led to a State court decision prohibiting the use by parochial school children of publicly purchased textbooks, and in 1938 (another constitution-revision year) to a decision invalidating a bus transportation law. The new constitution adopted by the people in 1938 overruled the bus decision by adding to the quoted section of Article XI the words "but the legislature may provide for the transportation of children to and from any school or institution of learning."

In 1966, on the recommendation of Governor Nelson Rockefeller and in disregard of the State attorney-general's opinion of probable unconstitutionality under Article XI, the legislature enacted a textbook loan law for nonpublic schools. A lower court judge agreed with the attorney-gen-

eral and ruled the law unconstitutional, but 1966 was another year for constitutional revision, and if the 1938
precedent were to be followed, textbooks would be added to
transportation as a permissible expenditure of public funds.

However, the Catholic Church in New York was now
after bigger game; it called for the complete repeal of
Article XI, Section 3, which it assailed as a product of 19th
century anti-Catholic bigotry. *America* gave it the name
"Blaine Amendment" and explained:

> The clause takes its name from Congressman (and later
> Presidential candidate) James G. Blaine, who in 1875 intro-
> duced a proposed amendment to the U.S. Constitution; it
> was designed to freeze the then Protestant-dominated public
> school system in a position of permanent superiority by
> prohibiting the states from aiding church-related (i.e.,
> Catholic) schools. The Blaine Amendment failed to pass Con-
> gress but found its way into many state constitutions in the
> late 19th century, when the tide of anti-Catholic nativism
> was still strong. . . . Is it not time to recognize this clause
> for what it is: an outmoded, archaic relic of 19th century
> prejudice?

There was another reason for attaching the name
Blaine to the clause. During the presidential campaign of
1888, a Protestant minister speaking for Blaine at a New
York rally, referred to the Democrats as the party of "Rum,
Romanism and Rebellion," and since then "Blaine" became a
symbol for anti-Catholicism in American politics.

Recognizing that an outright appeal of Article XI,
Section 3, without any substitute would not likely be accepted, the Church proposed that in its place the language of
the First Amendment be adopted. The State constitutional
convention agreed, and the proposed new constitution contained no "Blaine Amendment" but forbade "any law respecting an establishment of religion or prohibiting the free
exercise thereof." It was assumed that this language would
give the legislature far greater latitude in providing aid for
parochial schools than mere bus transportation and text-

books. The Supreme Court had announced the purpose-effect test in the *Schempp* decision of 1963 and Congress had relied on this to provide generous benefits for parochial school children in the 1965 Elementary and Secondary Education Act. Moreover, State Attorney-General Louis Lefkowitz, who had ruled against the textbook law, rendered an opinion that the State could administer funds received under the Federal law since they were not State funds and therefore not subject to the more rigid restrictions of Article XI, Section 3.

The new constitution was presented to the people in November 1967, but was rejected overwhelmingly; the ratio was 3 to 1 against it. The "Blaine Amendment" was by far the most debated single provision in the proposed constitution. (The opposition had been led by a broad alliance of educational, libertarian, Protestant, and Jewish organizations called the Committee for Public Education and Religious Liberty or, for short, PEARL.) The Church spent a great amount of effort and large sums of money in the campaign for its adoption. Nevertheless, it claimed that the referendum was not a fair test and argued that the rejection was based upon other provisions. It announced, therefore, that it would seek to prevail upon the legislature to present the repeal and substitution to the people as a separate and independent constitutional amendment. The legislature complied quickly. For a New York constitutional amendment to be presented to the people it must first be passed by the legislature in two successive sessions. With little debate the proposal was approved at the 1970 session of the legislature, but surprisingly never reached the second session. Between the two sessions, the Church announced that it would no longer seek repeal of "Blaine," for to do so would cause divisiveness and exacerbate interreligious tensions. Instead, it would work within the confines of "Blaine" on a more liberal interpretation of that clause by the New York courts.

What made the Church's change of position surprising was the fact that the *Allen* decision upholding the constitutionality of New York's textbook law seemed to validate the most optimistic expectations on the elasticity of the purpose-effect test to encompass far more liberal aid to parochial schools than merely textbooks. The language of the Court's opinion, even more than the decision itself, presented a great incentive to push forward in the campaign to replace "Blaine" with the Establishment Clause language and, implicitly, with its liberal interpretation in the *Allen* decision. The Church, nevertheless, seemed to have given up the battle when victory appeared to be in sight. What may help to explain this is that, in the interim, Nebraska had voted down in popular referendum a similar proposal to liberalize that State's "Blaine Amendment," and that in Michigan the voters had gone further and, overruling a pro-aid decision of their State court, tightened their constitutional prohibition against aid. The Church in New York may well have reconsidered its previously optimistic expectation of victory at the polls, and decided to operate within "Blaine," particularly after Governor Rockefeller assured it that, notwithstanding "Blaine," means would be found to provide State funds for parochial schools.

Federal Aid

Education in the United States has traditionally been a matter of State and local concern. Nevertheless, from the beginnings of our nationhood the Federal government has participated to some degree in its financing. At first the Federal contribution took the form of turning over to the States government-owned land or its proceeds to establish public schools or colleges. Later Congress from time to time adopted a variety of programs for Federal aid to special types of educational activity, such as nautical education, aeronautical education, nurses' training, veterans' aid, and specific research projects. It was, however, not until the 1880s that serious efforts began to be made to enact legislation providing general Federal aid to education.

These efforts were strongly contested not only by conservative business interests, represented by such organizations as the United States Chamber of Commerce, but also by the Catholic Church. Opponents of the Church charged that its opposition was motivated by the fear that added funds to public schools would enhance the competitive attraction of public schools for Catholic children, who—according to Catholic teaching—belonged exclusively in parochial schools. The Church, however, stated that its principal ground for opposition was fear of centralized control of education in Washington, which, the Church argued, was an inevitable consequence of Federal financial support. This coalition of conservative business interests and the Catholic Church frustrated all efforts to obtain Federal funds for public schools for some sixty years.

In 1937, however, a change in the position of the Church was indicated, almost accidentally and unnoticed. In testifying before a Congressional committee on a Federal aid measure, the General Secretary of the National Catholic Welfare Conference demanded that the bill be amended to include parochial schools as beneficiaries. Although the rest of his testimony was apparently in unqualified opposition to all bills for Federal aid, it was not long before it became evident that his impromptu interpolation would mark a new position of the Church, and that Federal aid, instead of being a threat to the Church, would be a possible source of badly needed financial assistance to parochial education. The turnabout was complete in 1949, when the National Catholic Welfare Conference issued a formal statement that "By authority of the general-welfare clause of the Constitution, the Federal Government has an obligation to secure for every American child, regardless of his place of residence, an opportunity for an adequate education."

Unfortunately, the defection of the Church from its alliance with big business accomplished no more than to replace one roadblock with another. Catholic endorsement of Federal aid to education was conditional upon inclusion of parochial schools as beneficiaries, and this was strongly opposed by the Protestant-Jewish-humanist (civil liberties and public education) alliance. Neither side was politically powerful enough to work its will on Congress, but each was able to prevent the other side from doing so. Not until 1965 was a breakthrough achieved in the Elementary and Secondary Education Act of that year.

A number of factors contributed to the victory: the earlier partial breakthroughs in the National Defense Education Act of 1958, the Higher Education Facilities Act of 1963, and the Economic Opportunity Act of 1964, each of which made some provision for participation by nonpublic institutions: the political astuteness of President Johnson; the Vatican II ecumenism which placed upon many Protestants an imperative to meet Catholicism halfway; and the fact that the bill did not purport to grant Federal aid to education generally but only to provide educational services for disadvantaged children living in urban slums and low-income rural areas. In any event, the measure was supported by most Protestant denominational leaders, the Catholic Church, the National Education Association, organized labor, and practically every major newspaper in the country. Jewish organizations were about the only dissenters; and even there the formerly united ranks had split, with the Orthodox wing expressing its support for the measure. In these circumstances it was hardly surprising that the bill soon passed with little difficulty.

Basically, the Elementary and Secondary Education Act of 1965 authorizes the expenditure of large sums of Federal funds to provide special educational services and books for educationally deprived children of low-income families. The act is administered in each State by its public educational agencies, which decide how the funds should be used. (In practice, most of the State agencies have elected to use the funds primarily to provide remedial reading and arithmetic to pupils below grade level in these subjects.) The major church-state problem raised by the act is the provision that, in order for a public educational agency to receive a grant, it must satisfy the United States Commissioner of Education

> that, to the extent consistent with the number of education-ally deprived children in the school district of the local educational agency who are enrolled in private elementary and secondary schools, such agency has made provision for including special educational services and arrangements (such as dual enrollment, educational radio and television, and mobile educational services and equipment) in which such children can participate.

(Dual enrollment, sometimes called shared time, is a program under which children can enroll simultaneously in both public and nonpublic schools, taking some courses in one and the balance in the other.)

Apparently, this means that if 15 percent of the disadvantaged children in a particular neighborhood attend nonpublic (including parochial) schools, then 15 percent of the Federal funds granted for that neighborhood must be used to provide "special educational services and arrangements" in which the nonpublic school children can participate.

Standing to Sue

Congress was not unaware of the church-state problem raised by the act. Separationists, recognizing that they could not prevail in their efforts to limit its scope to public schools, urged that, at the very least, Congress add a provision to make possible a judicial resolution of the problem. It was assumed that without such a provision the Federal courts, and ultimately the Supreme Court, would be unable to review the law and pass judgment on its constitutionality since in 1923, the Court, in the case of *Frothingham* v. *Mellon*, had ruled that a mere taxpayer did not have standing to challenge in the Federal courts a Congressional expenditure alleged to be in violation of the Constitution. Senator Sam

Ervin strongly urged the inclusion of a provision allowing judicial review, but it was opposed by the spokesmen for the Catholic Church, who argued that such a judicial review of Congressional expenditures should not be limited to one particular measure but should be made a rule of universal applicability. Persuaded of the validity of this objection or, perhaps, not overly confident that the act would survive judicial scrutiny, Congress turned down Senator Ervin's proposed amendment and passed the bill without any provision for judicial review.

Undaunted, Senator Ervin did introduce a measure providing generally for judicial review of Congressional expenditures in suits by taxpayers challenging their constitutionality. Public hearings were held on the proposal and expert witnesses testified for and against it. Sometimes, however, the mills of the legislatures grind even more slowly than those of the judiciary, and before the Senate had an opportunity to vote on the Ervin bill, the Supreme Court, in 1968, handed down its decision in the case of *Flast* v. *Cohen*.

In the *Frothingham* case (also known as *Massachusetts* v. *Mellon*), a taxpayer brought suit in a Federal court challenging the constitutionality of a law passed by Congress providing for payments to help poor mothers pay the medical costs attendant upon giving birth. The plaintiff, Mrs. Frothingham, contended that if any part of her tax-money was used to pay for bringing other people's babies into the world, then she was being deprived of her property without due process of law. The Supreme Court threw her case out on the ground that while a person who was directly affected by a law could sue to have it declared unconstitutional, such a suit could not be brought by one whose only relationship to the law lay in the fact that she paid taxes into the general treasury and that the costs of administering the law came out of the general treasury.

With few exceptions, the State courts did not follow the *Frothingham* decision and did allow taxpayers to sue. It was not clear whether, if a State allowed such a suit but ruled the challenged law constitutional, the taxpayer-plaintiff could appeal to the Supreme Court. However, it was universally taken for granted that a taxpayer could not sue initially in a Federal court and that there was no way to challenge the constitutionality of a Federal law, including the Elementary and Secondary Education Act of 1965, other than by a suit brought initially in a Federal court.

Nevertheless, in 1967 a group of taxpayers, under the sponsorship of the American Jewish Congress, the American Civil Liberties Union, the United Parents Association of New York, and the United Federation of Teachers, started a suit in a Federal court in New York for judgment declaring unconstitutional that part of the Elementary and Secondary Education Act which included parochial schools as beneficiaries. The court dismissed the complaint on the ground that under the rule in the *Frothingham* case the plaintiffs as taxpayers did not have standing to sue. The plaintiffs appealed to the Supreme Court and, in June 1968, that Court handed down its landmark decision in the case of *Flast* v. *Cohen.*

It was a landmark decision because the Court, while not expressly overruling the *Frothingham* decision, held that taxpayers would be allowed to sue in the Federal courts to prevent use of Federal funds in violation of the Establishment Clause. The Court thereby opened the door which Congress had thought it had kept firmly closed when it turned down Senator Ervin's amendment. (The Supreme Court did not pass on the constitutionality of the act itself, since the lower court had not done so, and at present writing the constitutional issue has still not been definitively passed on by the Supreme Court.)

The Supreme Court, however, did more than merely open the door for suits against the Elementary and Secondary Act or even other Federal laws appropriating funds for the benefit of sectarian institutions (such as the Higher Education Facilities Act of 1963). It opened the door wide enough to allow similar suits aimed at State laws. With a few exceptions, all of the cases which will be examined in the rest of this chapter were made possible by the Court's decision in *Flast* v. *Cohen*.

Parochial Bus Transportation and Indirect Aid

On the same day that the Court announced its decision in the *Flast* case it also handed down its decision in the *Allen* case. The net result of the two cases taken together—and so it was widely interpreted—was that litigating separationists were welcome to come into the Federal courts but would not find anything worthwhile when they did. However, before we consider the *Allen* case, we must consider in more detail the specific holding of the *Everson* case in which the Court passed upon the use of governmental funds to support, directly or indirectly, the operations of parochial schools.

An earlier case, *Quick Bear* v. *Leupp*, decided in 1908, should be noted briefly. During the course of American history considerable Indian-owned land had been taken over by the Federal government and more or less paid for by it. Not being convinced that the Indians were really sufficiently mature to take care of their own money, the government held it in trust for them. In the *Quick Bear* case the Court held that the government as trustee could constitutionally pay from these moneys the tuition at private religious schools which the Indians wished their children to attend. The expenditures were valid because the funds belonged to the Indians and not to the government, and they had the right to use their own money to educate their children in the schools of their own choice, even if the government could not disburse its own money to the same schools. (The same reasoning is applicable to the World War II G.I. Bill of Rights, under which the government paid the tuition of veterans at schools of their own choice, including even theological seminaries.)

Bus transportation, the question involved in the *Ever-*

son case, stands on a different footing. The funds used for it came from the State's treasury and got there through taxation of all citizens. The suit brought by Arch Everson, resident and taxpayer in the Trenton suburb of Ewing, was based on the claim that under the Establishment Clause his tax payments, no matter how small, could not be used to finance the operation of religious schools.

All nine members of the Court agreed with his basic premise; but they disagreed sharply on whether the premise was relevant to the question before them. Five of the justices were of the view that this was not at all the purpose of the New Jersey law. Its purpose was to enable children to "ride in public buses to and from schools rather than run the risk of traffic and other hazards incident to walking or hitchhiking," and this obviously was within the State's constitutional power. It served the same purpose as stationing policemen or traffic lights at busy intersections.

It is true, Justice Black continued for the majority, that if the State did not provide transportation to the parochial schools the latter might have to do so themselves or parents might be unwilling to send their children to the schools. But the same would be the case if the State did not place traffic lights or station policemen at intersections adjacent to the church schools, and nobody would contend that it would be unconstitutional for the State to do this not only at church schools but at churches themselves. The purpose of the law is to protect children; whatever aid inures to the schools is indirect.

The difficulty with Justice Black's rationale, as pointed out by Justices Jackson and Rutledge in their dissenting opinions, was that it was unrealistic. The law did not provide transportation for children on the streets, but only for those going to school, public or private. A child going to visit a friend or to a motion picture theater is just as much subject to the hazards of the road as one going to school. The Ewing board of education did not supply buses to transport children to schools; it simply paid their fare on public buses, but only if they were on their way to school.

It would therefore seem fallacious to equate—as Justice Black did—bus transportation and police protection. The purpose of supplying traffic police is to protect children from accidents; all children are protected, Catholic and Protestants, believers and nonbelievers. But the purpose of supplying bus transportation is to get children to school, not (at least, primarily) to protect them from traffic hazards. Transportation to schools is generally provided in rural rather than urban areas, which indicates that distance rather than traffic hazards is the motivating consideration. The New Jersey statute under attack did not mention traffic hazards, but provided only for transportation "whenever in any district there are children living *remote* from any schoolhouse. . . ." If the purpose of supplying bus transportation is to protect children from traffic accidents, the State can constitutionally supply free transportation not merely to church schools but to churches as well—just as it can constitutionally supply traffic police protection on the streets leading to churches.

As Justice Rutledge pointed out, the logical application of the Court's approach would nullify the First Amendment guaranty of the separation of church and state. If transportation to church schools can be justified under the state's police power to provide for the welfare of children, so also can many other expenditures. Fire hazards are not less dangerous than traffic hazards. Why then may not the state provide for the fireproofing of all schools which children attend? Why too may it not pay for the repair of unsafe walls and ceilings—and where repair is impracticable, for their replacement? When the *Everson* decision is coupled with the *Allen* decision they lead logically to the conclusion that a State may, notwithstanding the First Amendment, finance practically every aspect of parochial education, with the exception of such comparatively minor items as the pro-

portionate salaries of teachers while they teach the catechism and the cost of holy fonts and junior missals.

As we have already seen, many protagonists of aid to
parochial schools did in fact so interpret the *Everson-Allen*
combination. So, too, as we will shortly see, did Justice
White, the author of the *Allen* opinion. The rest of the Court,
however, has refused to go along. Indeed, in the *Engel* case,
Justice Douglas, whose vote helped make up the five-man
majority in the *Everson* case, expressed regret for his action
and indicated that had he another opportunity he would
vote the other way. The other members of the Court, however, have not accepted the invitation, and on several occasions have turned down appeals from State court decisions upholding bus transportation on the basis of the
Everson decision. It is fair to say that the constitutionality of
bus transportation under the Establishment Clause is now
the law of the land and likely to remain so for some time to
come. (This does not mean that bus transportation may not
be held invalid under State constitutions. As a matter of
fact, in the majority of cases which have arisen since *Everson*
was decided, the State courts ruled that parochial bus
transportation laws did violate their State constitutions.)

Textbooks and the *Allen* Decision

The question whether it is constitutional to use public funds for the purchase of textbooks supplied for use by
pupils of private schools first came to the Supreme Court
in 1930. In that year, the Court held in *Cochran* v. *Louisiana
State Board of Education* that such use did not violate the
Constitution. The suit was brought seventeen years before
the Court ruled in the *Everson* case that the Establishment
Clause was applicable to the States as well as to the Federal
government. The basis for the suit, therefore, was not the
First Amendment but, as in the *Pierce* case, the provision in
the Fourteenth Amendment forbidding States from depriv-

ing persons of life, liberty, or property without due process of law. The plaintiff argued that use of public funds for a private purpose deprived taxpayers of their money unlawfully to the same extent as it would if the State had forcibly taken their money and turned it over to private persons or institutions.

The Louisiana court rejected the argument and upheld the law on the basis of what later became known as the "child benefit" theory. It was well expressed by the court in the following language:

> One may scan the acts in vain to ascertain where any money is appropriated for the purchase of school books for the use of any church, private, sectarian, or even public school. The appropriations were made for the specific purpose of purchasing schoolbooks for the use of the school children of the State, free of cost to them. It was for their benefit and the resulting benefit to the State that the appropriations were made. True, these children attend some school, public or private, the latter sectarian or non-sectarian, and that the books are to be furnished them for their use, free of cost, whichever they attend. The schools, however, are not the beneficiaries of these appropriations. They obtain nothing from them, nor are they relieved of a single obligation because of them. The school children and the State alone are the beneficiaries.

The Supreme Court in the *Cochran* case quoted these paragraphs and adopted them as its own. The legislation, it added, did not segregate private schools, or their pupils as its beneficiaries, or attempt to interfere with any matters of exclusive private concern. Its interest was education, broadly; its method, comprehensive. To the extent that individual interests were aided, it was only as part of the general or common interest.

Since the *Cochran* case did not raise any church-state issues and none was decided by the Court, the decision was not a binding precedent when the *Allen* case reached it. The

attack on the New York textbook law in the latter case was
based exclusively on the claim that it violated church-state
separation as constitutionally protected by the Establishment
Clause of the First Amendment. The *Everson* case did, of
course, deal with church-state separation and was decided
on the basis of the Establishment Clause, but the plaintiffs
in the *Allen* case claimed that transportation and books were
constitutionally different; the former related to welfare, the
latter to education.

The Supreme Court, in an opinion by Justice White,
disagreed. Of course, he said, "books are different from
buses. Most buses have no inherent religious significance,
while religious books are common." However, the New
York law did not authorize the loan of religious books; all
books loaned had to be approved by the public school authorities and only secular books could receive approval. Put
somewhat differently, the view of Justice White was that,
regarding the First Amendment, there was no difference
between a nonsectarian book and a nonsectarian bus.

The test to be applied, said Justice White, was the
purpose-effect test set forth in the *Schempp* case. Under that
test, the New York law was constitutional, for neither its
purpose nor its primary effect was to advance religion.
Moreover, no funds or books were furnished to parochial
schools; the books were loaned by the State to the children,
and the financial benefit was to parents and children, not to
schools. Perhaps, Justice White continued, free books made it
more likely that some children would choose to attend a
sectarian school, but that was also true of free bus service in
the *Everson* case, and the Court there held that this alone
did not indicate an unconstitutional support of the school.

Justice Black, the author of the *Everson* decision (a fact
which he pointedly noted in his dissenting opinion), did not
agree. To him there was a vital distinction between books
and buses:

> Books [he said] are the most essential tool of education
> since they contain the resources of knowledge which the

educational process is designed to exploit. In this sense it is not difficult to distinguish books, which are the heart of any school, from bus fares, which provide a convenient and helpful general public transportation service. With respect to the former, State financial support actively and directly assists the teaching and propagation of sectarian religious viewpoints in clear conflict with the First Amendment's establishment bar; with respect to the latter, the State merely provides a general and nondiscriminatory transportation in no way related to substantive religious views and beliefs.

The Significance of *Allen*

What did the *Allen* decision signify? Looked at one way, it denoted very little if anything at all. It held that a State could lend secular textbooks to children attending parochial schools, but it had already held that in the *Cochran* case almost forty years earlier; all that the *Allen* decision added was another justification for the same ruling. That, indeed, is how opponents of parochial school aid publicly interpreted the decision in the three-year interim between it and the *Lemon-DiCenso* cases.

This, however, was whistling in the dark. By their interpretation of the *Allen* decision, the anti-aid forces apparently accepted the child-benefit theory as part of our constitutional law. But applied logically and consistently—and as we will see, this is what Justice White intended—there is very little aid to the operations of parochial schools that could not be justified under it. It was the child-benefit theory that the proponents of the Elementary and Secondary Education Act of 1965 used to defend its constitutionality, and it was the acceptance by the National Council of Churches of this theory that enabled it to support the measure and thus assure its adoption.

However, the special services authorized by the act and the textbooks provided for under the New York law were not the only benefits received by pupils in schools. Since everything that goes on in both private and public schools is presumably for the benefit of the children, practically everything (exclusive of religious "benefit") in the private schools can be financed with public funds, as is everything in the public schools.

It was at this point that the decision appeared most devastating to the claims of the anti-aid partisans, for Justice White expressly and emphatically rejected the assertion that all education in parochial schools is permeated with religion. We cannot assume, he said, "either that all teaching in a sectarian school is religious or that the processes of secular and religious training are so intertwined that secular textbooks furnished to students by the public are in fact instrumental in the teaching of religion." In the *Pierce* case the Court had ruled that while a State may require all children to receive a basic elementary secular education, it could not forbid them to receive it in parochial schools. That ruling constituted a recognition by the Court "that religious schools pursue two goals, religious instruction and secular instruction."

What followed from this was even more devastating. If, said Justice White, a State must accept the secular education available in parochial schools as meeting the standards required of public schools, it has the same power to finance the former as the latter. Then came the following testimonial for parochial school education:

> Underlying these cases, and underlying also the legislative judgments that have preceded the court decisions, has been a recognition that private education has played and is playing a significant and valuable role in raising national levels of knowledge, competence, and experience. Americans care about the quality of the secular education available to their children. They have considered high quality education to be an indispensable ingredient for achieving the kind of nation, and the kind of citizenry, that they have desired to create. Considering this attitude, the continued willingness to rely on private school systems, including parochial systems, strongly suggests that a wide segment of informed opinion,

legislative and otherwise, has found that those schools do an acceptable job of providing secular education to their students. This judgment is further evidence that parochial schools are performing, in addition to their sectarian function, the task of secular education.

The pro-aid groups could hardly have expected more. They might have hoped for a ruling upholding their claim that the *Pierce* decision *required* the States to finance the secular operations of parochial schools to the same extent as public schools. Such a ruling would have removed the barrier of State constitutional prohibitions since they would have to yield to the superior command of the Federal Constitution, but most pro-aid realists recognized that it was not in the cards. However, notwithstanding the defeat of the proposed New York 1967 constitution which omitted the "Blaine" provision, it was still widely felt that with added effort and persistence many State constitutional prohibitions of aid to parochial schools could be repealed, and the Supreme Court's warm endorsement of private schools in the *Allen* decision would surely be a valuable weapon in the campaigns for repeal. Moreover, the ease with which the Elementary and Secondary Act of 1965 sailed through the Congress and the textbook law through the New York legislature, notwithstanding grave constitutional doubts in both instances, evidenced a widespread legislative willingness to cooperate in avoiding or evading "Blaine" restrictions.

Even before the *Allen* decision, the pro-aid forces, particularly the Catholic Church, had added another string to their bow. Previously they had asserted that "Blaine" restrictions were the product of anti-Catholic bigotry, that parochial school children were the victims of discrimination, and that double taxation was unjust. Implicit (and sometimes explicit), in addition, was the political power of the Catholics and their allies; the names of those who voted for and against aid would not be forgotten on the first Tuesday after the first Monday in November. The new string was economy. These legislators, as well as voters at the polls, who were reluctant to approve aid measures because they feared the added burden on taxpayers were warned that should lack of funds force the parochial schools to close and send their children into the public schools, the added financial burden on the taxpayers would far exceed the cost of grants to parochial schools to enable them to stay open and keep operating. There is no doubt that this warning carried great weight with legislators. The Pennsylvania law invalidated in the *Lemon* case included in its preamble the dire prediction that

> should a majority of the parents of the present nonpublic school population desire to remove their children to the public schools of the Commonwealth, an intolerable added financial burden to the public would result, as well as school stoppages and long term derangement and impairment of education in Pennsylvania.

Teachers' Salaries, *Lemon* and *DiCenso*

The optimism of the pro-aid forces was well-founded. The *Allen* decision opened a floodgate of State bills for the financing of private school operations. The first of these adopted was the Pennsylvania law, approved by the governor of the State on June 19, 1968, exactly nine days after the *Allen* decision was announced. That decision, as we have noted, did not affect "Blaine" restrictions in State constitutions, including the stringent one in Pennsylvania which forbade appropriations to or use of public funds for the support of any sectarian institution. It was therefore necessary to devise some means whereby the operations of the parochial school could be financed without granting funds directly to the school or using them for its support. The framers of the Pennsylvania law accomplished this, or thought they did, by a purchase-sale arrangement.

The rationale was quite simple and logical. The State of

Pennsylvania, like all the other States in the Union, had undertaken to provide all children with a secular education. In most cases this was done by assembling the children in publicly owned buildings and providing the instruction through publicly employed teachers. But there was no reason it could not be done in another way, such as providing the instruction in places other than the publicly owned buildings. All that need be done was to make a contract with private school authorities under which they would sell their secular educational services to the State and deliver these services by teaching secular subjects to the children in their particular schools. To make sure that the services purchased were entirely secular, the law limited the subjects taught to mathematics, modern foreign languages, physical science, and physical education, and provided that the necessary textbooks and other instructional materials had to be approved by the State superintendent of public instruction. The transaction did not violate the Establishment Clause, since both the purpose and effect were secular and neither advanced religion. Nor did it transgress upon Pennsylvania's "Blaine Amendment," since a purchase of secular teaching services was not a grant of funds any more than a purchase of painting, heating, cleaning, or repair services would be.

Rhode Island, for whatever reason, adopted a more direct and less ingenious method of accomplishing its secular purpose. Its law, enacted in May 1969, authorized supplementing the salaries of teachers of secular subjects in nonpublic schools by paying directly to each teacher 15 percent of his current annual salary. Only teachers in poor schools (i.e., where the average per-pupil expenditure on secular subjects was less than the public school average) were eligible for salary supplements, and in addition they were required to sign an agreement that they would not teach religion so long as they received salary supplements.

Taxpayers in both States sued in the Federal courts to declare the laws unconstitutional. Initially they succeeded in Rhode Island but failed in Pennsylvania, and in both cases the losing parties appealed to the Supreme Court. The appeals in both cases, *Lemon* v. *Kurtzman* in Pennsylvania and *Earley* v. *DiCenso* in Rhode Island, came to the Supreme Court at the same time and a single opinion, written by Chief Justice Burger, covered both cases. With only Justice White dissenting, both laws were held unconstitutional.

According to the purpose-effect test that had been announced in the *Schempp* case and applied in the *Allen* case, a law is valid under the Establishment Clause if its purpose is secular and its principal or primary effect neither advances nor inhibits religion. The *Walz* tax exemption case, however, had added another dimension; it required also that the law must not foster excessive government entanglement with religion. It was this late addition that proved to be the insurmountable barrier. The Court accepted the statement of the legislatures in both Pennsylvania and Rhode Island that their purpose was only to aid the secular education of children attending parochial schools and in no way to advance religion. In the Pennsylvania case, the lower court had ruled that the primary or principal effect of the law was the same as its purpose; that the law did no more than help children get better secular instruction, and that it was therefore constitutional. In the *DiCenso* case, on the other hand, the lower court ruled to the contrary and held that by helping finance the operations of the religious schools a primary or principal effect of the Rhode Island law was to advance religion.

The Chief Justice and his colleagues, with the exception of Justice White, found it unnecessary to resolve this conflict between the two lower Federal courts. At the trial in the Rhode Island case (there was no trial in the Pennsylvania suit), the plaintiffs had introduced evidence, to which we have referred earlier in this chapter, that religion permeated all the teaching in the parochial schools, including that which was nominally secular, and therefore aid even to the secular teaching advanced religion. On the other hand, several teachers had testified that they did not inject religion into their secular classes, and the lower court itself had found that religious values did not affect the content of the secular instruction.

The Chief Justice accepted this finding. We need not and do not assume, he said, that teachers in parochial schools will be guilty of bad faith or any conscious design to evade the limitation imposed by the First Amendment.

> We simply recognize that a dedicated religious person, teaching in a school affiliated with his or her faith and operated to inculcate its tenets, will inevitably experience great difficulty in remaining religiously neutral. Doctrines and faith are not inculcated or advanced by neutrals. With the best of intentions such a teacher would find it hard to make a total separation between secular teaching and religious doctrine. What would appear to some to be essential to good citizenship might well for others border on or constitute instruction in religion.

The only way to avoid this was by subjecting the parochial school teachers to a comprehensive, discriminating, and continuing State surveillance. Unlike textbooks, involved in the *Allen* case, a teacher could not be examined once and for all to determine the extent of his or her commitment either to religion or to the First Amendment; nothing less than continuing surveillance would assure that the restrictions of the amendment were honored and complied with. But that very surveillance would involve the excessive entanglement between state and church which the Court in the *Walz* decision held violated the Establishment Clause. In the *Lemon* case, for example, in order to assure that the State funds would not be used to finance religious instruction, the law subjected the financial records of the parochial schools to State inspection so that it could be determined which expenditures were religious and which secular, thereby creating "an intimate and continuing relationship between church and state."

The Chief Justice referred also to another type of entanglement which, he said, the Establishment Clause was intended to prevent. Ordinarily, political debate and division, though vigorous or even partisan, were normal and healthy manifestations of our democratic system of government; political division along religious lines, however, was one of the principal evils against which the First Amendment was intended to protect. To have States or communities divide on the issues of aid to parochial schools would tend to confuse and obscure other issues of great urgency. The history of many countries attested to the hazards of religion's intruding into the political arena or of political power intruding into the legitimate and free exercise of religion. The Establishment Clause forbade political as well as other forms of entanglement between church and state.

Justice White was the lone dissenter. He could see no difference between what the Court allowed in the *Allen* case and what it barred in the *Lemon* and *DiCenso* cases. He wrote the opinion in the *Allen* case and there can be little doubt that he intended it to give the States practically *carte blanche* in aiding parochial schools, so long as the aid was designated secular.

The *Lemon* and *DiCenso* decisions were handed down on June 28, 1971. Two days later, in the case of *Sanders* v. *Johnson*, the Court affirmed without opinion a lower Federal court ruling that a Connecticut law similar to those of Pennsylvania and Rhode Island violated the Establishment Clause.

Within perhaps an hour or two after the *Lemon-DiCenso* decision was reported over radio and television, Governor Nelson Rockefeller of New York signed into law without comment a measure identical with the Pennsylvania, Rhode Island, and Connecticut laws. PEARL, the organization that led the campaign against the repeal of the "Blaine Amendment" and continued in existence and operation after achieving success, promptly brought suit in a Federal court to declare the new law unconstitutional, and to the surprise of no one, won its suit. The State of New York did not even bother to appeal, recognizing that it would be a futile effort, but the governor had made his gesture. The incident is reported here only to show how quickly was validated the Chief Justice's opinion in respect to religiopolitical entanglement. (Even more clear validation is manifested by the report in the *New York Times* of Congressman Mills' tax credit proposal, which we quoted in Chapter Two of this book.)

Game Plan After *Lemon-DiCenso*

Two years after the *Lemon-DiCenso* decision, Justice White declared that he was "quite unreconciled" to it. His disappointment was shared, undoubtedly even more deeply, by the Catholic Church, Orthodox Jewry, and other supporters of aid to parochial schools. The high hopes raised by the *Allen* opinion were, if not dashed, certainly gravely threatened. Justice White had based his decision on two pillars: the rejection of permeation, and the assertion that parochial schools serve a secular purpose independent of their religious functions. From this dual premise it followed, according to him, that government could constitutionally finance the schools' secular purpose. In the *Lemon-DiCenso* cases, however, all the other members of the Court rejected the conclusion without disturbing the premises. They accomplished this by holding that in order to prevent possible permeation and insure the independence of the secular functions, the government would have to engage in comprehensive and continuing surveillance, and this by itself would bring on excessive entanglement of state and church and therefore unconstitutionality under the Establishment Clause.

While disappointed, neither the school-aid proponents nor cooperative legislatures were ready to give up the struggle. The lawyers went back to the drawing boards and came up with quite a number of variations on the same theme. In the *Lemon* decision the Court said that it would not allow the

Everson and *Allen* decisions to be "used as a platform for yet further steps" in aid to institutions "whose interests have substantial political support." What the Court meant by this was that political pressure notwithstanding, bus transportation and textbooks were about as far as it would allow the States to go.

Still, there was no harm in trying, and even if all particular efforts ultimately proved unsuccessful the game could nevertheless show a profit. Theoretically, at least, an unconstitutional law is no law, and those who receive money from the government under it are legally liable to repay it after the law is declared unconstitutional. But after the *DiCenso* and *Sanders* cases were decided by the Supreme Court, the attorneys-general in Rhode Island and Connecticut found that it would cost more money to try to get the funds back from the parochial schools than to forget about the whole thing. In Pennsylvania, the attorney-general went even further; not only did he not call upon the schools to return the money they had received, but he sought and received permission from the Court to pay to them the balance of the money that had been appropriated for the school year following the *Lemon* decision.

A game plan emerged. Pass a law providing aid to parochial schools and start paying immediately or as quickly as possible. Continue paying until the Supreme Court finally declares the law unconstitutional. It may take a year or more before a suit is started to challenge the law, and perhaps another two years until the case gets to the Supreme Court. In the meantime, keep paying. When the law is finally struck down by the Supreme Court, rush some variation through the legislature and start over again. This pattern was followed in New York, Pennsylvania, Ohio, and Connecticut, among others.

Mandated Services

In New York the game started even before the *Lemon-DiCenso-Sanders* decisions. In 1970 the legislature passed a law appropriating some $28 million to pay parochial schools for the expenses incurred by them in maintaining records and conducting examinations. The money was to be distributed among the schools at the rate of $27 for each pupil in grades 1 through 6, and $45 per pupil in grades 7 through 12. The theory of the law was that since the State mandates all schools, private no less than public, to maintain records of the pupils' attendance, health, grades, etc., and to conduct examinations from time to time to measure the pupils' achievement, and since the State pays these expenses for pupils in public schools, it would be only fair to do the same for pupils in private schools.

Why was this particular method chosen to subsidize the operations of parochial schools? After all, the State mandated not only that records be kept and examinations conducted, but also that teachers teach, and the State paid for the teachers in public schools as well as for record keeping and examinations. The answer lies in the language of the "Blaine Amendment," which forbade appropriations in aid of sectarian schools "other than for examination or inspection." Governor Rockefeller and the legislative leaders assumed that if the State constitution permitted payment "for examination or inspection," it also allowed payment for recording and reporting the results of the examinations and inspections.

How was the $27/45 formula arrived at? Nobody but Governor Rockefeller and his close advisers knew for sure. The court records show that prior to the enactment of the law, a conference had been held in which the governor's counsel asked representatives of the State department of education whether the formula was "reasonable" and the latter replied that it was, and that "no record of the conference was made." The most probable explanation is to be found in the promises made by the governor to the representatives of the Catholic Church that he would find some means to provide funds to the parochial schools, that he determined that he could spare $28 million from his 1970–71 budget and instructed his aides to work out a formula by which that amount could be distributed to the schools, and that out of their computations came the $27/45 formula.

After the law was passed, the State department of education instituted a cost analysis of mandated services in the nonpublic schools and concluded that the $27/45 figures were fully justified. It should be noted, though, that the analysis accepted items such as $10,000 to maintain a convent at one school and $7,000 to pay for Sisters' transportation at another.

All for naught; the Federal district court in New York declared the law unconstitutional and the Supreme Court affirmed its decision. Yet, the schools began receiving money under the law in 1970 and continued to receive it until April 1972, when the district court acted. Moreover, after this happened the State legislature passed a new law authorizing the schools to sue the State and recover the amounts payable for the second half of the 1971-72 school year.

The Supreme Court decision declaring the mandated service law unconstitutional, *Levitt* v. *Committee for Public Education and Religious Liberty* (PEARL), was handed down on June 25, 1973. Only Justice White dissented. The cost analyses had shown that most of the moneys paid under the law were used to finance the conducting of the usual teacher-prepared tests and examinations with which all pupils are familiar, and only a small part, not more than one-third, to finance other mandated services, such as the conducting of objective, State-prepared tests, and the maintenance of attendance and health records. As can be seen from the examples of tests prepared for use in parochial schools which we set forth earlier in this chapter (and which were presented to the Supreme Court in the plaintiffs' brief in the *Levitt* case), tests and examinations can be a very effective means of teaching religion, as well as, of course, other subjects, and since the State allowed the tax-raised funds to be used for this purpose, the law was unconstitutional. Internally prepared tests, the Court said, are an integral part of the teaching process, and since no means are available to assure that they are free of religious instruction and avoid inculcating students in the religious precepts of the sponsoring church, the law cannot stand in view of the *Lemon-DiCenso* decision and of the decision, handed down the same day as the *Levitt* decision, in *Committee for Public Education and Religious Liberty* (PEARL) v. *Nyquist.*

Parenthetically, it should be noted that in the *Levitt* case as in every other aid-to-parochial-schools case decided by the Court on June 25, 1973, and two years earlier when it decided *Lemon-DiCenso*, the Court accepted at face value the declaration of the legislatures that their purpose was exclusively secular. The Court simply refused to recognize what every newspaper reader knew, namely that sectarian pressures play a significant if not determinative role in the enactment of aid-to-parochial-school measures. The practical effect of this refusal is to remove purpose from the purpose-effect test.

Maintenance and Repair

The Court in the *Levitt* decision, rejecting the attempted justification that since the State mandated testing and recording in parochial schools it could pay for them, noted that the State also mandated minimum lighting and sanitary facilities in all buildings, and that consequently the logic of the State's argument would enable the State to pay for those costs in parochial schools. That was exactly the proposition presented to the Court in the *Nyquist* case.

On May 22, 1972, New York Governor Rockefeller signed into law an act which provided "health and safety" grants to nonpublic schools, reimbursement of tuition to low-income parents of children in nonpublic schools, and a modification of gross income in computing State income taxes of middle-income parents whose children attend nonpublic schools. Cognizant of what had happened in Pennsylvania, Rhode Island, and Connecticut, and what appeared to be an emerging game plan, PEARL instituted suit challenging the law within three hours after the governor announced that he had signed it. By diligently prosecuting the suit and avoiding all procedural delays, PEARL was able to get a definitive decision from the Supreme Court just thirteen months after the law was signed.

The first part of the law provided that, in order to assure the health and safety of children attending nonpublic schools in low-income areas, grants were to be made to each of those schools at the rate of $30 per pupil in schools less than 25 years old and $40 in older schools. The funds were required to be used by the schools for "maintenance and repair," and this term was defined to include costs of heat, light, water, ventilation, and sanitary facilities; cleaning, janitorial, and custodial services; snow removal; necessary upkeep and renovation of buildings, grounds, and equipment; fire and accident protection; and such other items as the State commissioner of education might deem necessary to ensure the health, welfare, and safety of enrolled students. The schools were required to account annually for the proper expenditure of the funds, and in no event could the total payment to a nonpublic school exceed one-half the actual costs of comparable services in the public schools.

With only Justice White dissenting, the Supreme Court held this part of the law unconstitutional. No attempt, the Court said, was made to restrict payments to those expenditures related to the upkeep of facilities used exclusively for secular purposes, nor would it be possible to do so in religious-oriented schools. Nothing in the law, for example, barred a school from using the tax-raised funds to pay the salaries of employees who maintained the school chapel or for renovating classrooms in which religion was taught or for lighting and heating them. In view of this, the law was struck down as having a primary effect which advanced religion since it subsidized the religious activities of sectarian schools.

There is a subtle but highly significant difference between the purpose-effect test as applied in the *Allen* case and in the *Nyquist* case. The *Allen* decision assumed that there could be only one primary effect, and if that effect was secular the law was safe. Advancement of religion was not *"the"* primary effect of the textbooks law and therefore the law did not violate the Establishment Clause. Relying on this premise, the New York law limited the maintenance and repair grants to no more than one-half the average comparable costs in public schools, on the assumption that at least half of the educational services in parochial schools were secular. The *Nyquist* decision, however, was based on the premise that there can be more than one primary effect and if one of the primary effects is to advance religion the statute is unconstitutional, even if the religious effect is quantitatively secondary to the secular one. "It simply cannot be denied," the Court said, "that this section has *a* primary effect that advances religion."

Tuition Grants

The above premise was the foundation for the Court's invalidation of the second part of the New York law. In October 1972, the Court, in the case of *Essex* v. *Wolman*, affirmed without opinion a lower court decision holding unconstitutional an Ohio law providing for grants to parents of pupils in parochial schools to reimburse them for part of the tuition paid by them. The New York law was basically the same. It allowed grants of $50 to $100 to low-income parents (those earning less than $5,000 a year in taxable income) who presented a receipted tuition bill from a nonpublic school. The law, however, provided that in no case could the amount paid to a parent exceed 50 percent of the tuition actually paid by him.

This restriction was again obviously based on the assumption that certainly more than 50 percent of the tuition in parochial schools went to cover the cost of the secular instruction the pupils received and therefore the primary effect of the law was secular. Again, however, the Court refused to accept this justification. Since at least part of the tuition could be used to finance the religious aspect of parochial school education and the law contained no effective means of guaranteeing that the State funds would be used exclusively for secular, neutral, and nonideological purposes, the law could not stand.

Only Justice White had dissented in the *Levitt* case and in that part of the *Nyquist* decision which held unconstitutional the maintenance and repair provision of the New York law. In this part of the *Nyquist* case, however, and in *Sloan* v. *Lemon*, in which on the same day the Court invalidated a similar Pennsylvania tuition law, he was joined in dissent by Chief Justice Burger and Justice Rehnquist. Here we come to a second highly significant aspect of the *Nyquist* decision.

In the *Lemon-DiCenso* cases the Court had ruled invalid laws which granted public funds directly to parochial schools or (in the case of *DiCenso*) their teachers. In the *Levitt* case and in the maintenance and repair part of the *Nyquist* decision, the invalidated laws likewise granted funds directly to parochial schools. On the other hand, in the *Everson* and *Allen* decisions the Court had upheld laws in which the direct benefits went to children or their parents, and the aid to the schools was indirect. The three dissenters in the *Nyquist* case asserted that this difference should be observed and that laws under which the aid to parochial schools is indirect should be upheld.

The majority of the Court refused to do this. In the opinion by Justice Powell they indicated that they were not prepared to uphold aid to parochial schools beyond bus transportation and loans of textbooks, and as far as they were concerned the fact that the aid was furnished to the children or their parents did not automatically immunize them from constitutional challenge. By reimbursing parents for a portion of their tuition bill the State was unmistakenly providing financial support for parochial schools and the effect of its action was to advance religion.

Tax Benefits and Credits

The third part of the law before the Court in the *Nyquist* case also involved indirect aid to parochial schools. The tuition part applied to parents with taxable income below $5,000; the third part covered parents with income above that amount. One can only speculate as to why different methods were used for the two classes. Most probably it was because the governor was not too sure about the constitutionality of tuition grants; similar laws had been uniformly declared unconstitutional by State courts under their own "Blaine Amendments," and in some cases under the Establishment Clause of the United States Constitution. On the other hand, in the *Walz* case the Court had decided in favor of the constitutionality of tax exemption for churches, and therefore the tax approach seemed to offer better prospects of success. Since most parents with incomes below $5,000 do not pay State income taxes, a less subtle method, that of tuition, had to be used for them. (In Minnesota the legislature tried to bring both classes under the tax umbrella. It provided that if a parent paid no State income tax, then he would be entitled to a negative tax; that is, payment from the State as if he had overpaid his tax to the extent of the tax credit which other parent-taxpayers received.)

The New York law was not a tax exemption statute; the properties of churches and church schools were already exempt from taxation in New York, and the 1972 law did not change this in any way. Operating on a direct/indirect assumption (or hope), the legislature sought to furnish the tax benefit to the parents rather than to the parochial schools. It did not do so in the form of tax "credits," that is, allowing parents to take off from the amount they owed the State for taxes an amount representing all or part of their tuition bill. It spoke in terms of tax "benefits," "deductions," "subtractions," "exclusions," and "modifications."

Under the law, parents were permitted to subtract from their adjusted gross income for State income tax purposes a designated amount for each child for whom they paid at least $50 tuition. If a parent's adjusted gross income was less than $9,000 he could subtract $1,000 for each of up to three children attending nonpublic school. The higher the income, the lower the subtraction; if the income exceeded $25,000, no subtraction was allowed. As worked out by the legislative leaders, a parent of three children in nonpublic schools would receive a tax benefit of $150 ($50 for each child) if his income was less than $9,000, and proportionately lower amounts if his income exceeded $9,000.

Though called "deductions," the benefits were not deductions in the usual sense. Ordinarily, one who makes a contribution to a charity can deduct the amount from his gross income and pay taxes on the balance. Thus, if a parent of three children with an income of $9,000 paid $150 in tuition for them, he could deduct (if tuition payments were tax deductible) $150 from his income and pay his tax on the remaining $8,850. Under the New York law he could deduct $3,000 and pay his tax on $6,000, and he could do so even if he did not itemize his deductions but took the standard deduction available to all taxpayers. What the State did was simply to figure out for each eligible taxpayer what he had to deduct in his tax return in order to effectuate the tax credit intended by the legislature.

Why did the governor and legislature use this round-about method of achieving their purpose? In all probability because they entertained doubts about the constitutionality of an out-and-out tax credit law. In any event, it did not work. The Supreme Court, with the same three justices dissenting, would not buy the package. In his brief to the Court, counsel for PEARL stated that he was unable to discern any difference, in law or fact, between a situation in which a person sent to the State a check for the amount he owed on his tax return and independently thereof sent the

State his tuition receipt and got back a check for all or part of the amount shown thereon (tuition reimbursement), and the situation in which he computed his tax liability and sent the State his tuition receipt (tax credit) instead of sending the State a check for the amount. Two persons with the same income and the same allowable deductions owed the same amount to the State; one who had no children attending parochial schools sent the State a check for the amount he owed. The other sent a receipt from the school attended by his children. How could it be said that the State had not paid the tuition for him?

The majority of the Court too could not see any basic difference between tuition reimbursements and tax credits, nor between the latter and the type of benefits provided in the New York law. All three types had the effect of advancing religion, whether the tuition grant, the credit, or the benefit covered all or only part of the tuition; and all, said the Court, were equally unconstitutional.

To make sure that there was no mistake as to what it meant, the Court at the same time, in the case of *Grit* v. *Wolman*, affirmed without opinion the decision of a Federal court in Ohio declaring unconstitutional that State's usual type of tax credit for parochial school tuition. However, the Court did not have occasion to pass on, nor did it express any opinion regarding, the validity of a bona fide deduction statute, that is, one under which a parent could deduct from his gross income the amount of tuition he paid to a parochial school to the same extent and in the same way as he could deduct a contribution to the school or to any other religious, educational, or charitable institution.

Finally, in the *Nyquist* case the Court noted that although it found all three parts of the law unconstitutional under the purpose-effect test, and therefore did not find it necessary to consider whether they also failed the entanglement text, it nevertheless felt it appropriate to emphasize again the danger of political entanglement and religious divisiveness raised by the New York law and other measures seeking to aid parochial schools. In such situations, the Court said,

> where the underlying issue is the deeply emotional one of church-state relationships, the potential for serious divisive political consequences needs no elaboration. And while the prospect of such divisiveness may not alone warrant the invalidation of State laws that otherwise survive the careful scrutiny required by the decisions of the Court, it is certainly a warning signal not to be ignored.

College Aid

None of the "Blaine Amendment" provisions in the various State constitutions distinguishes between grants to sectarian educational institutions at elementary and secondary level on the one hand and college or university level on the other. Nor do the State court decisions interpreting and applying these provisions indicate any difference between the two levels. However, in two decisions of the United States Supreme Court, *Tilton* v. *Richardson* in 1971 and *Hunt* v. *McNair* in 1973, the Court appears to have applied different and more lenient standards in ruling on the constitutionality under the Establishment Clause where the beneficiary of governmental financing was an institution of higher education.

The issue was first brought to the Court in 1966 in the case of *Horace Mann League* v. *Board of Public Works*. The State of Maryland had passed four separate laws granting funds to each of four church-related colleges, two Protestant and two Catholic, to build or expand its facilities. At the trial of a suit by taxpayers challenging the grants, considerable evidence was produced to show the extent of church control of the colleges and the degree to which religion affected their admission practices, curriculum content, and general operations. On the basis of this evidence, Maryland's highest court ruled that three of the four institutions, the two Catholic and one Protestant, were sectarian, while the relationship of the fourth to the sponsoring church had become so attenuated and religion played so minimal a role in its operations that it could not be adjudged sectarian. The court further held that none of the grants violated the Maryland constitution since it did not contain a "Blaine Amendment" prohibition of aid to sectarian schools, but that the grants to the three sectarian colleges did violate the Establishment Clause of the First Amendment and therefore must be struck down. Both the plaintiffs and the defendants appealed to the Supreme Court but it refused to take the case and rejected both appeals.

Two years later, however, the Court did accept the appeal in the *Tilton* case. That suit challenged the inclusion of sectarian colleges in the Higher Education Facilities Act, adopted by Congress in 1963. That law provided Federal construction grants for college facilities, public and private, except facilities to be used for sectarian instruction or religious worship or which were part of a school or department of divinity. The law also provided that if this exclusion were violated within twenty years the government could recover the amount of its grant, but after that period the institution could use the facility for any purposes it wished, including religious purposes.

The law was based on a legal memorandum of the Department of Health, Education, and Welfare which appears to be the first serious effort to differentiate constitutionally between grants to colleges and those to elementary and secondary schools. While grants to the latter would violate the Establishment Clause, governmental financing of construction and expansion of academic facilities in colleges could be constitutional. The following factors, the memorandum stated, distinguish American higher education: the fact that the connection between religion and education is less apparent and that religious indoctrination is less pervasive in a sectarian college curriculum; the fact that free public education is not available to all qualified college students; the desirability of maintaining the widest possible choice of colleges in terms of each student's educational needs in a situation no longer limited by the necessity of attending schools located close to home; the extent to which particular skills can be imparted only by relatively few institutions; the disastrous national consequences in terms of improving educational standards which could result from exclusion of, or discrimination against, certain private institutions on grounds of religious connection; and the fact that, unlike elementary and secondary schools, collegiate enrollment does not have the power of state compulsion supporting it.

In the *Tilton* case, the Supreme Court appears to have accepted the distinction. It ruled unconstitutional that part of the act which allowed governmentally financed facilities to be used for religious purposes after twenty years. It could not be assumed that the facilities had no further substantial value after that period, and that therefore allowing them to be used for religious purposes would violate the Establishment Clause.

The Court, however, refused to strike down the rest of the law; since the use of the financed facilities was strictly limited to secular instruction, the primary effect of the law was not to advance religion. As for entanglement, the Court held, religion does not necessarily so permeate the secular education provided by church-related colleges nor so seep into the use of their facilities as to require a ruling that in all cases excessive surveillance would be necessary to assure that the facilities were not used for religious purposes. We must consider, said Chief Justice Burger, the skepticism of college students, the nature of college and post-graduate courses, the high degree of academic freedom characterizing many church-related colleges, their nonlocal constituencies, and the fact that the Federal grants under the law were one-time expenditures as opposed to the continuing subsidization of teachers which was held unconstitutional in the *Lemon-DiCenso* cases—all these factors indicated that the construction grants under the act did not foster excessive governmental entanglement with religion in violation of the First Amendment.

This does not mean that every grant to a church-related college is necessarily constitutional. If the institution is truly sectarian—if, for example, it imposes religious restrictions on admissions, compels obedience to the doctrines and dogmas of the faith, requires instruction in theology and doctrine, and does everything it can to propagate a particular religion—then a grant to it could probably not be upheld, for it would require considerable surveillance and hence excessive entanglement to make sure that the governmentally financed facility was not used for religious purposes.

In the *Tilton* case, four Catholic colleges in Connecticut were made defendants. As in the *Horace Mann League* case, a trial was held in which the control, operation, and curriculum of each college was examined in detail. However, unlike the three Maryland colleges, none of the Connecticut colleges was deemed to be sectarian, and each was therefore held to be qualified to receive funds under the Federal law. An examination of the trial records in the two cases does not show significant differences between the Maryland colleges on the one hand and the Connecticut colleges on the other. Consequently, it appears that in any case challenging aid to a church-related college the highest court to act on it would be the final judge as to whether the college manifested enough aspects of religiosity to disqualify it under the Establishment Clause.

Two years later, on the same day that the Court decided the *Nyquist-Sloan-Levitt* cases, it followed its *Tilton* case ruling in *Hunt* v. *McNair*. That case involved a South Carolina law that authorized a State agency to issue bonds whose proceeds were to be used to finance college facilities. As in the Federal and Maryland statutes, the facilities so financed could not be used for sectarian instruction or religious worship. The bonds were to be paid off out of the tuition and other income of the particular college, and could not be enforced against the State. The only benefit the college received under the law was that it could pay a lower interest on the bonds than it would have to pay if it borrowed the funds from banks, because income on the bonds was tax-exempt.

The Supreme Court could have held that the aid thus made possible by the law was so minimal (even the expense of floating the bonds had to come out of the college's income) that the advancement of religion was not the primary effect of the law. The Court did not do so; instead it applied the *Tilton* test and examined the record of the particular institution involved. This was a Baptist-related college of which, however, only 60 percent of the students were Baptists, a percentage about the same as the percentage of Baptists in the area in which it was located. The record showed no religious qualifications for faculty membership or student enrollment or any other evidence to show that the operations of the college were oriented significantly toward sectarian rather than secular education. As in the *Tilton* case, the Court concluded that the trial record did not establish religious permeation of the college to a degree that would require such surveillance by the State to assure that the bonded facilities were not used for a religious purpose as would amount to excessive entanglement of church and state.

To sum up: the present posture of the Supreme Court seems to indicate that it will strike down any law granting aid to parochial elementary and secondary schools beyond the narrow confines of bus transportation and textbook loans, but will require proof of sectarianism in each particular case in which a challenge is made to aid, at least in the form of construction grants or loans, to a church-related college or university. The difference in treatment is based on the assumption that there is not much difference between parochial schools, but that church-related colleges and universities vary substantially among themselves and each must therefore be judged individually in determining whether it is sufficiently secular to qualify for governmental aid under the Establishment Clause.

Chapter Seven

The Community and Its Welfare

The People's Peace

From time immemorial the hosts of God have been known to war among themselves. Had statistics been available in 1787, when our godless Constitution was written, they probably would have shown that throughout history more people had been killed in God's name than in any other cause. Often the forces of Caesar have had to be called in to keep peace among the forces of God.

The shedding of blood in God's name was not unknown on the shores of what was to become the United States; nor was Caesar's intervention. Complaints regarding the treatment of Quakers in New England led to an investigation by the king's commissioners who reported, in 1661, that "Puritans have put many Quakers to death" (actually four were executed). Twelve years earlier, the Maryland assembly enacted a law imposing fines, whipping, and imprisonment on any person calling another "an heretic, schismatic, idolator, Puritan, Independent, Presbyterian, papish priest, Jesuit, Jesuited papist, Lutheran, Calvinist, Anabaptist, Brownist, Antinomian, Barrowist, Roundhead, Separatist, or any other name or term in a reproachful manner relating to matters of religion." (While this "Act of Toleration" sought to maintain peace among the people of God according to the Trinitarian truth, it drew lines between the Children of Light and the Children of Darkness; the act imposed the penalty of death and forfeiture of estate on any person who "shall blaspheme

God, that is curse Him, or deny our Savior Jesus Christ to be the Son of God, or shall deny the Holy Trinity the Father the Son and Holy Ghost, or the Godhead of any of the said three persons of the Trinity or the unity of the Godhead.")

Compulsion in the area of religious doctrine survived until the eve of the Revolutionary War. In 1774 Madison wrote to a friend that "there are at this time in the adjacent county not less than five or six well-meaning men in close jail for publishing their religious sentiments, which in the main are very orthodox." However, the wave of humanist deism that swept across the country during the last quarter of the 18th century and culminated in the Establishment and Free Exercise clauses brought an end to Caesar's intervention on the side of God in His struggles against those who would deny His truths. Congress, within seven years after adopting the First Amendment which guaranteed freedom of speech and press no less than of religion, enacted a sedition law that imposed serious penalties for political unorthodoxy; but, as far as is known, it has never enacted any law proscribing or limiting religious unorthodoxy.

The record of the States has not been quite so clear. As we have seen, during the 1920s, three "Bible-belt" States did enact anti-evolution statutes, and as late as 1950 some fourteen States still had on their books laws making blasphemy a crime. The last time such a law appears to have been enforced was in 1928, when an atheist was convicted in an Arkansas court of "ridiculing the Christian religion." The latter-day justification for such laws was that they were necessary to protect not the Christian truths but the people's peace, and the same reason was asserted later to justify curbs on the activities of Jehovah's Witnesses and other evangelists whose missionary exhortations included verbal attacks upon other religions. Ridiculing religion or attacking particular religions, it was argued, was likely to provoke acrimonious reaction and even violence, and this the State had the power and duty to prevent.

The Supreme Court has not manifested any substantial

degree of sympathy to this rationale or other attempted justifications of governmental restrictions on religious or anti-religious expressions. In the 1952 case of *Joseph Burstyn, Inc.* v. *Wilson*, it ruled that New York could not constitutionally deny a license for the exhibition of a motion picture called *The Miracle* on the ground that it was "sacrilegious" in its treatment of religion with "contempt, mockery, scorn and ridicule." (The plot of the film was the seduction and impregnation of an Italian peasant girl by a bearded stranger whom she imagined to be St. Joseph. Cardinal Spellman and other Catholics attacked the film because they deemed it to cast doubts on the truth of the divine birth of Jesus.) "It is not," the Court said, "the business of government in our nation to suppress real or imagined attacks upon particular religious doctrine, whether they appear in publications, speeches, or motion pictures."

In *Kunz* v. *New York*, decided a year earlier, the Court ruled that New York City could not deny a permit to hold a religious meeting in a public park merely because the applicant, an ordained Baptist minister, had in previous meetings preached that "the Catholic Church makes merchandise out of souls," that Catholicism is "a religion of the devil," and the Pope is "the anti-Christ," that Jews are "Christ-killers," and that "All the garbage that didn't believe in Christ should have been burnt in incinerators. It's a shame that they all weren't." The fact, the Court held, that these meetings had caused disorder did not justify denial of a permit; there were, it said, appropriate public remedies to protect the peace and order of the community if speeches should result in disorder or violence, but these remedies did not include advance suppression.

These cases held that religious expression could not be curbed in advance for fear that it might disturb the peace. Might the speaker be arrested and punished after he has spoken? Yes, the Court answered in 1942 in *Chaplinsky* v. *New Hampshire*, where it upheld the conviction of a Jehovah's Witness who in a public street called a police officer "a God damned racketeer and a damned Fascist." But in order to sustain a conviction, the Court must be convinced that the circumstances were such that the religious expression constituted a clear and present danger to the people's peace. For that reason, the Court, in the 1940 case of *Cantwell* v. *Connecticut*, nullified the conviction of a Witness who was arrested on a public street in New Haven after playing a phonograph record that attacked the Catholic Church and offering to sell a book containing "conclusive proof that for more than fifteen hundred years a great religious system, operating out of Rome, has by means of fraud and deception brought untold sorrows and suffering upon the people."

In this case, the Court found, there was "no assault, or threatening of bodily harm, no truculent bearing, no intentional discourtesy, no personal abuse." On the contrary, there was "only an effort to persuade a willing listener to buy a book or to contribute money in the interest of what Cantwell, however misguided others may think him, conceived to be true religion."

> In the realm of religious faith [the Court continued] and in that of political belief, sharp differences arise. In both fields, the tenets of one may seem the rankest error to his neighbor. To persuade others to his own point of view, the pleader, as we know, at times, resorts to exaggeration, to vilification of men who have been, or are, prominent in church or state, and even to false statement. But the people of this nation have ordained in the light of history, that, in spite of the probability of excesses and abuses, these liberties are, in the long view, essential to enlightened opinion and right conduct on the part of the citizens of a democracy.

Peace in the Prisons

The Black Muslims are a group whose legitimacy as a religion is still under challenge. Although they profess to adhere to the faith of Islam, consider the Koran their holy book, maintain temples of Islamic worship, and observe the dietary and other laws of Islam, they are not accepted by the traditional Moslem churches. That fact, however, does not support the claim made in some cases that the Black Muslims are not a bona fide religious group but are instead racial extremists acting under the guise of religion. After all, today's heresies often become tomorrow's orthodoxies. Moreover, as the Supreme Court said in *Watson* v. *Jones*, in the United States the law knows no heresies. Hence, their rejection by orthodox Islamic churches does not disqualify the Black Muslims from recognition as a full-fledged member of the family of recognized faiths.

Nor are they ineligible to membership in the family of faiths by reason of their belief in the supremacy of blacks over whites, any more than Mormons are disqualified because the tenets of the Church of Jesus Christ of Latter-Day Saints include a belief in the inferiority of blacks. Even if Bob Jones University should be unsuccessful in its efforts to regain its tax-exempt status, it is unlikely that the decision will be based on the unacceptability of its belief or even teaching that God has commanded the separation of the races; more likely, it will be based on its actions in denying admission to black applicants and expelling whites who date blacks.

The Black Muslims are known to engage in violence of words, and are widely believed to engage in violence of deeds. The assassination of Malcolm X and the killing of other blacks whose assassins have not been identified have been widely attributed to internecine warfare between the followers of the accepted leader, Muhammad Elijah, and various groups of schismatics. But in this the Black Muslims are following an ancient tradition, the only difference being that their religious wars take place (as in Northern Ireland) in urban streets rather than on the more conventional battlefields.

For these reasons, the courts have with few exceptions rejected claims that Black Muslims are not entitled to the religious liberty guaranteed by the First Amendment nor to equal treatment with recognized religions. These cases have by and large arisen out of the complaints by Black Muslim prison inmates that they are not permitted to practice their religion to the same extent as members of the more conventional faiths, that they are deprived of the opportunity to read the Koran, to hold religious meetings, to obtain pork-free meals, and to obtain the services of Black Muslim religious advisers.

In *Cruz* v. *Beto*, decided in 1972, the Supreme Court ruled, somewhat briefly, on the religious rights of prisoners. The case, interestingly, involved not Black Muslims as did most of the cases which came to the lower courts, but a Buddhist inmate of a Texas prison. He claimed that while members of other religious sects were allowed to use the prison chapel, he was not; that because he shared his Buddhist religious materials with other prisoners he was placed in solitary confinement on a diet of bread and water for two weeks, and that he was forbidden to correspond with his religious adviser in the Buddhist sect. He claimed further that while Texas authorities encouraged inmates to participate in religious programs, provided Christian and Jewish chaplains and Bibles at State expense, and gave points of good merit for attendance at religious services which enhanced a prisoner's eligibility for desirable job assignments and early parole consideration, none of these privileges was accorded him.

The lower Federal court dismissed the complaint without hearing any evidence to support it, holding that the judiciary should not interfere with how prison officials maintain discipline and security within the walls. The effect of its decision was that neither the First Amendment's guaranty of the free exercise of religion nor the Fourteenth Amendment's requirement of the equal protection of the laws was applicable to prison inmates.

The Supreme Court rejected the lower court's ruling and reasoning. While obviously a prisoner cannot enjoy the free exercise of religion to the same extent as nonprisoners, he is protected by the Free Exercise Clause subject only to the necessities of prison security and discipline, and he may not be discriminated against simply because his religious beliefs are unorthodox. This does not mean that every religious sect or group within a prison, no matter how few in number, must have identical facilities or personnel. But reasonable opportunities must be afforded to all prisoners to exercise their religious freedom without fear of penalty.

Cruz v. *Beto* is a complement to *Laird* v. *Anderson*, discussed in Chapter Four of this book. In that case the Court rejected a claim that by reasons of national security it could not pass judgment on what takes place within the walls of West Point, and therefore could not interfere with the military officers' decision that all cadets must attend chapel. In the *Cruz* case it refused to accept domestic security as a barrier to its passing judgment on what happens within the walls of any State or Federal prison. In both cases it held that the guaranty of the free exercise of religion applies to all places, subject only to such modifications in application as are strictly necessary by reason of the particular situation and circumstances.

Prevention of Fraud

It is often difficult to draw the line between religion and magic. Moses, in his appearance before Pharaoh, sought to establish his credentials as the true spokesman of Jehovah by having Aaron turn his stick into a serpent; but Pharaoh's magicians, who obviously did not speak for the Hebrew deity, were able to duplicate the act. It is no less difficult to distinguish between religion and fraud. Every prophet in ancient Israel prefaced his oracle with "Thus saith the Lord," but had no hesitation in charging that other self-proclaimed prophets were false.

It has not been unusual throughout history for contending claimants to appeal to the state to decide between them as to who speaks God's true word and who speaks falsely and fraudulently. The Archbishop of Canterbury enthrones the British monarch, but it is the monarch who decides who shall be the Archbishop of Canterbury. In his monumental Memorial and Remonstrance against religious assessments, Madison labeled the implication that "the civil magistrate is a competent judge of religious truth" an "arrogant pretension falsified by the contradictory opinions of rulers in all ages, and throughout the world."

Yet, in modern times at least, it is the responsibility of the state not only to preserve the peace among its citizens but to protect them from fraud. A person can be prosecuted and convicted of fraud if he sells you for a large sum of money a vial of liquid which, he says, can cure you of all your ills because it is made by a secret formula that he alone knows. He can be convicted because competent chemists and physicians can testify at the trial that the supposedly secret formula is H_2O and that it can cure you permanently of nothing and only temporarily of thirst. But suppose he tells you that its curative powers derive from the fact that it is holy water and was blessed by a priest or guru or hassidic rabbi. Will the prosecution produce another priest, guru, or rabbi who will testify that holy blessed water has no curative powers not possessed by unholy and unblessed water? If so, will not the civil magistrate be called upon to decide between competing claims to religious truth?

The Supreme Court was confronted with this dilemma in 1944 in the case of *United States* v. *Ballard*. It involved the "I Am" movement and the prosecution of its organizers, Guy W., Edna W., and Donald Ballard, for using the mails to defraud. The indictments charged that the defendants had falsely and fraudulently represented "that Guy W. Ballard . . . alias Saint Germain, Jesus, George Washington . . . had been selected and designated . . . as a divine messenger"; that the words of "ascended masters and of the divine entity Saint Germain" would be communicated to the world through the "I Am" movement; that the Ballards had supernatural powers to heal the incurably ill, and that they had in fact cured hundreds of afflicted persons. The indictments charged that the Ballards knew that these representations were false, and made them solely for the purpose of obtaining for themselves the moneys of the credulous.

During the course of the trial, it was testified that the Ballards had represented that the teachings of the "I Am" movement had been dictated from Heaven to the Ballards who took down and transcribed them, and that Jesus had shaken hands with them. The trial judge instructed the jury that they should not decide whether or not these statements were literally true, but only whether the defendants honestly believed them to be true.

The majority of the Supreme Court, in an opinion written by Justice Douglas, agreed with the trial judge. They held that under the constitutional principles of the separation of church and state and religious freedom, neither a jury nor any other organ of the state had the power or competence to pass on whether certain alleged religious experiences actually occurred. The jury could no more constitutionally decide that Guy Ballard did not shake hands with Jesus than they could determine that Jesus did not walk on the sea. The Court said:

> . . . Heresy trials are foreign to our Constitution. Men may believe what they cannot prove. They may not be put to the proof of their religious doctrines or beliefs. Religious experiences which are as real as life to some may be incomprehensible to others. Yet the fact that they may be beyond the ken of mortals does not mean that they can be made suspect before the law. Many take their gospel from the New Testament. But it would hardly be supposed that they could be tried before a jury charged with the duty of determining whether those teachings contained false representations. The miracles of the New Testament, the Divinity of Christ, life after death, the power of prayer are deep in the religious convictions of many. If one could be sent to jail because a jury in a hostile environment found those teachings false, little indeed would be left of religious freedom. . . .

> The religious views espoused by respondents might seem incredible, if not preposterous, to most people. But if those doctrines are subject to trial before a jury charged with finding their truth or falsity, then the same can be done with the religious beliefs of any sect. When the triers of fact undertake that task, they enter a forbidden domain.

What the Court held, in effect, was that no agency of the secular state, including a jury, may pass judgment upon the factuality of religious beliefs or religious experiences. On the other hand, it also held that it was constitutionally permissible to allow a jury to decide whether the Ballards actually *believed* that what they recounted was true, and if the jury determined that they did not, they could convict them of obtaining money under false pretenses.

There were two dissenting opinions, one from what may be called the right, the other from the left. The former, by Chief Justice Stone, argued that if the Ballards obtained money from elderly or infirm persons by stating that through their spiritual powers they had cured hundreds of persons afflicted with diseases and ailments, the prosecution should be allowed to prove that no such cures had been effected. From the left, Justice Jackson urged that the prosecution should not have been instituted in the first place. Few juries, he said, could find that the Ballards honestly believed in something which the jury felt was unbelievable.

The decision by the majority of the Court seems to have been a pragmatic compromise. Acceptance of Chief Justice Stone's approach would threaten the long-established legitimacy not only of Christian Science practitioners, but also of all other teachers of the efficacy of prayers to heal physical ailments. Acceptance of Justice Jackson's approach, on the other hand, would leave the aged and infirm at the mercy of charlatans.

The majority of the Court could not accept either approach; yet, it may have felt uncomfortable with the compromise it had adopted, for logically it sanctioned prosecution for fraud not only of Elmer Gantry but at least theoretically of thousands of real-life ministers, priests, and rabbis who weekly preach the literal historicity of the Bible even though they themselves may not believe it. Moreover, it required juries to read the minds of defendants or guess whether they were sincere in what they professed. It is a relatively simple matter for a judge or jury to determine whether a certain brick sold for a large sum of money is gold or lead and, if the latter, whether the defendant knew that fact when he made the sale; it is not so simple a matter· to determine whether a solicitor of funds to build a spiritualist temple had actually communed with the dead or, if he had not, whether he honestly believed that he had.

Nevertheless, sincerity of belief has become the test for distinguishing between faith and fraud. Basically it is the way, imperfect as it may be, to ascertain whether an applicant for conscientious objection exemption from the draft is entitled to it. At the same time, it has become the shield of innumerable charlatans who find it easy to extract money from persons only too willing to believe in supernatural relief from ills and anxieties when natural means have failed. Yet, this may be a necessary price to pay for freedom of religion, and a worthwhile one as well. Justice Jackson stated the point eloquently in his dissenting opinion in the *Ballard* case:

> The chief wrong which false prophets do to their following is not financial. The collections aggregate a tempting total, but individual payments are not ruinous. I doubt if the vigilance of the law is equal to making money stick by over-credulous people. But the real harm is on the mental and spiritual plane. There are those who hunger and thirst after high values which they feel wanting in their humdrum lives. They live in mental confusion or moral anarchy and seek vaguely for truth and beauty and moral support. When they are deluded and then disillusioned, cynicism and confusion follow. The wrong of these things, as I see it, is not in the money the victims part with half so much as in the mental and spiritual poison they get. But that is precisely the thing

the Constitution put beyond the reach of the prosecutor, for the price of freedom of religion or of speech or of the press is that we must put up with, and even pay for, a good deal of rubbish.

The People's Morals

America's traditional moral standards and values were the product of New England Puritanism. The standards of Virginian Anglicanism were vastly different. As Justice Frankfurter noted in *The Miracle* case, when Anglicanism controlled New England's churches James I's *Book of Sports* was required reading in the churches, while under the Puritans all copies were consigned to the flames. But Anglicanism had little influence in shaping America's morality or culture. It was the Puritan scale of moral values that prevailed with the virtues of honesty, industry, thrift, austerity, and Godliness, while the major evils were frivolity, gambling, extravagance, dishonesty, sexual immorality, and Sabbath-breaking.

Not all these evils could be translated into terms of secular law. Although idleness of the poor, called "vagrancy," has been decreed a misdemeanor in some State penal codes, it is not feasible, for example, to make frivolity or thriftlessness a penal offense. To the extent, however, that the compulsory arm of the law could be employed to impose Puritan moral values upon the community at large, it was done. The countless laws against drunkenness, traffic in obscene books, gambling and lotteries, licentiousness and Sabbath-breaking, all witness to the monopolistic domination that Puritan Protestantism exercised over America's penal codes.

Protestantism entered the field of moral censorship in 1802 with the establishment of the Society for the Suppression of Vice, followed by the Society for the Reformation of Morals in 1813, and the American Tract Society in 1825. In 1821, New England Protestantism prevailed upon the Vermont legislature to enact the first State law in the United

States making it a criminal offense to publish or exhibit obscene matter. Shortly thereafter two other New England States, Massachusetts and Connecticut, followed suit. From New England the anti-obscenity crusade spread throughout the nation so that today just about every State in the Union has some kind of anti-obscenity law on its books. On the national level a provision was added to the Tariff Act of 1842 prohibiting the import of obscene books, and in 1872, as the result of a militant Protestant crusade led by Anthony Comstock, the first of a series of laws was passed barring obscene matter from the mails and from interstate transportation.

Some time during the second quarter of the 20th century, Catholicism entered the field of anti-obscenity censorship. The Catholic bishops established a scale of ratings for motion pictures on the basis of their moral acceptability and, in 1938, organized the National Office for Decent Literature. By that time there were more than enough laws on the books of both the Federal and State governments to combat obscenity; the problem lay in their enforcement. At this point, Catholicism took over the mission first launched by Protestantism. Diocesan newspapers called upon the police for stricter enforcement of the laws, and parish priests often cooperated with the police or instigated police action against purveyors of pornography.

It was not until 1957 in the case of *Roth* v. *United States* that the Supreme Court was first confronted with the task of reconciling anti-obscenity laws with the First Amendment's guaranties of freedom of speech and press. In the *Chaplinsky* case the Court had stated that there were "certain well-defined and narrowly limited classes of speech, the prosecution and punishment of which has never been thought to raise any Constitutional problem." These, it said, included "the lewd and obscene, the profane, the libelous, and the insulting or 'fighting' words—those which by their very utterance inflict injury or tend to incite an immediate breach of the peace." The reason for their exclusion from the protection of the First Amendment was that they "are of such slight social value as a step to truth that any benefit that may be derived from them is clearly outweighed by the social interest in order and morality."

The difficulty with the pronouncement lay in the fact that the Court did not say who was to determine what was "lewd and obscene" nor what standards were to be used in making the determination. It was these questions the Court sought to anwer in the *Roth* case. It answered the first question by ruling that it was up to the jury to decide whether the material was in fact obscene. If it decided that it was not, it found the defendant not guilty and that ended the matter. Should it, however, find the defendant guilty he could appeal up to the Supreme Court, which would be the final judge of whether or not the matter was obscene. This meant that the Court, in every case in which it accepted an appeal, would have to read the particular book or magazine or sit through a showing of the film. And this, indeed, is what the Court did for some fifteen years after the *Roth* decision.

The answer to the second question was more difficult and, in the end, was found by the Court to be equally unsatisfactory. During the Victorian period, in a criminal prosecution against one Hicklin, an English court ruled (in 1868) that if any excerpt from a book or other publication was obscene the whole was obscene, and in determining whether the part was obscene the jury must decide what effect it might have on the minds of the most susceptible persons in the community. That meant, that if a particular page, paragraph, sentence, or even word in a book would arouse sexual desires or impure thoughts in the mind of a young, immature, or highly prudish person, the whole would have to be condemned.

In the *Roth* case the Court rejected the *Hicklin* ruling. Sex and obscenity, it said, were not synonymous. The true test was whether to the average person, applying contemporary community standards, the dominant theme of the material taken as a whole appealed to prurient interest. By "contemporary" standards the Court intended that a book should not be judged by prudish Victorianism but could honestly reflect changing and more liberal current approaches to sex. By "community," the Court meant the nation as a whole and not any particular rural, easily shockable town or village. And "material taken as a whole" meant that a solid piece of literature could not be outlawed because it included a four-letter word which many people might find objectionable.

The *Roth* test was a liberal one, far more liberal of course than the *Hicklin* rule. It did not, however, accord *carte blanche* to hard-core pornographers, as proven by the fact that the Court upheld the conviction of Roth. But the Court did more in the *Roth* case than adopt a new test. In its opinion, written by Justice Brennan, the Court said that "all ideas having even the slightest redeeming social importance" enjoy the protection of the First Amendment. In subsequent cases the Court interpreted this to mean that if a publication or a film had "even the slightest redeeming social value" it was not obscene, and therefore was constitutionally protected. No great feat of the imagination is required to find some slight redeeming social value in practically anything written or depicted. Some lawyers have contended that anything written necessarily has some social value, for, by reading, the reader reinforces his reading ability and capacity. The net effect of these decisions—or at least so it seemed to many—was to accord constitutional protection to almost anything short of the hardest of hardcore pornography.

This is illustrated by the 1966 case of *Memoirs* v. *Massachusetts* wherein the Court reversed a State court ruling that *Fanny Hill* was obscene. At the trial, literary experts testified that the book, the fictitious memoirs of an 18th century prostitute, displayed a skill of characterization and a gift for comedy, played a part in the history of the development of the English novel, and contained a moral, namely, that sex with love was superior to sex in a brothel. The Massachusetts court based its ruling on the assumption that the mere fact that a book had a minimal literary value did not mean it was of any social importance. The Supreme Court held that in order for a book to be adjudged obscene and hence not constitutionally protected three things had to be proved: (a) the dominant theme of the material taken as a whole appealed to a prurient interest in sex; (b) the material was patently offensive because it affronted contemporary community standards relating to sexual matters; and (c) the material was utterly without redeeming social value. In view of the testimony of the experts, the Court held, it could not be said that *Fanny Hill* was utterly without redeeming social value.

The Supreme Court decisions did not cause the sexual revolution of the 1960s and '70s; it is closer to the truth to say that they reflected it. They did, however, accord it constitutional sanction and thereby contributed to its acceptability. For instance, in the 1962 case of *Manual Enterprises* v. *Day*, the Court held that a magazine catering to homosexual patronage and consisting of photographs of nude males was protected by the First Amendment; this decision undoubtedly contributed to growing public acceptance of homosexuality as a way of life for those who choose it. In any event, conservative voices, particularly but by no means exclusively Catholic, were heard in strident criticism of the Court's obscenity decisions. What effect they had upon the Court can only be a matter for speculation. Probably the effect was minimal, and what caused the Court in 1973 to call a halt and try somewhat to retrace its steps was more likely its own disgust with the trash that its decisions must have encouraged and its weariness of reading and watching much of it. Most significant, in all probability, was that by 1973 four of the members of the Court were appointees of President Nixon, and a fifth, Justice White, shared their general conservative philosophy.

Whatever the cause, these five justices (Burger, Blackmun, Powell, Rehnquist, and White) handed down a number of decisions which in effect said that enough was too much, and that the Court would no longer accept what it called an "anything goes" view of the First Amendment. The leading case was *Miller* v. *California*, in which the Court passed on a conviction for mailing an illustrated brochure describing four books entitled "Intercourse," "Man-Woman," "Sex Orgies Illustrated," and "An Illustrated History of Pornography," and a film entitled "Marital Intercourse." Chief Justice Burger, speaking for the majority of five, said that the threefold *Roth-Memoirs* test had not worked and had to be revised. The new test would require the jury in each case to determine: (a) whether the average person, applying contemporary community standards, would find that the work, taken as a whole, appealed to the prurient interest; (b) whether the work depicted or described in a patently offensive way, sexual conduct specifically defined by law; and (c) whether the work, taken as a whole, lacked serious literary, artistic, political, or scientific value.

The first part of the *Miller* threefold test seems to be much the same as its counterpart in the *Roth-Memoirs* test, but there is one significant difference. In explaining the meaning of "community standards," the Chief Justice made it clear that under the new test the phrase would no longer be taken to mean national standards, but rather local ones; the First Amendment, he said, did not command that the people of Maine or Mississippi accept public depiction of conduct found tolerable in Las Vegas or New York City.

In respect to the second part of the new test, the Chief Justice gave as examples of what might constitutionally be forbidden: (a) patently offensive representations or descriptions of ultimate sexual acts, normal or perverted, actual or simulated; and (b) patently offensive representations or descriptions of masturbation, excretory functions, and lewd exhibitions of the genitals. (Elsewhere in his opinion the Chief Justice rather grudgingly conceded that the "'sexual revolution' of recent years may have had useful byproducts in striking layers of prudery from a subject long irrationally kept from needed ventilation," but his use of the word "perverted" in characterizing some sexual acts indicated that he was not quite reconciled to the "sexual revolution.")

In formulating the third part of its new test, the Court expressly discarded the "utterly without redeeming social value" aspect of the *Roth-Memoirs* test. Without saying so, the Chief Justice was probably mocking that aspect when he denied in *Paris Adult Theater I* v. *Slaton*, decided on the same day as the *Miller* case, that "a 'live' performance of a man and a woman locked in sexual embrace at high noon in Times Square is protected by the Constitution because they simultaneously engage in a valid political dialogue."

In a sense, the "utterly without redeeming social value" test was the direct opposite of the *Hicklin* rule. Under the latter any obscenity in a work, no matter how slight, contaminated the whole; under the former, any slight redeeming trait purified it. The *Miller* test represented a compromise. Under it the jury would have to determine in each case whether a book or film, taken as a whole, lacked serious literary, artistic, political, or scientific value. The practical implication of this would seem to be that each jury decides by itself whether the people in its community should be allowed to read a particular book or see a particular film. This conclusion is justified by the Court's 5 to 4 decision in *Kaplan* v. *California*, also decided on the same day as the *Miller* case, that a jury could reach its determination without the benefit of any expert testimony. The net effect of this, when coupled with the equation of community standards with local standards, would appear to be that the First Amendment guarantees no more than the right to say or print what the local community, represented by twelve of its citizens, thinks the people should be allowed to hear or read.

The only alternative to this rather frightening conclusion would be to allow each defendant a right to appeal the jury's decision, up to the Supreme Court. But if so, the Court would be back again to the situation it found so distasteful and does not wish to repeat; namely, being required to read every book or watch every film found by a jury to be obscene.

There is another aspect of the 1973 obscenity decisions which may have serious implications. In 1969 the Court had held, in the case of *Stanley* v. *Georgia*, that a person could not be punished for reading an obscene book or watching a film in the privacy of his home. In the *Paris Adult Theater* case the Court refused to extend this principle to a situation in which the film was exhibited in a commercial theater even though there was an outside sign reading "Adult Theater—You must be 21 and able to prove it. If viewing the nude body offends you, Please Do Not Enter." The Court "categorically" rejected the contention that conduct which only involves "consenting adults" is constitutionally immune from governmental regulation or prohibition. Government, the Court said, had the right to take action necessary to maintain "a decent society," to protect "the quality of life and the total community environment," and to preserve "the tone of society." How far government could go for this purpose the Court did not say, but in *United States* v. *Orito*, another of the 1973 obscenity cases, it held that a passenger on a plane (and, presumably therefore a pedestrian in the streets) could be punished for merely carrying with him an obscene film (and, presumably an obscene book). The "quality of life" is a broad, open-ended concept. It is one thing when it is used to justify governmental steps to protect the environment from physical pollution; it is something radically different, notwithstanding the Court's apparent analogizing of the two situations, when applied to "moral" pollution. There must be good reason for the fact that the First Amendment guarantees freedom to speak but not to pollute the air or waters.

The Health of the Community

Governmental action to protect the health of the people is taken for granted and is no longer challenged in the courts as it was in 1925 when, as we noted in the previous chapter, Mrs. Frothingham brought her unsuccessful suit to stop the Federal government from using taxpayers' money to help pay the lying-in expenses of indigent women. Constitutional problems within the context of this book arise when the state, in the interests of protecting the people's health, commands what religion forbids or forbids what religion commands.

Where the health of the community at large is concerned, the Supreme Court has not hesitated in ruling that the government can act even if its action may violate the religious conscience of individual citizens. In 1905, in the case of *Jacobson* v. *Massachusetts*, the Court upheld a compulsory immunization law enacted to protect the people against particular communicable diseases. While Jacobson, who challenged the law, did not do so on the basis of any religious objections to inoculation, the Court in later cases made it quite clear that the result would have been the same had he done so, and that individual religious conscience must yield to the paramount obligation of the state to protect the people's health.

Compulsory immunization involves the Free Exercise Clause of the First Amendment. Where the health of the community is concerned, the Establishment Clause too may have to yield. In *Bradfield* v. *Roberts*, decided in 1899, the Supreme Court rejected a taxpayer's suit challenging the payment of Federal funds to construct a hospital operated by a corporation formed by members of the Catholic Sisters of Charity. The Court held that the corporation was a legal entity separate and distinct from the stockholders, and though they were all nuns, the corporation itself was secular and nonsectarian.

Bradfield v. *Roberts* is the constitutional basis of the Hill-Burton Act of 1946, under which many hundreds of millions of dollars from Federal funds have been poured into denominational hospitals. But if the only rationale of the decision was the fact of legal incorporation, the parochial schools could easily adopt the same device; they could form a corporation in each diocese with all the stock held by the diocesan bishop—a practice in fact used by the Catholic Church in a number of States, turn over the schools to it, and thereby qualify them to receive governmental funds. There is, however, a major difference between hospitals and schools. Providence Hospital, the beneficiary of Federal funds in the *Bradfield* case, neither taught nor practiced religion; it taught nothing and practiced only medicine. While religion may motivate the establishment and operation of a hospital as well as of a school, education is inherently more closely related to the propagation and practice of religion. A governmental subsidy to a religious educational institution is a use of tax money which directly supports an institution formed and operating for the providing of religious education rather than merely for the secular function of healing the sick.

In the *Bradfield* case the Court did not rely exclusively on the fact that the hospital was owned and operated by a corporation. "There is no allegation," the Court said, "that its hospital work is confined to members of [the] church or that in its management the hospital has been conducted so as to violate its charter in the smallest degree," i.e., that it has been conducted as anything other than a nonsectarian hospital. In 1973, Congress enacted a law directing that no hospital receiving Federal funds should by reason of that fact be required to make its facilities available for the performance of sterilizations or abortions in violation of its religious beliefs or moral convictions. Conversely, this means that a hospital which for religious or moral reasons refuses to allow sterilization or abortion does not lose its right to receive Federal funds.

Initially, it should be noted that this law is somewhat inconsistent with the principal rationale of the *Bradfield* decision. The 1973 law also provides that no individual may be required to perform or assist in any sterilization or abortion contrary to his religious beliefs or moral convictions. (It provides also that no hospital receiving Federal funds may discriminate against physicians or other health care personnel because they either performed or assisted or refused to perform or assist in lawful sterilizations or abortions.) As to this, there is no problem. But if a church-related hospital is legally incorporated, and it may be assumed most are, it is a separate, secular entity and therefore has no religious and perhaps no moral convictions. However, in post-*Bradfield* cases, the Supreme Court has ignored differences between legally incorporated and non-incorporated groups in respect to application of the Establishment Clause.

A more difficult problem is presented by the second ground for the *Bradfield* decision, namely, that Providence Hospital admitted patients without regard to religion and was administered like any other hospital. The 1973 law does not distinguish between therapeutic and nontherapeutic abortions, or even between those indispensable for the mother's survival and those which are not. Even in respect to nontherapeutic abortions, a constitutional problem exists. A hospital may decide that it will not provide facilities for nontherapeutic operations, such as face lifting or similar purely cosmetic procedures, and no constitutional obstacle would bar continued governmental financing. The same answer could not so confidently be offered if the decision were based exclusively on religious considerations; the First Amendment mandates the separation of religion and state, not of aesthetics and state.

It is doubtful that the Court would uphold governmental financing of hospitals which limit their admissions on the basis of religion. In the *Bradfield* case it stressed that Providence Hospital did not do so. Even Justice White, in his dissent from the ruling in the *Lemon-DiCenso* cases invalidating governmental aid to parochial schools, agreed that aid would be unconstitutional in respect to any school that excluded pupils on the basis of religion. There is something inherently wrong in taxing citizens of all religions to finance services available only to persons of a particular religion, and that wrong may well be a constitutional one even if Congress refused to make it a statutory one.

If this is so, it could well be argued further that there is no basic difference between a hospital's restricting services by reason of the patient's religion and its own. If it bars use of its facilities for abortions solely because it deems them sinful, it effectively excludes patients to whom abortions are religiously acceptable. In the *Epperson* case, which we considered in Chapter Five of this book, the Supreme Court held that the Establishment Clause forbade publicly funded schools from excluding on religious grounds the teaching of evolution. Does not the same reasoning impel a conclusion that under that clause a publicly funded hospital may not for religious reasons exclude abortion procedures?

At the present writing, the Supreme Court has not yet been called upon to decide this difficult question, but it may confidently be assumed that it will soon find it necessary to do so. Cases against hospitals, church-related and secular, which refuse to allow their facilities to be used for sterilizations and abortions have already been started in a number of States, and one or more of them should reach the Supreme Court before long. Consistency with the principles stated and applied in the *Bradfield* and the parochial school decisions would seem to point in the direction of a ruling by it that the 1973 law conflicts with the First Amendment.

The Health of Children

Where the health of children is involved, the Supreme Court has shown little reluctance in bending the restrictions of the Free Exercise Clause to accommodate the concerns of the state. The leading case in this area is *Prince* v. *Massachusetts*, decided in 1944. There, a member of the Jehovah's Witnesses sect was convicted of violating the State's child labor law by allowing her children and nine-year-old niece to accompany and help her while she sold the sect's religious literature in the city's streets. The Court rejected the defense that Mrs. Prince and the children considered themselves ordained ministers of God and believed it was their religious duty to perform this work and that neglect would bring condemnation "to everlasting destruction at Armageddon." Under long-established law, children are deemed wards of the state, and it has the power and duty to protect them, when necessary, even from their parents and their God.

> Parents [the Court said] may be free to become martyrs themselves. But it does not follow that they are free, in identical circumstances, to make martyrs of their children before they have reached the age of full and legal discretion when they can make that choice for themselves.

On the basis of this decision the Court has consistently refused to upset lower court rulings allowing hospitals to perform blood transfusions necessary to save the lives of children whose Jehovah's Witnesses parents refused to consent because they believed it was forbidden by God's command that blood shall not be eaten and that violation would entail eternal damnation. So too the Court has upheld decisions allowing communities to fluoridate their water supplies to prevent tooth cavities notwithstanding objections by Christian Scientists and others that the drinking of fluoridated water is sinful.

Some State legislatures have appeared to be more

tolerant of religious convictions affecting the health of children than has been the Supreme Court. Notwithstanding *Jacobson* v. *Massachusetts*, they have enacted laws exempting from compulsory immunization statutes Christian Scientists and others to whom the practice is religiously unacceptable. Many have gone even further and have exempted Christian Scientists and other practitioners of faith healing from laws forbidding the unlicensed practice of medicine and their children from attendance at public school classes in which the germ theory of illness and other aspects of health education are taught. There is, however, little doubt that should the States elect to repeal these laws and impose upon the children of believers in faith healing the same requirements regarding immunization and health education to which other children are subject, the Court would not interfere and would reject any claim based upon the Free Exercise Clause of the First Amendment.

The Health of Adults

Although the Court said in the *Prince* case that "parents may be free to become martyrs themselves," it is by no means certain that this is always so. In one case a lower court authorized a compulsory blood transfusion for a woman who, as a member of the Jehovah's Witnesses sect, would not consent to it, but the court justified its action on the fact that she was 32-weeks pregnant. In another, justification was found in that the woman had a seven-month-old child who would suffer by becoming motherless and whose welfare the State had a right to protect. It may be assumed that the same reasoning could be applied in the case of a father of dependent children. The reasoning could be extended further to the case of a young man who, though unmarried, is a member of the armed forces, or even further to one who is of draft age. It could well be argued, as in some of the cases discussed in Chapter Four of this book, that the interests of national defense are superior to the claims of religious liberty. The rationale could be further extended to the concededly unlikely case of a great brain surgeon who is a member of the sect, or even to the more likely but no less logically sound example of an ordinary carpenter or bricklayer. The point in all these instances is that the community as a whole has an interest in the continued life of a person that may be superior to his own Free Exercise rights.

Lest it be thought that this reasoning is far-fetched and unlikely of acceptance by the Supreme Court, it should be noted that the Court did in fact accept it as a matter of course almost a century ago. In disposing of the religious liberty defense in the Mormon polygamy case of *Reynolds v. United States*, the Court asked rhetorically whether "if a wife religiously believed it was her duty to burn herself upon the funeral pyre of her dead husband, would it be beyond the power of civil government to prevent her carrying her belief into practice?"

On the other hand, the proposition that the state can constitutionally authorize compulsory blood transfusion to save the life of an adult presents its own difficulties. Is it constitutional for the state to override a patient's decision not to undergo a lifesaving operation that would result in permanent paralysis of much of the body? Or even to order against the patient's will an operation which most competent surgeons deem quite safe but a few or even the patient alone considers risky? Why should the state be allowed to override his decision when it is based on religious belief, which after all is protected by the First Amendment?

The Supreme Court has never directly grappled with the question, perhaps because by the time the few cases sought to be appealed actually reached it the transfusion had already been given. This fact alone would not stop the Court from deciding the case if it had wished to do so; *Roe* v. *Wade*, one of the 1973 abortion decisions, was decided 13 months after it was argued and long after the pregnancy had terminated or been terminated. Jehovah's Witnesses are a growing sect and have given no indication of any intention to alter their doctrine regarding blood transfusions. It is therefore safe to predict that transfusion cases, involving both children and adults, will continue to come to the Court, and sooner or later will be decided by it. With respect to children it is highly improbable that the Court will rule that parents' religious convictions are superior to the state's interest in preserving the lives of children. Where adults are involved the Court's decisions are not so easily predictable. The statement from the opinion in the *Reynolds* case would support a holding against the claim of religious freedom. So too would the Court's 1949 dismissal, in the case of *Bunn* v. *North Carolina*, of an appeal from a decision upholding the constitutionality of an anti-snake handling law even though the defendant in the case, a member of a religious sect whose doctrines required snake handling as witness of faith, was an adult. On the other hand, some of the Court's more recent decisions, such as the *Yoder* case discussed in Chapter Three and *Sherbert* v. *Verner* discussed later in this chapter, manifest a more sympathetic concern for the claims of religious liberty than do the earlier ones.

Prediction is risky where the countervailing value is life; but suppose it is only health. Can the state disregard an adult's religious convictions where the alternative would be no more than injury to his health? Obviously, a line must be drawn somewhere. The government certainly cannot force a Christian Scientist to take cough medicine when he has a cold, and of course it cannot forbid him from praying when he is ill. It is equally obvious that neither can it prohibit salaried priests and rabbis from praying for the recovery of their sick congregants. Then, what about State laws prohibiting paid or professional "faith healing"? The constitutionality of such laws has generally been upheld in State courts, and in 1952 the Supreme Court refused to review the one such case appealed to it. On the basis of the *Ballard* decision, discussed earlier in this chapter, it would seem that the law could constitutionally be enforced on proof that the faith healer himself did not have faith in his own healing powers or, in other words, that he was guilty of deliberate fraud.

A related problem arises from the use of hallucinatory and other drugs as part of a religious sacrament. Here, too, the question of sincerity may be critical. If the guise of religious belief is falsely used to immunize users of the drugs from prosecution, the *Ballard* decision would seem to allow criminal prosecution. If, however, the motivations are found to be bona fide, does the First Amendment protect the user? In 1964 California's highest court upheld the right of members of the Native American Church, a bona fide religious group, to use peyote as an integral part of its religious ceremonies; but the ruling was based on the court's determination that there was no clear proof that peyote was harmful to its users. On the other hand, members of a rural commune in Tennessee were convicted of cultivating marijuana and the State's highest court ruled that since government can regulate religious practices for the good of society, the defense of religious liberty could not be upheld. The defendants appealed the decision to the United States Supreme Court, but in 1973 the Court, in *Gaskin* v. *Tennessee*, dismissed the appeal on the ground that the judgment was clearly correct.

The People's Welfare: Sabbath Rest

Six days, the Hebrews' Bible told us, you shall work, but the seventh day is the sabbath of rest. The Christians changed it somewhat by making the first day the sabbath of rest. In either case it was a command of God enforced by Caesar, first in the form of the theocratic state of Judea, later of Constantine and other Roman emperors, then of Christian governments in Europe and the American colonies, and most recently in the States of the United States. Until the time this nation launched the experiment of separating church and state there was no reason why Caesar should not help God out in assuring compliance with His command.

Indeed, as late as 1861 a New York court, in enforcing a State Sunday closing law, said that "it would be strange that a people, Christian in doctrine and worship, should in their zeal to secure to all the freedom of conscience which they valued so highly, solemnly repudiate and put beyond the pale of the law, the religion which is as dear to them as life."

Exactly a century later, a more sophisticated United States Supreme Court felt it necessary to examine in depth and not take for granted the propriety under the First Amendment of governmental enforcement of sabbath rest. The question came to the Court in four cases known collectively as the *Sunday Law Cases*. Two of them, *McGowan* v. *Maryland* and *Two Guys from Harrison-Allentown, Inc.* v. *McGinley*, concerned owners of highway discount stores which were open for business seven days a week. The other two, *Gallagher* v. *Crown Kosher Super Market* and *Braunfeld* v. *Brown*, involved stores owned by Orthodox Jews who, by reason of religious convictions, abstained from all business activity on Saturdays.

In all four cases the prevailing opinions were written by Chief Justice Warren. In meeting the attack based upon the principle of separation of church and state he said that if it were the present purpose of a Sunday law to use the State's coercive power to aid religion the law would be unconstitutional as a violation of the Establishment Clause. He conceded further that this indeed was the original purpose of the Sunday laws under attack. There was no question, he said, that historically these Sunday laws (of Massachusetts, Pennsylvania, and Maryland) were enacted during colonial times as religious laws whose purpose was to insure the observance of the Christian sabbath as a religious obligation. However, he held, the religious origin of these statutes did not require that they be held invalid today, if in fact, the religious purpose was no longer in effect.

This, he said, was the case in respect to these laws. The present purpose of the legislation was to set aside a day not for religious observance, but for rest, relaxation, and family togetherness; and the motivation was therefore secular rather than religious. As evidence to support this conclusion the Chief Justice pointed out, for example, that the Maryland statute permitted such Sunday activities as the operation of bathing beaches, amusement parks, and even pinball and slot machines as well as the sale of alcoholic beverages and the performance of professional sports. Such exemptions from the law obviously were directly contrary to the religious purpose of the sabbath and thus indicated clearly that the present purpose of the statutes was not religious but secular.

Since these were now welfare or secular statutes, the fact that to a certain extent their operation coincided with religious purposes did not make them religious laws, according to the Chief Justice. In this respect, he referred to the *Everson* case. The purpose of that statute, the Chief Justice said, was to protect children from the hazards of traffic; the fact that the parochial schools benefited indirectly thereby did not transform what was basically a secular or welfare law into a prohibited law respecting an establishment of religion. For the same reason, he concluded, the fact that the Christian religion might benefit by the State's decision to choose Sunday as the day in which people were required to abstain from labor and to rest and relax did not transform these purely secular and welfare laws into laws prohibited by the First Amendment.

Realistically, it is difficult to quarrel with the Court's conclusion. Although the compulsory day of rest is Sunday, the Christian sabbath, rather than a neutral day such as Tuesday or Thursday, this is no more than a recognition of the reality that Americans are accustomed not to work on Sundays; as Justice Frankfurter noted in his concurring opinion, Sunday is also the official day of rest in godless Soviet Russia. There was a time when Sunday closing laws were enforced because of pressure by such religious organizations as the now almost-forgotten Lord's Day Alliance;

today the pressure comes from secular labor unions or owners of city stores facing the serious competition of highway discount stores and shopping centers.

Sabbath Rest: But Whose Sabbath?

More difficult to accept is the Court's decision in the *Crown Kosher* and *Braunfeld* cases. While only Justice Douglas dissented in the other two cases, Justices Brennan and Stewart joined him in dissenting in these two cases. The major constitutional question in these cases was whether even a secular law could be enforced in violation of religious convictions where the secular purposes of the law could be achieved without such violation. As far as the human body is concerned, one day is no different from another, and if Jewish and Seventh-Day Adventist Sabbatarians rest on the seventh rather than the first day of each week, the health and welfare objectives of the law are fully satisfied. Refusal to accept Saturday rest as a substitute for Sunday rest would appear to be a violation of the Free Exercise Clause.

The majority of the Court, however, rejected this contention. Freedom to hold religious beliefs, Chief Justice Warren said in his opinion, is absolute; however, freedom to act, even when motivated by religious considerations, is not totally free from legislative restrictions. Thus, in the *Reynolds* case the Court had held that the fact that polygamy might be a positive command of the Mormon religion did not prevent the government from declaring it illegal and making its practice criminal. Similarly, in the *Prince* case the Court upheld a statute making it a crime for girls under the age of eighteen to sell newspapers and other periodicals in public despite the fact that a child of the Jehovah's Witnesses felt it was her religious duty to perform this work.

In the present cases, the Chief Justice continued, the statutes did not even go as far as those involved in the *Reynolds* and *Prince* decisions, for there they forbade conduct which religion commanded, whereas the Jewish religion did not command engaging in business on Sunday. The restriction on religious freedom was merely indirect and consequential; and just as indirect aid to religion did not invalidate a law under the Establishment Clause, neither did indirect restriction invalidate it under the Free Exercise Clause.

The States, the Chief Justice and Justice Frankfurter in his concurring opinion conceded, could perhaps have fulfilled their objectives by enacting laws requiring one day of rest each week for all workers but leaving it up to each employer to decide which day it should be. Or they could, as a number of them did, designate Sunday as the day of rest but provide an exemption for those whose religious convictions required them to rest on another day. However, the justices said, it was not unreasonable for the State legislatures to take another road. They could, for example, have determined that allowing the exemption would have frustrated their goal of eliminating the atmosphere of commercial noise and activity (note the anticipation of the "tone of society" concept); or that it would make enforcement of the law more difficult (for how could a passing policeman be sure that the owner of a store doing business on Sunday was a bona fide Sabbatarian); or that it would discriminate against non-sabbatarian employees inasmuch as the Sabbatarian storekeeper would probably hire only Sabbatarians.

The reasoning of the Court is not entirely persuasive. The legislatures could have based a refusal to exempt Jewish Sabbatarians on any or all of these considerations, but the fact is that they did not. The only reason they were not exempted was the one stated in the 1861 New York decision, namely that we are a Christian nation and it is therefore entirely proper to require all to comply with Christian standards. It is quite likely that the majority of the Supreme Court were uncomfortable with their own decision, for within two years they handed down the decision in *Sherbert* v. *Verner* which is quite difficult to reconcile with the decisions in the *Crown Kosher* and *Braunfeld* cases. However, before we consider the *Sherbert* case it is appropriate to take a brief look at nonjudicial responses to the *Crown Kosher* and *Braunfeld* decisions.

Ten years before these decisions were handed down, the Court, in the case of *Friedman* v. *New York*, upheld, without opinion, a State conviction of an Orthodox Jewish storekeeper for violating the Sunday closing law notwithstanding his claim that the conviction violated the Free Exercise Clause. After the Court disposed similarly of the claim in the Massachusetts *Crown Kosher* and Pennsylvania *Braunfeld* cases, all three States amended their Sunday closing laws to grant Sabbatarians the exact exemption to which the Court held they were not constitutionally entitled, and other States, both before and after 1961, enacted similar exemptions.

One of these exemption statutes was challenged in 1962. The argument presented in that case, *Arlan's Department Store* v. *Kentucky*, was that in allowing Sabbatarians to keep their stores open on Sunday while compelling nonsabbatarians to close theirs, the State was preferring religion over nonreligion and was thus violating the Establishment Clause. There is a certain degree of logic to the argument; the preceding year the Court had ruled, in *Torcaso* v. *Watkins*, that a law which disqualified nonbelievers in God from public office violated the Establishment Clause by according to believers a privilege denied to nonbelievers. On the other hand, acceptance of the argument would invalidate the exemption of conscientious objectors for war service; and as far back as 1918, the Court, in the *Selective Draft Law Cases*, summarily rejected a challenge to the exemption. In any event, the Kentucky State courts refused to accept the department store's claim and the Supreme Court dismissed an appeal from that decision.

Religion and the Rights of Workers

The *Sunday Law Cases* dealt with the Free Exercise claims of storekeepers. However, *Sherbert* v. *Verner* concerned employees; a Seventh-Day Adventist was discharged by her employer because, when the plant changed from a five-day to a six-day week, she would not work on Saturday. When she was unable to obtain other employment because of her unwillingness to work Saturday, she filed a claim for unemployment compensation benefits under the compensation law of the State (South Carolina). The law disqualified from benefits a person who "without good cause" refused to take a suitable position offered him. The State unemployment compensation commission ruled the claimant's refusal to accept a position requiring Saturday work was "without good cause." The ruling was affirmed by the State courts, and the claimant appealed to the United States Supreme Court.

With only two justices dissenting, the Supreme Court reversed the decision and ruled that the denial of benefits to the claimant constituted an infringement of her constitutional rights under the First Amendment. The disqualification for benefits, the Court held, imposed a burden on the free exercise of religion. The consequence of such a disqualification to religious principles and practices, it continued, may have been only an indirect result of the State's action, but this fact did not necessarily render it immune from the invalidation under the First Amendment. Here not only was the claimant's declared ineligibility for benefits derived solely from the practice of her religion, but the pressure upon her to forgo that practice was unmistakable. The ruling forced her to choose between following the precepts of her religion and forfeiting benefits on the one hand, and abandoning one of the precepts of her religion in order to accept work on the other. Governmental imposition of such a choice put the same kind of burden upon the free exercise of religion as would a fine imposed against the claimant for her Saturday worship, and both were equally unconstitutional.

The majority opinion was written by Justice Brennan, one of the dissenters in the *Crown Kosher* and *Braunfeld* cases.

He paid lip service to the decisions in the cases and did not indicate any intention to overrule them, but it is not easy to reconcile them with the spirit if not the words of the *Sherbert* decision. In the first place, in the earlier decisions Chief Justice Warren relied heavily on the fact that the effect of the Sunday laws on the Sabbatarians' exercise of their religion was indirect, while in the *Sherbert* case Justice Brennan held that indirect inhibitions of religion were not immune from challenge under the Free Exercise Clause. Secondly, and more important, in a major respect *Sherbert* v. *Verner* went further than the *Crown Kosher* and *Braunfeld* decisions; in the latter cases the Sabbatarians asked only to be let alone, whereas Mrs. Sherbert demanded that the State pay her money and the Supreme Court held she was entitled to it.

Sherbert v. *Verner* manifests a greater degree of concern for Free Exercise claims than any previous decision of the Supreme Court. Similar concern was indicated during the same year in the case of *In re Jennison*. Mrs. Jennison, a resident of Minnesota, was summoned to serve on a jury but refused to do so because, she said, the Bible commanded "Judge not that ye be not judged." The Minnesota courts refused to accept this as a valid excuse, and she was held to be in contempt of court. She appealed to the United States Supreme Court, which directed the State court to reconsider its decision in the light of *Sherbert* v. *Verner*. The latter court did so and came to the conclusion that the assertion of this claim to religious liberty did not constitute a grave danger to the administration of justice in Minnesota. Accordingly, it reversed itself and dismissed the charge against her.

The most recent instance of the Court's sympathetic concern with the claims of religious freedom is found in *Wisconsin* v. *Yoder*, discussed in Chapter Three. The willingness of the Court in that case to allow Amish children above the age of fourteen to discontinue attendance at school because it violated their religious conscience contrasts markedly from its 1944 decision in the *Prince* case refusing to allow Jehovah's Witnesses children to sell literature in public even though their consciences dictated that they do so.

In the light of this recent change of attitude on the part of the Supreme Court we might expect that at some future time it will overrule its *Crown Kosher* and *Braunfeld* decisions. This, however, may not be necessary. Aside from the fact that many States have provisions in their Sunday closing laws exempting Sabbatarians is the additional fact that these laws are themselves rapidly becoming dead-letter laws and are only sporadically enforced. In New York City, for example, the police department publicly announced that summons for violation of the sabbath would not be issued by police officers as a matter of course, but only where a specific complaint is made by some citizen against a particular violator. While this publicly announced policy of non-enforcement is not usual, in reality it reflects the *de facto* situation in most cities all over the nation.

State legislative sympathy toward the free exercise of religion is indicated not only by the provisions exempting Sabbatarians from Sunday closing laws but in many other respects. *Sherbert* v. *Verner*, although not unique, was an unusual case. In the overwhelming majority of States Sabbatarians were not disqualified from receiving unemployment benefits because of their refusal to accept positions requiring Saturday work. Exemptions of believers and practitioners of faith healing from immunization and health-education laws and laws forbidding the unlicensed practice of medicine to which we have referred in this chapter are other examples, as are the ubiquitous "Church Entrance—No Parking" signs, and laws allowing pupils in public schools to be absent on their particular holy days.

Congress, too, has long manifested a sympathetic approach to the needs of religious conscience. The best-known example, of course, is the conscientious objection exemption from military services which goes back at least to the nation's first universal military service law of 1917. A more recent and less well-known instance is the action taken by Congress in respect to the rights of employees.

The Civil Rights Act of 1964 prohibited discrimination in employment on grounds of race, color, religion, national origin, and sex. In 1972 the law was amended to add the following definition:

> The term "religion" includes all aspects of religious observance and practice, as well as belief, unless an employer demonstrates that he is unable to reasonably accommodate to an employee's or prospective employee's religious observance or practice without undue hardship on the conduct of the employer's business.

The purpose of the amendment was to overrule the holding by a Federal court, in *Dewey* v. *Reynolds Metals Company*, that an employer could legally discharge an employee who refused for religious reasons to work on his sabbath. The company was willing to permit, and in the past had permitted, the employee to arrange for changes of shifts with fellow workers. The employee, however, refused to continue this practice because his conscience would not allow him to induce others to violate the sabbath; he therefore insisted that the company make the arrangements. The court rejected his demands, noting that no such arrangements were required by the provisions of the Civil Rights Act of 1964. The effect of the 1972 amendment thus was to require an employer to take affirmative action to meet his employees' religious needs, and it excused him from doing so only if he could prove that this would result in undue hardship on the conduct of his business.

Under the amendment an employer may not refuse to hire a worker nor discharge him because he will not work on his sabbath or other holy days unless he can show that allowing the worker this privilege would result in "undue hardship" to the business; mere inconvenience is not enough. The law does not define "undue hardship," so that it cannot be predicted with any certainty how it will work out. A likely case will be one where nonsabbatarian workers object to the privilege enjoyed by a Sabbatarian co-worker who is relieved of taking the Saturday shift, and their union files a grievance in their behalf. Suppose the union threatens a strike if all workers are not treated equally, would that fact constitute "undue hardship" under the law?

Even in the absence of any "undue hardship," the constitutionality of the amendment is not entirely beyond question. It is one thing for Congress to say that an applicant may not be denied a job in private industry merely because he is a Jew (or Negro or Puerto Rican); it is another thing to say that the employer must inconvenience himself or his business or suffer a hardship less than "undue" so that the Jew can observe his own religion.

Support for upholding the constitutionality of the law may perhaps be found in two cases not involving religion. In 1952 the Supreme Court in *Day-Bright Lighting Inc.* v. *Missouri* upheld the constitutionality of a State law forbidding employers from deducting wages for four hours' absence in order to enable workers to vote on Election Day. In 1973, in the case of *Dean* v. *Gadsden Times Publishing Corp.*, it made the same ruling in respect to a statute which required employers to pay employees serving on juries the difference between their jury pay and their regular wages. These cases are somewhat different from one involving a privately employed Sabbatarian who refuses to work on Saturdays, since in the former cases the community as a whole benefits when workers vote and serve on juries, whereas in the latter case only the Sabbatarian is benefited. Yet the Supreme Court's recent liberality in Free Exercise cases may well induce it to uphold the 1972 amendment of the Civil Rights Act, as consistent with the spirit if not the letter of the laws involved in the *Day-Bright* and *Dean* cases.

The 1972 amendment, referring as it does, to "all aspects of religious observance and practice," is obviously not limited to abstention from work on the employee's particular sabbath and other holy days. Its all-inclusive language would seem to encompass such "accommodations" as providing kosher food for Jewish employees in the company lunchroom, allowing male employees, including sales personnel, to keep their heads covered by *yarmulkes* (skull caps), adding prayer-breaks to coffee-breaks, and permitting employees to wear beards, if required by their particular religions. These accommodations, particularly the last, are minimal and not likely to cause serious problems to the employer, but others may, especially when they invoke hostility on the part of co-employees or go counter to union policies, as sabbath-absence.

Another example is union membership, or more accurately nonmembership. Among the more fundamentalist Seventh-Day Adventists, at least, union membership with nonbelievers is forbidden ("be ye separate, saith the Lord," 2 Corinthians 6:17). On the other hand, many collective bargaining agreements with employers require all workers to join the contracting union within a specified time after getting their jobs if they were not already members when they were hired. In a number of cases, Seventh-Day Adventists thus barred from employment brought suit claiming that governmental enforcement of the exclusion through the National Labor Relations Act violated the Free Exercise Clause. In at least one of the cases, *Linscott* v. *Miller Falls Company*, the Adventist, to manifest his good faith, offered to contribute regularly to charity the amount of his union dues. Nevertheless, with only Chief Justice Burger and Justice Douglas dissenting, the Supreme Court refused to upset the lower court decision upholding the exclusion.

The *Linscott* case, as well as other cases similarly decided, arose before the 1972 amendment of the Civil Rights Act. Whether a different result should be reached under the changed law would depend on whether the Court considers union opposition as constituting "undue hardship." A reasonable argument can be made either way. Certainly, it would be an "undue hardship" on an employer to require him to suffer a strike in order to accommodate the Adventist's religious observance or practice. On the other hand, unions as well as employers are subject to the Civil Rights Act, and the employer or the Adventist could perhaps get an injunction forbidding the union to strike or take other retaliatory action. Yet, even if this is so, workers and unions can express their displeasure through means which, though less conspicuous than a work stoppage, can nevertheless be damaging to an employer; and it may well be argued that the employer thereby suffers "undue hardship." How the Supreme Court will resolve this conflict cannot be predicted, but it is safe to predict that it will soon be called upon to do so one way or the other.

The People's Streets and Parks

In the *McCollum, Engel,* and *Schempp* cases, discussed in Chapter Five, and in *Tilton* v. *Richardson* in Chapter Six, the Supreme Court held that publicly owned or financed buildings could not constitutionally be used for sectarian instruction or religious worship. On the other hand, in the *Kunz* case discussed earlier in this chapter, it held that publicly owned streets and parks could not be closed to religious meetings. At least one member of the Supreme Court, Justice Jackson in his dissent in the *Kunz* case, found these decisions to be inconsistent with each other. There is, however, a historically justifiable difference. Streets and parks have from time immemorial been used not only for the transportation or relaxation of people but also for the communication of ideas. The use of streets by pedestrians has always been considered as free as the use of the air above it. The function of the municipality in respect to streets has been primarily that of policing and regulating so as to assure their free use by all. Unpaved paths and open places are in some respects the gift of nature; and though technically the state as sovereign may have ultimate title to the land, so too does it have ultimate title to the land on which rest churches and private houses. In neither case does the state's ultimate ownership of the land warrant the prohibition of its use to communicate religious ideas.

If the state may not prohibit missionary activity on unpaved highways and open places, it may not remove these from the domain of communication by paving and finishing them. Such improvements merely make them serve their original purpose better, but do not change their basic character or nature. The same is true of the landscaping which makes an open place into a park.

The same, however, is not true of public buildings. An unpaved path is usable to carry people from place to place; but a building until it is built is nothing at all. Buildings, whether publicly or privately owned, are property in the sense of economic assets. Public buildings are frequently sold and leased, like private buildings; public streets and parks are rarely sold or leased. The use of a public building is not free unless the state makes it so; and when it does so it acts in the same way as any other proprietor who permits the free use of his property. It is true that the state may—and frequently does—grant the free use of its buildings for political debates, dancing lessons, or group singing. This is constitutional, not because it does not constitute a grant of public funds, but because the Constitution permits a state to grant public funds to promote political discussion, dancing, or group singing. The state may not grant the free use of its buildings to propagate religion, because the constitutional requirement of separation bars a state from granting public funds for that purpose.

In any event, the difference, whether logical, historical, or pragmatic, is well settled. Under the decisions of the Supreme Court the Establishment Clause forbids free use of publicly owned buildings for religious teaching or worship, while the Free Exercise Clause requires free use of publicly owned streets and parks for such use. Indeed, in 1946 the Court ruled, in *Marsh* v. *Alabama*, that free use was required even in the case of streets in a town completely owned by an industrial company, which, but for the fact that it was privately owned, was indistinguishable from any other town of similar size.

While use of streets and parks for religious meetings and worship may not be forbidden, it may be regulated; and the Court therefore held in the 1941 case of *Cox* v. *New Hampshire* that a municipality could require a prior license or permit to conduct parades, including religious ones, in its streets. Regulation, however, must deal only with the time and place of the meeting, not with its content; as the Court held in the *Kunz* case, it may not be used as a means of censorship. Nor may it be discriminatory; in the 1953 case of *Fowler* v. *Rhode Island* the Court held that a community which allowed its parks to be used for religious meetings by conventional religious groups could not deny them to Jehovah's Witnesses for the same purpose.

It is a frequent, if not usual, practice to exhibit a cross or other religious symbol at religious meetings, just as an American flag is exhibited at patriotic or political meetings. What happens if the cross or symbol is left on the public property or placed there without a meeting; does its presence there violate the Establishment Clause? A number of cases raising this question have come to the courts and have received differing answers. In *Paul* v. *Dade County*, in 1968, Florida's highest court upheld the action of the Miami city council in allowing the lights in the municipal building to be kept on in the form of a cross during the Christmas season, so long as the added electricity cost was not borne by the city but was paid from private contributions. In *Lowe* v. *City of Eugène*, the highest State court in Oregon held, in 1969, that a 50-foot concrete cross placed in a public park and illuminated during the Christmas season had to be removed even though the cost of the electricity was paid by private citizens. In *Meyer* v. *Oklahoma City*, the highest court of Oklahoma reached the opposite conclusion in an identical case decided by it in 1972.

All three cases were appealed to the United States

Supreme Court, and were refused; the Court gave no reasons for its refusals. A fourth case was decided by the Federal court of appeals in Washington, D.C., in 1973. In this case, *Allen* v. *Morton*, the court held that the government could not participate in the presentation of the Christmas Pageant of Peace which was held annually in the Ellipse, a park adjacent to the White House, and which included a crèche depicting the Nativity Scene. In view of the fact that the crèche was clearly a religious symbol, governmental participation would constitute entanglement with religion in violation of the Establishment Clause as spelled out in the *Walz* and *Lemon-DiCenso* cases. On the other hand, the court determined that the purpose and effect of the pageant as a whole were secular, and therefore the government could allow the Ellipse to be used and could even contribute to the cost, so long as it made it clear, by a suitable plaque or otherwise, that its role was entirely secular in both sponsorship and participation.

Neither side chose to appeal this compromise decision to the Supreme Court. Instead the government discontinued contributing to the cost of the pageant. However, it still permitted the pageant to be maintained on government property, thus leaving the basic constitutional question unanswered.

Had an appeal been taken by either side, the Court's disposition of other appeals indicates that it would probably have refused to accept this one too. It may be that the Court does not consider the controversies of sufficient national importance to merit review by it, although it did take other Establishment and Free Exercise cases, as for example the *Epperson* evolution case, which seemed to be of even less importance. But even if the Miami and Ellipse cases, temporary as the religious symbolism was, may be considered relatively unimportant, the same cannot be said of the Oregon and Oklahoma cases, which involved the permanent appropriation of publicly owned property for a religious purpose. When James Madison, the author of the First Amendment, was President he vetoed a bill which would have given a certain piece of land to a Baptist church because, he said, it constituted "a principle and a precedent for appropriation of funds of the United States for the use and support of religious societies, contrary to the article of the Constitution which declares that 'Congress shall make no law respecting a religious establishment.'" We do not know how large a piece of land was involved, nor what was its value. But even if it be assumed that both were greater than those in the Oregon and Oklahoma cases, and that the latter were small both in size and value, it is appropriate to note that in *Flast* v. *Cohen* the Court itself quoted from Madison's Memorial and Remonstrance that "the same authority which can force a citizen to contribute three pence only of his property for the support of any one establishment, may force him to conform to any other establishment in all cases whatsoever."

More than a small piece of land was involved in these cases. Crosses are a symbol of the Christian religion, and their presence on governmental property is a symbol of established Christianity; crosses and crucifixes are to be found in courtrooms, municipal offices, and public school classrooms throughout such countries as Spain, Portugal, Italy, and many Latin American countries, where Catholicism is the established religion. On the other hand, because we do not and cannot have an established religion in the United States, crosses on public places are rare in this country. There are perhaps more crosses in a typical south Italian village or a moderately sized public building in Spain than on all governmental premises in the United States. While we do have many thousands of crosses visible in the United States, with very few exceptions they are all on private property—an implicit but nevertheless cogent expression of the constitutional truth that in our nation religion is a private, not a public, concern.

Absence of crosses from publicly owned property is

itself a symbol—a symbol of the separation of church and state. For that reason, the question, presented not only in the Oregon and Oklahoma cases but in the Miami and Washington ones as well, is a substantial and important one. It is to be hoped that the next time such a case again comes to the Supreme Court, its importance will be recognized by the Court and a decision will be handed down consistent with the principles of the separation of church and state.

Chapter Eight

Where Do We Go from Here?

Where Are We Now?

The year 1976 marks two centuries from the signing of the Declaration of Independence. Eleven years thereafter the American people will celebrate the bicentennial of the adoption of the Constitution. The former short document contains no less than four references to the Deity; the latter, much longer one, contains none. The omission was by no means the result of an oversight. It was a deliberate decision to establish what one great American jurist later called "a state without religion and a church without politics." The Constitution itself makes only one reference to religion, and that an exclusionary one: the provision in Article VI forbidding religious tests for public office. The First Amendment makes explicit what is implicit in the Constitution, and there too, by exclusionary language forbidding both the establishment of religion and prohibitions of its free exercise.

How faithful has the American nation been to this original commitment? The answer must necessarily be to some extent subjective and impressionistic. There are, however, some more or less objective criteria by which an evaluation can be measured. One of these is a comparative examination with another of the commitments of the First Amendment—the guaranty of the freedom of speech.

Seven years after the adoption of the First Amendment, Congress enacted a sedition act which was irrecon-

cilable with both the spirit and the letter of its Freedom of
Speech Clause. Although the law was promptly repudiated
by the American people and came to an end two years after
its enactment, this did not mark the end of Federal legislation aimed at political unorthodoxy. Congressional action
in this area was manifold even before World War I, and the
period since then witnessed the enactment of such major
laws aimed at political heresy as the euphemistically named
Espionage Act of 1917, the Espionage Act of 1918, the Smith
Act of 1940, the Subversive Activities Control Act of 1950,
and the Communist Control Act of 1954, as well as a host
of lesser-known but similarly targeted statutes and legislative investigations.

Nor were the States inactive in this field. State anti-
subversion laws were legion, equaling if not exceeding in
number the Federal laws. To these must be added countless
municipal ordinances and State and municipal investigations,
all aimed at rooting out political unorthodoxy.

In sum, it is fair to suggest that the American consensus, measured by legislative action, has not reflected great
solicitude for political unorthodoxy or ascribed to it a high
social or constitutional value. The record of legislative action
—or, more accurately, inaction—in the field of religious unorthodoxy points in the opposite direction. As far as is
known, Congress has never enacted any law proscribing or
limiting religious unorthodoxy. Nor, with a few exceptions
such as the three "Bible-belt" anti-evolution laws of the
1920s which quickly became dead-letter laws, have the
States done so.

Even more significant than legislative action or inaction, has been the people's response to unorthodoxy. The
treatment of pacifists during World War I, socialists and
communists in the 1920s, and practically everybody left of
center during the McCarthy period is unmatched in the area
of religious nonconformity. True enough, there were two
religious sects—Mormons and Jehovah's Witnesses—who
suffered substantial persecution in post-revolutionary

American history. However, in neither case was religious unorthodoxy the cause of the mistreatment. In the former case, after the Mormons in 1890 renounced the practice of polygamy, a practice which in the eyes of many threatened America's monogamous family structure, they were quickly welcomed as respected members of the family of faiths. With respect to the Jehovah's Witnesses, persecution was limited to a short period of nationalistic fervor when their refusal to salute the flag seemed to threaten the security of the nation. Once the American people recovered their senses, the Jehovah's Witnesses were allowed to live in peace without any modification or restriction of their theological doctrines.

The converse of America's non-interference with the propagation of religious doctrine has been its abstention from supporting it. Both on the national and State levels, legislatures have until quite recently refrained from appropriating tax-raised funds for the maintenance of parochial schools. The almost universal constitutional and statutory prohibitions against such expenditures reflect the national consensus, and this inference is evidenced by the fact that, in the several occasions when the people were offered an opportunity to vote on the abolition or relaxation of these prohibitions, they have voted against it.

The conclusion from the foregoing, and from most of what is in this book, is that on the whole the American people have been faithful to the commitment that the business of God is not that of Caesar. This does not mean that there have been no deviations and lapses. Although the national Constitution contains no reference to God, practically every State constitution does invoke His name (usually in the preamble) and acknowledges the people's dependence upon Him. Christmas is a national holiday; legislatures, national and State, open their sessions with prayer; prayer meetings are sporadically held in the White House; "In God We Trust" is to be found on the currency of the realm, and "under God" in our Pledge of Allegiance.

These and similar instances of governmental religiosity are, however, marginal and of little significance. The chaplains and visiting clergymen who open legislative sessions with prayer do so almost in splendid isolation facing large rows of practically empty seats. The well-publicized prayer meetings in the White House are political and social events rather than religious experiences. Department store sales and office parties that precede the 25th day of December commemorate Mammon and Bacchus more appropriately than Jesus Christ.

All this proves is that in an imperfect world there are bound to be distances between the oughts and the is's. The validity of a rule of law is not negated by the fact that it may be violated in practice, else we should have neither Ten Amendments nor Ten Commandments, nor for that matter income tax or traffic laws. The question is one of degree: the Eighteenth Amendment could not survive because violations were so widespread and accepted that the conclusion was ineluctable that the amendment no longer expressed the will of the American people. The history not only of the Free Exercise but also of the Establishment Clause of the First Amendment leads to a directly opposite conclusion. The violations have been comparatively minor and marginal. Moreover, and perhaps more important, they are not defended, they are denied; advocates of prayer in the public schools or aid to parochial schools do not generally challenge the principle of church-state separation but assert that what they advocate does not violate it.

Why Are We Here?

The principle of separation has withstood the intensive attacks upon its application in the prayer and aid to parochial school decisions. It is as alive and well as it was in 1791, when the First Amendment was added to the Constitution. Indeed, there are many who claim that it is now more vigorous than its fathers intended it to be. They still adhere to the premise, oft rejected by the Supreme Court, that the intent of the framers of the amendment was to allow considerably more governmental intervention in religious matters than the Court today will tolerate, so long as it was benign rather than hostile, equal rather than preferential, and universal rather than particularistic.

Wherein lies the explanation for the viability of the ideal that Caesar has no business in God's business? Certainly it is not that the American people are hostile to religion. At the time our Constitution was adopted perhaps as few as one person in ten was formally associated with some organized religious group; today, about two-thirds of all Americans have some affiliation with organized religion. Nor is this friendliness limited to the conventional faiths. Caesar has not only welcomed the nonconforming religions into the family but has gone out of his way to make them comfortable, as by exempting them from required military service or Sunday closing laws.

Nor can responsibility or credit—depending on how you feel about it—justly be attributed to the Supreme Court. The Constitution wisely clothed the judiciary with a mantle of substantial independence from the executive and legislative branches of government and even from the people themselves. Nevertheless, the Court is in trouble when it allows itself to be too far ahead or too far behind the general American consensus, as is evidenced by its *Dred Scott* decision which sought to confer constitutional sanctification on slavery or the New Deal decisions which appeared to do the same for unbridled capitalism. The racial integration decisions of the 1950s and the church-state decisions of the '60s and '70s aroused controversy and opposition, some of it quite passionate. The difference between these and the earlier decisions lies in the fact that the reactions to the *Dred Scott* and New Deal rulings reflected general if not universal unacceptance, while the opposition to the integration and church-state decisions came principally from particularized interest groups (Southern die-hards and the Catholic

Church, respectively) which, while undoubtedly large, did not represent the American consensus.

What is the American consensus in the arena of church-state relations? No one stated it better than Thomas Paine during the Revolutionary War. "As for religion," he said in *Common Sense*, "I hold it to be the indispensable duty of government to protect all conscientious professors thereof, and I know of no other business which government hath to do therewith."

Where Do We Go from Here?

Prediction is a risky business, but sometimes the risk is worth taking. In any event, we have almost two centuries of history behind us as a basis for reasonable guesses, at least in regard to the near future. Turning to some of the subjects considered in this book, we offer the following:

The Contestants, the Rules, and the Referee. The secularization of religion in America, which first affected Protestantism, then Judaism, and most recently Catholicism, is likely to continue. Counteroffensives, such as Key '73, Jesus Movements, Pentecostalist upsurges, and papal encyclicals, come and go; but there is little reason to expect any substantial halt, much less any retreat, in the humanization of God and His mission in the immediate future. Even if we should experience another Great Awakening, its effects, at least in respect to the secularization of religion, are unlikely to be any more permanent than those of the original in the 18th century.

Nor is there any reason to expect a change in the role of the judiciary, and most particularly the United States Supreme Court, as the ultimate referee in the confrontation of God and Caesar. Perhaps never in the history of this nation has the Supreme Court been held in higher esteem than it is today, and never has its role as an independent, impartial arbiter of controversies of great pith and moment been more universally recognized and gratefully accepted. Supporting evidence for this conclusion can be found in the Senate's refusal to confirm two appointments to the Court made by President Nixon in 1969 because it believed that the nominees did not measure up to the high qualifications which the people had the right to expect; the universal adverse reaction to the President's short-lived threat to defy the Supreme Court's order directing him to turn over the Watergate tapes is another example. Until something better comes along, and at present this does not seem to be likely within the foreseeable future, the judiciary will continue its role as ultimate referee in church-state controversies.

Finally, there is also no reason to expect any imminent change in the basic rules of the contest in respect to either the Establishment or Free Exercise clauses. There have been semantic variations of the no-establishment test ("wall of separation" [*Reynolds* v. *United States*], "no-aid" [*Everson*], "purpose-effect" [*Schempp*], "entanglement" [*Walz*]); and of the free exercise test ("clear and present danger" [*Cantwell* v. *Connecticut*], "preferred position" [*Barnette, Sherbert*], "compelling interest" [*Sherbert, Yoder*]), although it must be noted that rejection, in the *Sherbert* and *Yoder* decisions, of the "belief-action" (*Reynolds*) and "general law" (*Minersville School District* v. *Gobitis*) formulations constituted something more than mere semantic reformulations. Variations will undoubtedly continue, since judges, like nearly everybody else, have pride of authorship and originality; but it is doubtful that they will affect the basic theme as formulated by Tom Paine, or, as more commonly expressed, that "religion is a private matter."

When it comes to application of the basic rules to specific confrontations, however, prediction cannot be quite so confident. Cases are not decided by tests but by judges, and any test, no matter how formulated, leaves the judges with considerable room for maneuvering. Changes in Court personnel undoubtedly affect the application of rules to which all the judges express commitment; a Court of nine Douglases will certainly arrive at different conclusions than one of nine Whites. Yet, the fact that in the abortion case three of President Nixon's four appointees to the Court voted against a position which he had strongly endorsed, and in the *Nyquist* decision on tax credits two of them followed suit, indicates that, even in the application of principles, changes in Court personnel may have less significant consequences than is usually assumed. In any event, the following suggestions are offered as reasonable probabilities.

The Church. A century has passed since the Court, in *Watson* v. *Jones,* expressed a strong policy against state involvement in church affairs. Since that time the policy has been reaffirmed and even extended. Intrachurch disputes often affect tangible assets, such as lands and buildings, and judicial intervention is therefore unavoidable; but the Supreme Court has emphasized that the intervention must be limited to the minimum necessary to resolve the secular aspects of the dispute, and the resolution must be made in accordance with neutral, rather than theological, rules. Nothing on the horizon gives any indication of a change in this hands-off policy in the near future.

In the *Lemon* and *Nyquist* cases, the Court indicated that the street between God and Caesar was closed in both directions, and that constitutional policy militated against church entanglement in political affairs as well as vice versa. Here the Court was on less sure ground. Religious groups have always expressed themselves on political issues. One of the documents presented to the Virginia legislature in opposition to the bill for religious assessments and in support of the principle later to be known as church-state separation was the Memorial of the Presbytery of Hanover; and similar protests were made by Baptists, the most separationist of the religious groups. Prohibition was the child of Protestantism, and so too were the laws against pornography and contraception. The context in which the statements were made in the *Lemon* and *Nyquist* decisions seems to point to the conclusion that they were aimed specifically at the Catholic Church, and Catholic spokesmen were justifiably disturbed. Whatever the case may be, it is safe to assume that the Court's strictures are not likely to discourage active involvement in political affairs by religious groups.

A far more effective deterrent is possible loss of tax exemption. The Court's refusal to review the action of the Internal Revenue Service in terminating the exemption of Christian Echoes is quite consistent with the attitude it expressed in the *Lemon* and *Nyquist* cases, and if it adheres to this hands-off position in future cases, the role of religion in the formation of national policy in areas which it has long felt to be within its concern may well be severely restricted. Yet, the role of religion here has been so firmly established and accepted that in particular cases it is unlikely either that the Internal Revenue Service will press for or the Supreme Court will sanction revocation of exemption for intervention in the political arena unless it is to a degree grossly disproportionate to the church's liturgical and sacerdotal functions.

As for tax exemption itself, its constitutionality is secure, at least so long as it is limited to property used exclusively for religious purposes. In *Diffenderfer* v. *Central Baptist Church*, the Court did not find it necessary to pass on the question whether exemption from taxation of church-owned property used for commercial purposes is consistent with the Establishment Clause. The reason for that was Florida's amendment of its laws to remove the exemption, and in this it conformed to the practice in most of the other States. However, since a few States still continue the exemption so long as the proceeds of the commercial enterprise are used exclusively for religious purposes, the question may again reach the Court for determination. However the Court should decide (and the chances are that a majority will vote against the exemption), the effect will be small since, Court decision or no, the fiscal needs of the States will require the few that still allow it to follow the action of the Federal government and most of the States in limiting exemption to property used exclusively for religious purposes.

The *Walz* decision was a compromise. The Court held that tax exemption did not violate the Establishment Clause but refused to hold that it was mandated by the Free Exercise Clause. It is not likely that the Court will change its position in the near future, and so tax exemption will remain what it has always been, namely, a matter for legislative rather than judicial judgment and decision.

The Family. The sexual revolution which we are now experiencing is certainly having its effects on family relations, and the repercussions have already reached the halls of the Supreme Court. It is by no means impossible that the Court will be called upon in the not-too-distant future to reconsider its decision in the *Reynolds* case, and to accord constitutional protection to other than monogamous heterosexual marital structures. While it is improbable that the Court will compel States officially to recognize and issue licenses for polygamous, polyandrous, or other nonconventional marriages, it is possible that the Court will impose restrictions upon State regulation of marital relations which may on the whole amount to *de facto* recognition of such marital structures. Criminal adultery statutes may be taken as an example. While they are today almost universally dead-letter laws, a prosecution may arise, and a consequent conviction may be appealed to the Supreme Court. Should this occur, there is better than an even chance that the Court would rule it unconstitutional. With even more confidence it can be predicted that sooner or later, and more probably sooner, the Court will adjudge illegitimacy illegitimate and will declare that under the Constitution all children are born equal in the eyes of the law.

In *Griswold* v. *Connecticut* the Court held that by reason of the constitutionally protected right of marital privacy, anti-contraception laws could not be applied to married couples. In *Eisenstadt* v. *Baird* it extended the principle to unmarried couples, in effect converting marital privacy to bodily privacy. There is little likelihood that the Court will retreat from these decisions; it is more likely that, notwithstanding Chief Justice Burger's emphatic denials, it will extend the principle even further and will rule unconstitutional criminal prosecutions against consenting adults engaging privately in homosexual practices, and may in time go even further and hold that government may not discriminate in public employment or otherwise against avowed homosexuals.

It is quite possible that the Court will modify its abortion decisions somewhat and allow the States greater freedom in regulating abortions. It may, for example, uphold regulations requiring that abortions, even during the first three months of pregnancy, be performed at licensed hospitals or clinics. Beyond such marginal modifications the Court is not likely to go.

The unconstitutionality of legal barriers to interreligious marriages is hardly open to question. State-imposed barriers to interreligious adoptions are almost as difficult to justify constitutionally. A Supreme Court ruling forbidding restrictions on interreligious adoptions is only a matter of time, and so too is a ruling forbidding discrimination against atheists and agnostics in the application of adoption statutes and procedures.

Wars Moral and Immoral. The constitutional law relating to conscientious objection to participation in war is by no means settled. As of now, all the Supreme Court has held is that there is no constitutional right to exemption, and that in granting the privilege of exemption Congress may distinguish between objectors to all wars and objectors to specific wars, and may limit exemption to the former. What is still undecided is whether Congress may constitutionally grant exemption to persons whose opposition to war is based upon religious beliefs while denying it to those motivated by ethical considerations. The Supreme Court avoided deciding the question by interpreting religious belief so broadly as to make it practically synonymous with ethical belief. Up to the present, Congress has not indicated any dissatisfaction with the Court's interpretation and has done nothing to redefine the term to make it conform more closely to its traditional understanding. In view of the fact that the secularization of religion is still going on and gives no evidence of an early reversal of direction, it may be assumed that Congress will not overrule the Court's decision short of a war more serious and considerably more acceptable to the American people than was the Vietnam conflict. Even if that should occur, it is more probable that Congress will repeal all religious exemptions (other than those of ordained clergymen and possibly bona fide seminarians) rather than narrow the definition to exclude all but traditional and liturgical faiths.

The Schools Public. The basic secularity of American public education was accorded constitutional protection by the Supreme Court in the *McCollum* case. There is little chance that this will be changed either by Court decision or constitutional amendment. The secularization of public education was no more than an aspect of the secularization of American life in general, and had been substantially achieved long before its recognition in the *McCollum* decision. Even in those areas where the Court has sanctioned some public school involvement in religious education, secularization has not been noticeably affected. Released-time programs of religious education offer an example. There is probably today considerably less enthusiasm for and participation in released-time religious education than there was in 1952 when the Supreme Court ruled it constitutionally permissible, and we use the word "probably" because there is today a telling dearth of statistics on enrollment and participation.

The objective study of religion and the study of the

Bible as a work of literature are similar instances. Both were declared by the Supreme Court to be within the ambit of constitutionality, but here too we lack reliable statistics as to the extent that public schools have availed themselves of the privilege. In any event, to the extent that they have been faithful to the Court's mandate, the result has been the further secularization of religion, so much so that, as we have seen, traditionalists have resorted to the courts in an effort to put a stop to it.

Prayer recitation and, to a lesser extent, devotional reading from the Bible stand on a different footing. Judicial retreat from the positions taken in the *Engel* and *Schempp* decisions does not appear to be in the cards at the present time, but change through constitutional amendment is quite possible since, as indicated by practically every public opinion poll, the overwhelming majority of Americans find nothing objectionable in prayer recitation or devotional Bible reading in the schools. Indeed, it is a fair assumption that many of them welcome it as a salve to their conscience for not engaging in the practices at home.

Despite this, efforts toward constitutional amendment have been unsuccessful up to the present writing; while most Americans favor the practices they do not feel sufficiently passionate to make a Federal case or a constitutional amendment of it. Moreoever, most establishment-type religious leaders have expressed opposition to amendment, and because of these facts the anti-amendment forces have been able to muster sufficient numbers of Senators and Representatives who could with comparative safety vote to table or defeat proposed amendments to prevent passage by the necessary two-thirds vote in each House of Congress. This will continue to be so even though the Catholic Church has again changed its position on school prayers and Bible reading (anti until 1948, pro from 1948 to 1963, anti from 1963 to 1973, now pro again) primarily because the matter is not one of high priority for the Church, taking third place after abortion and aid to parochial schools.

But even if this prediction is wrong, even if the necessary two-thirds vote in Congress will be attained, the proposed amendment is likely to be so attenuated (perhaps limited to silent prayer and meditation) in order to get the votes, that the total effect will be slight, perhaps hardly worth the effort. Certainly, the basic secularity of the American public school system will not be seriously affected.

The Schools Private. It is here that prospects for judicial change of position are most promising or threatening, depending on how you look at things. In the *Nyquist-Sloan-Levitt* decisions, only one justice dissented from the invalidation of direct grants to parochial schools, but three dissented from the same disposition of indirect aid in the form of tuition grants or tax credits. A change in personnel could effect a change in decisions. But even if this should occur, it is more likely than not that the change in position would be small or marginal rather than substantial or basic. The Supreme Court has reached a compromise stance—aid to church colleges yes, to elementary and secondary schools no. It is not easy to justify the compromise on constitutional logic, but the American people seem to have accepted it, and the Court will be reluctant to upset the applecart. In a series of cases (*McCollum, Zorach, Engel, Schempp*) the Court developed the constitutional law of church-state relations as they affect religion in public education, and gives no sign of any intent to change it in any substantial degree. It has done the same thing in the area of aid to church schools (*Everson, Lemon, DiCenso, Tilton, Nyquist, Sloan, Levitt, Hunt*), and is not likely to make any substantial changes in the foreseeable future.

Even less probable is change by constitutional amendment. Unlike prayer and Bible reading, the majority of Americans do not favor aid to parochial schools. Any serious effort in Congress to amend the Constitution so as to allow tax funding of parochial schools would almost certainly raise a storm of controversy, and few things are more distasteful to Congressmen than that.

The Community and Its Welfare. The permissive decisions of the Supreme Court in the area of obscenity, beginning with the *Roth* case in 1957, undoubtedly contributed to the sexual revolution of the 1960s and '70s, but the contribution was small. The revolution would have come had there been no *Roth* or *Fanny Hill* or similar decisions. In its 1973 decisions, the Court sought to put a rein on the permissiveness which in its previous decisions it held to be mandated by the First Amendment. But here, too, the effect will be relatively slight. While we may have a counterrevolution and a total or partial return to the Victorian era, this does not yet appear on the horizon. Should this happen, the 1973 revisionist decisions may become meaningful, and the Court may give the States even greater freedom in putting reins on obscenity and pornography. But there, as elsewhere, the Court will be reflecting rather than fundamentally fashioning the national ethos.

In the area of the people's health, the Court has not yet handed down a definitive decision on how far the state may go in preventing adults from sacrificing their lives rather than disobeying God's word. More specifically, can the state, for example, force a blood transfusion on an unwilling Jehovah's Witness? When such a case does come to the Court in circumstances which induce it to decide the question, it is a good guess that it will hold that society's interest in human survival outweighs individual rights protected by the Free Exercise Clause.

The Court may never get around to overruling its decisions in the *Sunday Law Cases*; there really is no need for it to do so. Sunday closing statutes are fast becoming dead-letter laws, in large measure because America's dynamic economy simply cannot tolerate one day in every seven in which consumption is at an abnormally low level. Until such time as the American people learn again to pray, meditate, and rest one day a week, they will continue to pass their time either in making money or in spending it, on Sunday as on all other days. In any event, Sunday closing controversies are no longer part of the struggle between God and Mammon, but rather between the Mammon of the cities and the Mammon of the suburbs, so that church-state considerations are hardly relevant.

To sum up not only this chapter but the entire book, it may be suggested that the American people have on the whole been faithful to the constitutional command to Caesar not to meddle in God's affairs, either to help Him or to hurt Him, that the Supreme Court has reflected this faithfulness, and that one can risk the prediction that there will be no substantial change in attitude or action by either the people or the Court in the proximate future. Beyond that even fools should not venture.

Bibliography

This bibliography is limited to books published within the last decade. A more comprehensive bibliography (including articles) covering the period 1940-1960, but limited to church-state relationships in education, was compiled by Brother Edmond G. Drouin and published in 1963 under the title *The School Question* by the Catholic University of America Press in Washington, D.C. Another comprehensive bibliography of earlier publications, critically annotated, is to be found in Volume 3, pages 769-836, of Anson Phelps Stokes, *Church and State in the United States*, published by Harper & Brothers (now Harper & Row) in 1950. Shorter bibliographies are to be found in Anson Phelps Stokes and Leo Pfeffer, *Church and State in the United States* (New York: Harper & Row, 1965), and Leo Pfeffer, *Church, State, and Freedom*, revised edition (Boston: Beacon Press, 1967), as well as in many of the books listed in this bibliography.

For the convenience of the reader wishing to engage in further study, the books in this bibliography are arranged by chapters according to the subject matter treated in the respective chapters. It must be recognized, of course, that there will be considerable overlapping, particularly in respect to Chapters Five and Six. Indeed, readers studying the subjects of either of these chapters would do well to consult the books listed for both.

Books covering all or most of the subjects considered in this book are listed at the beginning of the bibliography under the heading, General Studies.

General Studies

Antieau, Chester J., Arthur T. Downey, and Edward P. Roberts, *Freedom from Federal Establishment: Formation and Early History of the First Amendment Religion Clauses* (St. Paul, Minn.: Bruce Publishing Co., 1964).

> Written from a Catholic viewpoint, the authors' thesis is that the Supreme Court has misinterpreted the true intent of the framers of the First Amendment which was only to bar exclusivity, preference, and compulsion.

Antieau, Chester J., Phillip M. Carroll, and Thomas C. Burke, *Religion Under the State Constitutions* (Brooklyn, N.Y.: Central Book Company, 1965).

> A topical examination of how State courts have dealt with church-state confrontations in the light of their own constitutions. The Appendix is a useful compilation of the text of State constitutional clauses dealing with religion.

Fellman, David, *Religion in American Public Law* (Boston: Boston University Press, 1965).

> An expository summary of Federal and State court decisions by a separationist professor of political science who believes, however, that "a complete and uncompromising separation is, in the nature of things, altogether unattainable." And who would deny that?

Hook, Sidney, *Religion in a Free Society* (Lincoln, Neb.: University of Nebraska Press, 1967).

> A philosophical critique of Supreme Court decisions.

Howe, Mark D., *The Garden and the Wilderness: Religion and Government in American Constitutional History* (Chicago: University of Chicago Press, 1965).

> The author, late professor of constitutional law at Harvard, charges the Supreme Court with dishonoring the arts of the historian and degrading the talents of the lawyer in construing "the wall of separation" in a manner hostile to religion, rather than friendly to it, as Roger Williams, its author, intended.

Katz, Wilber G., *Religion and American Constitutions* (Evanston, Ill.: Northwestern University Press, 1964).

> Expository lectures favoring exclusion of religion from public education but not religious schools from public funding of secular education.

Kauper, Paul G., *Religion and the Constitution* (Baton Rouge, La.: Louisiana State University Press, 1964).

A series of lectures by the late constitutional law scholar and active Lutheran layman.

Konvitz, Milton R., *Religious Liberty and Conscience: A Constitutional Inquiry* (New York: Viking Press, 1968).

The term "religion" as used in the First Amendment has not and cannot be satisfactorily defined either by Congress or the Supreme Court. The meaning should be kept open-ended to encompass each man's conscience.

Marnell, William H., *The First Amendment: Religious Freedom in America from Colonial Days to the School Prayer Controversy* (New York: Doubleday and Co., 1964).

A mishmash by a professor of English who knows little about the subject of his book but is infuriated about the prayer decision, which he considers a victory for the minority over the majority.

Morgan, Richard E., *The Supreme Court and Religion* (New York: Free Press, 1972).

While agreeing with the Supreme Court decisions barring ritual practices in the public schools, the author believes the Court has gone too far both in the protection of religious minorities under the Free Exercise Clause and in barring aid to parochial schools under the Establishment Clause. The best solution would be adoption of Kurland's religion-blind approach.

Norman, E. R., *The Conscience of the State in North America* (London: Cambridge University Press, 1968).

A British historian's comparative study of the development of church-state relations in the United States and Canada.

Pfeffer, Leo, *Church, State, and Freedom*, revised edition (Boston: Beacon Press, 1967).

Pratt, John W., *Religion, Politics, and Diversity: The Church-State Theme in New York History* (Ithaca, N.Y.: Cornell University Press, 1967).

A historical study emphasizing political factors and recommending accommodation and compromise to preserve interreligious harmony.

Smith, Elwyn A., *Religious Liberty in the United States: The Development of Church-State Thought Since the Revolutionary Era* (Philadelphia: Fortress Press, 1972).

   Examines the subject in the light of the separatist, Catholic, and constitutional traditions.

Stokes, Anson P., and Leo Pfeffer, *Church and State in the United States* (New York: Harper & Row, 1964).

   A one-volume abridgment and update of A. P. Stokes' 3-volume work published in 1950.

Stroup, Herbert, *Church and State in Confrontation: A Sociological Study of Church-State Relations From Old Testament Times to the Present* (New York, Seabury Press, 1967).

Chapter I

Gleason, Philip, ed., *Contemporary Catholicism in the United States* (Notre Dame, Ind.: University of Notre Dame Press, 1969).

   Essays on Catholicism in transition.

Kelley, Dean M., *Why Conservative Churches Are Growing* (New York: Harper & Row, 1972).

   The reason why is not quite clear, but statistics show that they are doing well in membership and fund raising as compared to the social action churches.

O'Brien, David J., *The Renewal of American Catholicism* (New York: Oxford University Press, 1972).

   American Catholicism after the two Johns—XXIII and Kennedy—faces the challenge of joining the struggle against dehumanization and injustice.

Sanders, Thomas G., *Protestant Concepts of Church and State* (New York: Holt, Rinehart and Winston, 1964).

   Separation secures the integrity of a free church, but it must not be corrupted by anti-Catholicism.

Smith, Elwyn A., ed., *The Religion of the Republic* (Philadelphia: Fortress Press, 1970).

   Essays on civil religion.

Wogaman, Philip, *Protestant Faith and Religious Liberty: The Basis of Religious Freedom in Protestant Theology* (Nashville, Tenn.: Abingdon Press, 1967).

   Opposes aid to parochial schools and favors creative teaching about religion in public schools and released-time and shared-time programs.

Chapter II

Adams, James L., *The Growing Church Lobby in Washington* (Grand Rapids, Mich.: Eerdmans Publishing Co., 1970).

    Deals mainly with the Elementary and Secondary Education Act of 1965, also considers the Civil Rights Act of 1964, O.E.O., and Peace.

Alley, Robert S., *So Help Me God: Religion and the Presidency, Wilson to Nixon* (Richmond, Va.: John Knox Press, 1972).

    How religion affected the decisions of presidents, particularly in foreign affairs, and why "civil religion" is no good.

Balk, Alfred, *The Religion Business* (Richmond, Va.: John Knox Press, 1968).

    Unrelated business enterprises of churches should be taxed. Churches should make contributions in lieu of taxes for their houses of worship.

Coriden, James A., ed., *The Case for Freedom: Human Rights in the Church* (Washington, D.C.: Corpus Publications, 1969).

    Essays on individual freedom within the Catholic Church.

Geyer, Alan F., *Piety and Politics: American Protestantism in the World Arena* (Richmond, Va.: John Knox Press, 1963).

    Religion as a source and sanction for loyalty, conflict, and reconciliation of conflict.

Larson, Martin A., *Church Wealth and Business Income* (New York: Philosophical Library, 1965).

    A study of church property in four cities: Buffalo, Baltimore, Washington, and Denver, by one who believes exemption should be strictly limited.

Larson, Martin A., *The Great Tax Fraud* (New York: Devin-Adair, 1968).

    The fraud is that many of church-owned assets are used not for worship but for profit making and are nevertheless tax exempt. (Or were when this book was written.)

Larson, Martin A., and C. Stanley Lowell, *The Churches: Their Riches, Revenues, and Immunities* (Washington, D.C.: Robert B. Luce, Inc., 1969).

    How churches accumulate great wealth and are free from tax obligations.

Morgan, Richard E., *The Politics of Religious Conflict: Church and State in America* (New York: Pegasus, 1968).

>An analysis of the sources of tension, the pressure of interest groups, and the trigger issues underlying church-state discord in America. Includes a chapter on the "Blaine Amendment" controversy in New York.

Robertson, D. B., *Should Churches Be Taxed?* (Philadelphia: Westminster Press, 1968).

>A useful, balanced study.

Stedman, Murray S., *Religion and Politics in America* (New York: Harcourt, Brace & World, 1964).

>Churches should play an educational and judgmental role in politics but should not be active participants.

Strout, Cushing, *The New Heavens and New Earth: Political Religion in America* (New York: Harper & Row, 1974).

>A study of religious involvement in the political arena from the Puritans to the present.

Chapter III

Birmingham, William, ed., *What Modern Catholics Think About Birth Control* (New York: The New American Library, 1964).

>A symposium.

Bromley, Dorothy Dunbar, *Catholics and Birth Control* (New York: The Devin-Adair Co., 1965).

>Under sponsorship of the Planned Parenthood Federation, a Protestant journalist surveys contemporary Catholic opinion on birth control.

Callahan, Daniel, *Abortion: Law, Choice and Morality* (New York: Macmillan Company, 1972).

>Written by a liberal Catholic scholar, this book is objective, comprehensive (worldwide) in scope and treatment. Though published before the U.S. Supreme Court decision, it still is probably the best single book on the subject.

Feldman, David M., *Birth Control in Jewish Law* (New York: New York University Press, 1968).

>Encompasses abortion as well.

Rodgers, Harrell R., Jr., *Community Conflict, Public Opinion, and the Law: The Amish Dispute in Iowa* (Columbus, Ohio: Charles E. Merrill Publishing Co., 1969).

>A study of public attitudes and their effect on law enforcement.

St. John-Stevas, Norman, *The Agonizing Choice: Birth Control, Religion, and the Law* (Bloomington: Indiana University Press, 1971).

> How can the Catholic Church reconcile long-established doctrine with the demands of contemporary society?

Shannon, William H., *The Lively Debate: Response to Humanae Vitae* (New York: Sheed and Ward, 1970).

> The birth control controversy within Catholicism.

Chapter IV

Appelquist, A. Ray, *Church, State, and Chaplaincy* (Washington, D.C.: General Commission on Chaplains and Armed Forces Personnel, 1969).

> Expository, ecumenical, and defensive.

Cox, Harvey G., Jr., ed., *Military Chaplains: From a Religious Military to a Military Religion* (New York: American Report Press, 1971).

> A non-establishment collection of essays sparked by the dilemma of the Vietnam War.

Dohen, Dorothy, *Nationalism and American Catholicism* (New York: Sheed and Ward, 1967).

> From an examination of the lives and words of a half-dozen bishops and cardinals, from John Carroll to Francis Spellman, this professor of sociology at Fordham concludes that by and large the hierarchy has agreed with the essence of Cardinal Spellman's response to a question regarding his position on the United States in Vietnam: "I fully support everything it does."

Drinan, Robert F., S.J., *Vietnam and Armageddon: Peace, War, and the Christian Conscience* (New York, Sheed and Ward, 1970).

> The Christian conscience, particularly Catholic, has not been forthright.

Finn, James, ed., *A Case of Loyalties: The Case for Selective Conscientious Objection* (New York: Pegasus, 1968).

> Ecumenical symposium of nine essays.

Chapter V

Clayton, A. Stafford,, *Religion and Schooling: A Comparative Study* (Waltham, Mass.: Blaisdell Publishing Co., 1969).

A comparative study of the relation of government and religious education in England, Holland, and Sweden.

Costanzo, Joseph, S.J., *This Nation Under God* (New York: Herder and Herder, 1964).

Favors religion in the public schools and governmental aid to parochial schools.

Dolbeare, Kenneth M., and Philip E. Hammond, *The School Prayer Decisions: From Court Policy to Local Practice* (Chicago: Chicago University Press, 1971).

Impact of the decisions on five small Midwestern communities.

Douglas, William O., *The Bible and the Schools* (Boston: Little, Brown and Co., 1966).

A lecture, somewhat expanded, by the most separationist and prolific member of the Supreme Court.

Drinan, Robert F., S.J., *Religion, the Courts and Public Policy* (New York: McGraw-Hill Book Co., 1963).

Except for a short chapter on Sunday laws, this book deals with education, public and private, presenting dispassionately the Catholic position. The author, former dean of Boston College Law School, is now a member of the U.S. House of Representatives.

Freund, Paul A., and Robert Ulich, *Religion and the Public Schools* (Cambridge, Mass.: Harvard University Press, 1965).

Two short lectures, on the legal and educational issues respectively.

Johnson, Richard M., *The Dynamics of Compliance: Supreme Court Decision-Making From a New Perspective* (Evanston, Ill.: Northwestern University Press, 1967).

How a typical Midwestern town responded to the Supreme Court decisions barring the Bible and prayers from the schools.

McLean, Milton D., ed., *Religious Studies in Public Universities* (Carbondale: Central Publications, Southern Illinois University, 1967).

Papers delivered at a conference held at Southern Illinois University in 1965.

Michaelsen, Robert, *Piety in the Public Schools: Trends and Issues in the Relationship Between Religion and the Public School in the United States* (New York, Macmillan Company, 1970).

An exposition of the religio-historical, educational, and legal sources, concluding with a proposal for the critical and appreciative (objective, nonworshipful, and sympathetic) study of religion in the public schools.

Muir, William K., Jr., *Prayer in the Public Schools: Law and Attitude Change* (Chicago: University of Chicago Press, 1967).

A study of the response of a Midwest community to the Supreme Court's prayer and Bible decisions. Reaches the conclusion that the decisions could and did affect public attitudes.

Nielsen, Niels C., Jr., *God in Education: A New Opportunity for American Schools* (New York: Sheed and Ward, 1966).

The Supreme Court decisions do not require the public schools to ignore religious values.

Panoch, James V., and David L. Barr, *Religion Goes to School* (New York: Harper & Row, 1968).

What the Supreme Court allows the public school teacher to do in the area of religion.

Phenix, Philip H., *Education and the Worship of God* (Philadelphia: Westminster Press, 1966).

The Supreme Court has not deprived the public schools of their duty to deal responsibly and maturely with religion in the curriculum. Specifically religious subjects and devotional exercises are not the only or even primary means of discharging this duty. The concerns of faith are chiefly manifest in the regular subjects and should be treated there.

Sizer, Theodore R., ed., *Religion and Public Education* (Boston: Houghton Mifflin Co., 1967).

Papers presented at Conference on the Role of Religion in Public Education.

Chapter VI

Beggs, David W., III, and R. Bruce McQuigg, eds., *America's Schools and Churches: Partners in Conflict* (Bloomington: Indiana University Press, 1965).

An ecumenical collection of essays.

Berke, Joel S., and Michael W. Kirst, *Federal Aid to Education: Who Benefits? Who Governs?* (Lexington, Mass.: D. C. Heath & Co., 1972).

368   *God, Caesar, and the Constitution*

Sandwiched between a two-chapter introduction and a one-chapter summary are reports on the politics of Federal aid to education in six major States: California, Michigan, Massachusetts, Texas, Virginia, and New York. Except for a few random references to parochial schools, the book gives the impression that these schools play no role in the politics of who benefits from and who governs Federal aid to education.

Blum, Virgil C., S.J., *Catholic Education: Survival or Demise?* (Chicago: Argus Communications Co., 1969).

Catholic schools are good for America and for American public schools. Without public funds they cannot survive.

Callahan, Daniel, ed., *Federal Aid and Catholic Schools* (Baltimore: Helicon Press, 1964).

Compilation of articles appearing in *Commonweal*.

Erickson, Donald A., ed., *Public Controls for Non-Public Schools* (Chicago: University of Chicago Press, 1968).

Proceedings of a conference growing out of the Amish controversy but published before the Supreme Court's decision in *Wisconsin v. Yoder*.

Friedlander, Anna F., *The Shared Time Strategy: Prospects and Trends in the Growing Partnership Between Public and Church Schools* (St. Louis, Mo.: Concordia Publishing House, 1966).

Useful introduction, but should be used with caution. Reference to the "enthusiasm of some Jewish orthodox groups for Shared Time" could be more wrong only if the word "some" had been omitted. I know of no Jewish Orthodox groups who favor sending their pupils into public schools for any purpose. It's money they want.

Gellhorn, Walter, and R. Kent Greenawalt, *The Sectarian College and the Public Purse: Fordham—A Case Study* (Dobbs Ferry, N.Y.: Oceana Publications, Inc., 1970).

How a Catholic college can desectarianize itself and get a lot of public money—but may lose its soul in the process.

Greeley, Andrew M., S.J., *The Changing Catholic College* (Chicago: Aldine-Atherton, Inc., 1968).

Greeley, Andrew M., S.J., and Peter H. Rossi, *The Education of Catholic Americans* (Chicago, Aldine-Atherton, Inc., 1966).

Two scholars, a Catholic and a non-Catholic, conclude

that Catholic schools have worked very well for those who (by reason of a religious family milieu) would already be part of the religious elite, have worked less well for those whose religious backgrounds were less intense, and have been wasted on those with little or no religious family milieu.

Hassenger, Robert, ed., *The Shape of Catholic Higher Education* (Chicago: University of Chicago Press, 1967).

Johnstone, Ronald J., ed., *The Effectiveness of Lutheran Elementary and Secondary Schools as Agencies of Christian Education* (St. Louis: Concordia Seminary Press, 1966).

>Conclusion: effective for youths from marginal Lutheran families.

Kraushaar, Otto, *American Nonpublic Schools: Patterns of Diversity* (Baltimore: Johns Hopkins University Press, 1972).

>A study of American private schools, independent and parochial, which concludes that they are a necessary and valuable part of our educational system, which must be preserved.

La Noue, George R., ed., *Educational Vouchers: Concepts and Controversies* (New York: Teachers College Press, 1972).

>A useful compilation of pro and con views with some discussion of the legal and constitutional issues.

Larson, Martin A., *When Parochial Schools Close: A Study in Educational Financing* (Washington, D.C.: Robert B. Luce, Inc., 1972).

>An Americans United study reaches the conclusion that the public schools can absorb parochial school children without substantial additional cost to taxpayers, and that any increase which might ensue could be substantially lower than the cost of financing the parochial schools.

Locigno, Joseph P., *Education: To Whom Does It Belong?* (New York: Deselée Company, Inc., 1968).

>Shared time is a viable solution to the problems of Catholic parochial schools.

Lowell, C. Stanley, *The Great Church-State Fraud* (Washington, D.C.: Robert B. Luce, Inc., 1973).

>The fraud, or a major part of it, is that governmental subsidization of parochial schools is for the benefit of the children. The truth is that it is for the benefit of the Church. It was Americans United which single-handedly exposed

fraud to the American people and more important to the courts—at least, so it appears from this book written by the organization's associate executive director.

McGarry, Daniel D., and Leo Ward, C.S.C., eds., *Educational Freedom and the Case for Government Aid to Students in Independent Schools* (Milwaukee, Wisc.: Bruce Publishing Co., 1966).

15 contributed articles.

Neuwien, Reginald A., ed., *Catholic Schools in Action: The Notre Dame Story of Catholic Elementary and Secondary Schools in the United States* (Notre Dame, Ind.: University of Notre Dame Press, 1966).

Reaches a positive, though modest, conclusion on the effectiveness of parochial schools in furthering religious understanding.

Pattillo, Manning M., Jr., and Donald M. Mackenzie, *Church-Sponsored Higher Education in the United States* (Washington, D.C.: American Council on Education, 1966).

A statistical and analytical report prepared for the Danforth Commission.

Swomley, John M., Jr., *Religion, the State and the Schools* (New York: Pegasus, 1968).

Although a chapter is devoted to religion in the public schools, most of the book concerns aid to parochial schools; written by a staunch defender of strict separation.

Trent, James W., and Jenette Golds, *Catholics in College: Religious Commitment and the Intellectual Life* (Chicago: University of Chicago Press, 1967).

Wolterstorff, Nicholas, *Religion and the Schools* (Grand Rapids, Mich.: Eerdmans Publishing Co., 1966).

A pluralistic society committed to religious liberty requires that all schools, public and private, be governmentally financed.

Chapter VII

Clor, Harry M., *Obscenity and Public Morality: Censorship in a Liberal Society* (Chicago: University of Chicago Press, 1969).

Since pornography leads to anti-social behavior it should be restrained, and this can be done without endangering the values of a liberal society.

Coughlin, Bernard J., S.J., *Church and State in Social Welfare* (New York: Columbia University Press, 1965).

Reaches the conclusion that there should be greater, not less, cooperation between (a) church and state, and (b) church and church.

Hart, H. L. A., *Law, Liberty and Morality* (New York: Random House, 1966).

An English philosopher argues that law has no business in the arena of particularistic morality, but should concern itself exclusively with conduct harmful to others.

Mitchell, Basil, *Law, Morality, and Religion in a Secular Society* (London: Oxford University Press, 1970).

Basically a response to Hart, argues that religion, and particularly Christianity, has much to contribute to law in a secular society.

Rembar, Charles, *The End of Obscenity* (New York: Random House, 1968).

The optimism of the lawyer who argued some of the 1967 cases before the Supreme Court may have been somewhat premature.

Table of Cases

Index